Understanding Children

Donald Swan, *Margaret Donaldson* is reproduced by kind permission of the Scottish National Portrait Gallery, Edinburgh.

Understanding Children

Essays in Honour of Margaret Donaldson

Edited by
Robert Grieve and Martin Hughes

Basil Blackwell

First published 1990
Reprinted 1991, 1992

Blackwell Publishers
108 Cowley Road, Oxford, OX4 1JF, UK

3 Cambridge Center
Cambridge, Massachusetts 02142, USA

British Library Cataloguing in Publication Data
A CIP catalogue record for this book is available from the British Library.

Library of Congress Cataloging in Publication Data
Understanding children: essays in honour of Margaret Donaldson/edited by Robert Grieve and Martin Hughes.
    p. cm.
    Includes bibliographical references and index.
    ISBN 0–631–15387–X   ISBN 0–631–15388–8 (pbk.)
    1. Cognition in children.   2. Donaldson, Margaret C.
I. Donaldson, Margaret C.   II. Grieve, Robert.   III. Hughes, Martin.
BF723.C5U17 1991
153.4′13—dc20

90–36327
CIP

Typeset in 10 on 12pt Palatino
by Wearside Tradespools, Fulwell, Sunderland
Printed in Great Britain by
T.J. Press Ltd., Padstow, Cornwall

Contents

This volume is dedicated to Margaret Donaldson, with great respect and much affection.

Foreword

Jerome Bruner
New York University

There are some figures in intellectual history who, while they and their ideas have a widespread even worldwide impact, must also be understood as quintessentially local both with respect to the place and to the times in which they worked. Lev Vygotsky's life and thought, for example, cannot be fully grasped without reference to the intensely revolutionary parochialism of Moscow during the 1920s when a gifted group of 'visitors from the future' were trying to forge a new vision of human consciousness to match the audacity of the Revolution itself. But the Moscow of those years is perhaps too specialized an example of the point I want to make, for it was more a crucible than a home, and in the end it destroyed or dispersed the seething talents it had produced – Vygotsky himself, but also his circle of visionary friends, scholars like Mikhail Bakhtin, Roman Jakobson, Viktor Shklovsky, and poets like Akhmatova and Mandelstam.

Rather I have in mind more nurturing and less turbulent parishes that somehow manage to blend their local wisdom and local practice with the great universals of thought, all within the compass of a single personality. I know I will be accused of romanticism if I single out Edinburgh as a prime historical example of such a parish, but I could defend my choice if I had to. I could cite David Hume, and even better, Adam Smith. But I could also bring into evidence the Scottish students I have taught at Harvard and Oxford over the years – more than a few, and all from Edinburgh. Many of them plainly exhibited the 'Edinburgh effect' to which I shall come in a moment. But my trump card in such a discussion would surely be Margaret Donaldson. For while she is a world figure, she is ineluctably and irreversibly Edinburgh. It is not just the intellectual lucidity and depth of her work that brings her renown, but the richly parochial, Edinburgh-style common sense that pervades it.

Let me get down to cases. Psychologists are forever in search of universals – universal processes of growth, universal stages of development, universal principles of education. Consequently, they tend, if they can, to be acultural, ahistorical, acontextual. In order to achieve this high goal, they devise procedures and experimental testing situations through which they 'stabilize' their results. The procedures and situations that best withstand cultural, historical, and contextual influences on performance become the chosen instruments, the instruments that produce 'robust' and 'invariant' results. This is all in the spirit of nineteenth-century physics. Now, parishes are curious places. They are repositories of a kind of contrarian wisdom where 'human nature' is concerned. They survive and thrive not simply by accepting the ubiquitousness of 'exceptions to the rule,' but by trying to *account* for them. Indeed, parish 'gossip' is principally an exercise in accounting for 'eccentricities', an exercise that takes it as given that departures from the general case can be found to be, on close inspection, just as 'rational' as the general case itself.

But the 'Edinburgh' of which I speak is not just any old parish, something out of one of Mrs Gaskell's novels. For one thing, it is astonishingly high-minded which, of course, leads both to heightened moral consciousness and to a susceptibility to scandal. For another, it is strikingly mindful of its intellectual past. Not one but *two* postgraduates who have come to study with me mentioned Hume in our first conversation, the one in which one encourages new students to talk about their future hopes. And finally, in the 'Edinburgh' of which I speak, in contrast to New York or London, the scholarly life is seen as an idealistic route to 'self-improvement'. So, the Edinburgh effect combines, on the one side, high-mindedness, a tradition of intellectual distinction, and an idealistic aspiration to self-improvement, that is hemmed on the other side with all of the sceptical particularism one expects from a going parish.

This was the Edinburgh of Margaret Donaldson. It was not surprising, once she moved from French literature into psychology and education, that she would be attracted by the high intellectuality of Jean Piaget's work. Nor was it surprising that when she encountered the disturbing anomalies in cognitive growth that were part of the Piagetian account of mental development in children (the Genevan explanations for which, let it be said, she understood exquisitely well), she did not try to 'explain them away' or to sweep them under the rug as 'décalages' (slippages or inhomogeneities in the even flow of development). Rather, her strategy was to find a reasoned basis for them that would be just as compelling as, and indeed would throw light on, the regularities that they were alleged to violate. This was no sudden impulse either. For whereas most research workers in child development trundle themselves and their equipment off to a school here and a nursery there in order to do their experiments on their young 'subjects,' Margaret Donaldson had her children downstairs in a small nursery school she had established right in the Department. These were the children on whom she pre-tested her experiments before ever going out into the bustling city to find the necessary 'right N' to test the reliability of her results. I have walked around in that nursery school with her: the children knew her and she knew them. They were part of the parish of particularity. She knew when their replies were part of a rhetoric of courtesy – children trying to give her the responses they thought appropriate to the occasion. And she knew the children well enough to get them to give reasoned accounts of their 'non-standard' answers.

What she knew most deeply in conducting those studies is that all human beings, no matter what their ages, respond to the world according to how they define the situation in which they find themselves. And what she has taught us all is to find ways of discerning the sense children were making of the testing situations in which we exposed them. There is an odd anomaly in all this. Piaget's fame rested upon his demonstration that children have, as it were, a logic of their own, and that their logic is as well formed as adult logic, but different and dependent upon their stage of development. Yet somehow he did not extend that profound insight into the determination of how children were in fact viewing the tasks that he gave them. His ingenuity had led him to a set of robust procedures that yielded results pretty much as called for by his abstract view of how development moved from pre-operational to concrete operational to formal operational thinking. Yet, there were glaring problems: how could a child who had mastered the pronominal 'deictic shift' and knew how to handle such terms as 'I' and 'you' or 'here' and 'there' ('I' is you when you say it, me when I say it; 'here' is around me when I say it, around you when you say it), how could such a child be said to be 'egocentric' and incapable of taking another's perspective into account when tested on one of the Geneva procedures?

What Margaret Donaldson did, of course, is now history – stirring history. She showed that how children proceeded in any testing situation was a function of the context into which they fitted that situation. The meanings they imposed on the task before them were a function of that context, including its discourse requirements: what is this task about and what am I supposed to say under such circumstances? She was *not* anti-Piagetian. She was demonstrating, rather, that Piaget makes better sense when his theory is looked at in the light of the child's definition of the situation rather than the experimenter's.

Her views of schooling, it seems to me, follow from the same set of premises. There is no way of understanding how a child achieves mastery of a subject matter without taking into account his or her own mode of defining, analysing, relating, discoursing, etc. And if the child has difficulties in finding a way of his or her own, he or she will 'fail'. I put the word in inverted commas, because in some deep way (and here I refer back to my own journals and diaries of the 1960s), Margaret Donaldson (as I wrote then) 'believes that failure is a perverse inability of the teacher and student to come to terms with the communication problem'. And I noted (rather self-servingly) that she agreed with my conviction that pedagogy was an extension of conversation. In this respect, she was surely Vygotskian or Bakhtinian. But she was also, I am sure, working from her 'parish' model as well: that local knowledge, related to particular situations, always precedes general knowledge based on reflection or, as we say nowadays, upon meta-cognition.

I want to say a word about how Margaret Donaldson conducted her 'research group' in the years when I used to visit Edinburgh more regularly – officially as an external examiner in the 1960s and 1970s on this dissertation committee or that, or unofficially because Edinburgh has been something of a 'home away from home' for me. For one thing, her group was astonishingly diverse in talent and temperament; yet they always seemed to take a certain salty pleasure in just that diversity. At their research meetings, she was not one to hold back her opinions, yet she gave them forcefully and undogmatically as opinions – and got it back in the same coin. They were not a 'shy' and certainly not an intimidated group. And they were a genuine culture, not only as psychologists sharing a common discipline but as human beings participating in the life of a great university in a cultivated city. I do not recall a visit to Edinburgh in which I did not attend a brilliant lecture on Blake, an exiguous exposition of augmented transition networks, a chamber music recital, a performance of the Azumi Kabuki theatre, or an offbeat lecture on drama by, say, Jonathan Miller – with Margaret most often, but virtually always with some other member of the 'gang'. Conversation at the interval was just as likely to be about the latest 'shenanigans' at the Department (of which there was never a shortage and for the pacification of which Margaret was not infrequently recruited) as it was about the new Villa-Lobos or the interpretation of 'Der Wanderer'. I commented once to her and her husband Stephen Salter about the cohesiveness of the group. She reminded me that Scottish society is based on the concept of the clan, an extended family arrangement, not upon a class system, as in the 'South'.

The unifying, binding role of Edinburgh in the life of the 'group' had the effect of creating many little joint symbols for its members, many of them in the form of a kind of psychic geography – like certain favoured pubs in the Grassmarket where particularly arcane single malts could be found. But the most bizarre and wonderful of the mythic symbols was the belief that wherever you drove with Margaret in Edinburgh, there would always be a parking place waiting at (or very near) the destination. Let it be clear: I have reason to believe that this is indeed a *true* myth, for I have seen it played out on repeated occasions. Never mind that it strains my sense of statistical rigour. Besides, whether it is a Mosteller statistical anomaly or a gift from the *genii loci* hardly matters. Margaret Donaldson's uncanny access to the world of Edinburgh parking spaces stood magically for her students as an open sesame to all of Edinburgh. She was passing on not only the world of abstract universals but the equally intense one of parochial particulars.

Margaret Donaldson is a painter of some talent and also a gifted writer of children's stories. She told me once that she greatly regretted having so little time for painting. But her 'painterliness' flares up in the presence of work she loves. I hesitate to tell this tale, for I do not fully understand it. Over the years, we often visited the Scottish National Gallery of Modern Art, which was then housed in the old Cunard mansion in the Botanic Gardens and arguably the most beautiful little museum in the world. One afternoon, on one of our earliest visits, we came upon a painting by Joan Eardley, an exquisite and moving canvas entitled 'Children and Chalked Wall, 3', where we stood transfixed for what may have been five minutes. Finally, I looked over, embarrassed by my long preoccupation, only to discover that she was just as 'caught'. I mumbled something about it being very beautiful, and she said that it grew on you the more often you saw it. The end of the story is that I asked the Harvard University Press if they could get permission from the Scottish Modern Gallery to use the picture on the jacket of a book I then had in press, a plan I had already mentioned to Margaret who had offered any help she might be able to give. I have no idea whether its eventual appearance on the jacket of *Toward a Theory of Instruction* owes anything to her intervention. I learned years after that permission had been granted despite Eardley's estate being in litigation. Whether Margaret intervened or not, I want to thank her for this emblem from a Scottish parish.

Two young, rather ragamuffin girls are standing before a wall from which tattered notices and posters are hanging in some disarray. The girls are looking unshyly eye-to-eye at the painter. They have kindly faces and very wise eyes. In some hard-to-describe way they have the tender-toughness that goes with living in a parish, fantasy and realism hand in hand. Their grandfathers had probably thrown in their lot with Keir Hardie. I have always suspected (I met these two tough kids twenty-five years ago) that they are among the ones for whom Margaret Donaldson writes her children's stories. She has always been as respectful to the young whose erratic growth she studies so well as to those of us to whom she offers her reports on their doings.

I don't know in what 'tradition' I would place Margaret Donaldson. There is a robust functionalism that always runs through her think-ing. But it is not the hard-edged functionalism of the American School, with its emphasis on adaptive behaviour that made it so vulnerable to behaviourist revision. I would like to hear her on this matter. Her approach to meaning is very much in the pragmaticist tradition, and she has always (more implicitly than explicitly) been an adherent of the view that meanings are situationally mediated and negotiated – indeed, in certain situations, we have learned from her, less can be more. About all these matters I am uncertain.

But I would not hesitate for a moment to locate her intellectually in another way. In my view, and I say this with the deepest respect, her developmental psychology is pervasively feminine in gender. There is an avoidance of 'all-or-none' conceptions of growth, a shunning of fixed 'stages'. Her experiments, always subtle, avoid the 'sudden death' feature of pass-or-fail. They are designed to discover not what the child fails to understand, but what the child in fact understands. And they are concerned with the child's engagement in discourse. Many have criticized Piaget for treating the child as if he or she were forever solo, figuring the world out from scratch on his or her own. For Margaret Donaldson the child is not alone; he or she is in collaboration with others in dialogue, in a culturally definable situa-tion. Perhaps I am wrong in thinking of these aspects of the Donaldson *oeuvre* as 'feminine'. Yet I cannot escape the conclusion. The issue is *not* tender mindedness and tough mindedness. Rather, it is contextualism and negotiability of meaning on one side of the gender divide, versus hard-edged rules and derivational operations on the other. If developmental psychology (and developmental psycholinguistics) have become more feminine in gender character over the last quarter-century, it is surely partly Margaret Donaldson's doing, and partly too the doings of such others as Lev Vygotsky and the ladies and gentlemen who grace the pages of this volume. But then again, aren't these gender marks the very same ones I attributed earlier to an enriched parochialism?

1 An Introduction to Understanding Children

Robert Grieve and Martin Hughes

University of Edinburgh, University of Exeter

The present volume, in honour of Margaret Donaldson, has been written by contributors who have had the good fortune to have worked with her and been influenced by her during their academic careers.

Margaret Donaldson's own academic career began with her taking her Master's degree in French at the University of Edinburgh. She then embarked on study for a Diploma of Education, but converted to a Bachelor's degree which she gained with distinction in psychology and education. Thereafter, she completed her Doctor's degree. During her studies in psychology and education, she encountered the work of Piaget, and discovered the fascination of trying to study and understand the development of children's minds. She completed her Doctorate on 'The relevance to the theory of intelligence testing of the study of errors in thinking' in 1956, and proceeded to spend virtually the whole of her academic career teaching and researching within the Department of Psychology at the University of Edinburgh. She was appointed to a Readership in 1969, and was made Professor of Developmental Psychology in 1980. Thus while she may originally have thought of teaching children French, the bulk of her career has in fact consisted of teaching adults – her colleagues in developmental psychology, students, and teachers – how children's minds develop and how this development might best be studied.

Three main concerns are apparent in Margaret Donaldson's work. Her concern with the development of children's thinking has been present from the start of her academic career, when she was considerably influenced by the European School, and notably Piaget. This early work is exemplified in her book *A Study of Children's Thinking*, published in 1963. During the 1960s and 1970s, influenced in part by the work of the Russian School, and notably Vygotsky, she became increasingly aware of the importance of language, and its relationship to thought. Her work during this period was predominantly concerned with children's understanding of language and how this affected their interpretation of the tasks conventionally used to study their thinking. This work resulted in a series of seminal papers on topics such as word meaning, classification, processes of comparison, conservation, reasoning, verification, and egocentricity – e.g., Donaldson and Balfour, 1968; Donaldson, 1970, 1971, 1976; Donaldson and Wales, 1970; Donaldson and Lloyd, 1974; Donaldson and McGarrigle, 1974; McGarrigle and Donaldson, 1974; Donaldson and Hughes, 1979. Her third main concern has been with the educational implications of her work, and here the influence of developmentalists such as Bruner is apparent. This concern has expressed itself not only in papers on children's acquisition of literacy (e.g., Donaldson, 1984, 1989), but also in the publication of a number of children's stories and of a reading and language programme for children in primary classrooms (Reid and Donaldson, 1984). These three major concerns – with children's thinking, their language, and their education – are brought together in the book for which Margaret Donaldson is undoubtedly best known, *Children's Minds*, published in 1978. Like all her writings, *Children's Minds* combines great clarity and lucidity of expression with original and rigorous thought. It has served to illuminate and inspire many thousands of students, teachers and academics throughout the world.

What, then, are the lessons which Margaret Donaldson has tried to teach us? One important lesson concerns *the need to consider the whole child* when trying to discover what a child understands or is capable of. Traditionally, psychologists go about assessing children's capabilities by using some standardized experimental task. The children are removed from their normal surroundings and presented with a problem which has been specifically devised to assess their understanding. Such experimental evidence can of course be extremely valuable, but there may be occasions when it needs to be augmented by observations of children in more natural surroundings.

A good example of this arises in the study of children's reasoning, particularly in their ability to make what are known as transitive inferences. Suppose we make known to a child that we have three sticks, all of different length. The red stick is longer than the blue one; and the blue stick is longer than the yellow one. There are now two questions. First, does the child know that the red stick is longer than the yellow one? In other words, can the child make a transitive inference using rules such as 'If $a > b$; and if $b > c$; then $a > c$'? However, there is an additional aspect to this inferential process. From the premises $a > b$ and $b > c$, it does not simply happen to be the case that $a > c$. Given these premises, this conclusion *must* follow. From such premises, the conclusion is logically *necessary*. While in experimental studies we can observe when children draw the appropriate conclusion from the premises we present, how can we observe when children also appreciate the logical necessity of the conclusions they are drawing? Experimentally, this issue is far from tractable, and here Donaldson points out the advantage of supplementing experimental evidence with naturalistic observation (see Donaldson, 1978, Chapter 5). That is, while it may prove difficult or impossible to devise the appropriate experiment to get at young children's appreciation of logical necessity, they may reveal that they have a measure of understanding of logical necessity in what they say and do in everyday contexts.

The second important lesson which Margaret Donaldson has taught us is *the need to consider the situation from the child's point of view*. This lesson is particularly relevant to experimental contexts. Here the child is typically presented with various materials and asked various questions by an adult. The adult will usually accompany these questions by various manipulations of the materials. Traditionally, we have tended to see these situations from the adult's point of view. The adult is trying to find out what the child knows or understands, and the child's responses are interpreted accordingly. What Donaldson has taught us, however, is that at the heart of the experimental situation is a child who is actively trying to make his or her own sense of the situation – and in particular, trying to understand, from what the adult says and does, and from how the materials are manipulated, what the adult's motives and intentions might be. Crucially, the child's interpretation of these factors might be quite different from that intended by the adult.

This lesson has been illustrated in studies of conservation, classification, and word meaning. In studying children's ability to conserve number, when two rows of counters are initially lined up in one-to-one correspondence, the child will agree that the rows have the same number. Instructed to 'watch what I do', the child then observes the adult transforming the spatial arrangement of one of the rows – e.g., it is spread out. Asked again if the rows have the same number, four-year-olds will typically say 'no', that the spread-out row has more. From the adult point of view, the child has failed to conserve number, apparently failing to appreciate that the spatial rearrangement of a set has no effect on its numerosity. But from the child's point of view, what might be going on? The child has been shown two sets arranged in one-to-one correspondence, and agreed that they have the same number. The adult has then drawn attention to a deliberate change in the array, and asked again about the numerosity of the sets. Should the child match the adult's deliberate change in the array with a change in his or her answer? If this is how the young child construes what is happening, it could begin to account for the response that four-year-olds typically give. Further, if the transformation of the array is effected accidentally rather than deliberately, then the young child's construal of the context might differ. Apparently it does, as reported in the classic 'Conservation Accidents' study of McGarrigle and Donaldson (1974). Here, young children tended not to change their response about the numerosity of the sets following an apparently accidental transformation of the spatial arrangement of one of the sets by a now famous 'Naughty Teddy'.

Another aspect of trying to appreciate the task from the child's point of view is found in studies of class inclusion, which involve an ability fundamental to classification. In a class inclusion task, the child is presented with a class of objects (e.g., ten flowers), composed of two subclasses (e.g., seven roses and three daffodils). Asked if there are more flowers or more roses, four-year-olds will typically say that there are more roses, for there are only three daffodils. They compare the two subclasses of roses and daffodils, rather than the subclass (roses) and the total class (flowers) which includes the subclass of roses. But what Donaldson points out is that the young child's construal of the task is different from that of adults or older children. What influences the young child is not so much what is said or meant by the adult's question. Rather, the young child's response is determined by what the child thinks the adult's question must mean. Since the distinction between the two subclasses is immediately obvious, the adult's question must be referring to the relative numbers of roses and daffodils. When the perceptual salience to the child of the class and subclasses is manipulated, as in some of McGarrigle's experiments (McGarrigle, Grieve and Hughes, 1978), then four-year-olds' understanding of the referring expressions in the adult's questions improves.

Young children's changing interpretations of word meaning dependent on their construal of context is also apparent in Donaldson and McGarrigle's (1974) study of semantic development. Presented with a shelf of five cars, above another shelf of four cars, four-year-olds judge correctly that the top shelf has more. If six garages are now placed over the five cars on the top shelf (leaving one garage empty), and four garages placed over the four cars on the bottom shelf (all garages being full), then about one in three four-year-olds now maintain that the *bottom* shelf has more cars. Why? All the garages on the bottom shelf are full, but one of the garages on the top shelf is empty. Again we can appreciate the importance of trying to see the task from the child's point of view. The child has initially been asked to compare the number of cars on the two shelves, and has done so correctly. The adult has made a change to the array – introduced garages irrelevant to the number of cars. Yet it is the number of cars which is again queried. In working out how to answer, a considerable proportion of four-year-olds are influenced by the alternative basis of response that the 'irrelevant' introduction of the garages provides – i.e., the relative fullness of the two sets of garages, rather than the relative numerosity of the two sets of cars.

What Donaldson is drawing attention to is that the experimental context involves a complicated and subtle set of interactions between what is presented, said, and done by the adult. Further, a fundamental aspect of the context is the young child's construal of the adult's words and actions. This is why she places so much importance on the child's appreciation of the adult's motives and intentions in experimental tasks. If these cannot be readily appreciated by children – as is often the case with young children who are typically limited to understanding tasks which make immediate sense – then children will produce inappropriate responses and apparently lack the mental capacity in question.

A further important lesson conveyed by Donaldson concerns both *the necessity and difficulty of formal education* for the young child. Because of her sympathy with the child's point of view, and her belief that young children are frequently underestimated, Donaldson is sometimes associated with those educationalists who are opposed to formal education and who maintain that young children will learn all they need to know in informal contexts outside of school. This, however, is a grave misunderstanding of Donaldson's position. Her writings make clear her belief that it is vital that children acquire abstract modes of thought – in her terms, modes of thought that are 'disembedded' from the vicissitudes of immediate context. She argues that if thought remains context-bound or context-dependent, control over one's thought processes is thereby constrained. Since our culture places high value on thought which is abstract and independent, we need to gain a better understanding of how the transition is made from the embedded thought of the preschool child, to the disembedded thought of older children and adults – a process which is far from easy.

Here Donaldson draws attention to the importance of the new systems of representation that children encounter in school, in the acquisition of literacy and numeracy. While the abilities to read, write, and be numerate are essential for negotiating one's way in society, their acquisition also has a profound impact on the nature of mental life. Given the abstract nature of our alphabetic system for representing language, and the abstract nature of our wholly context-free numerical system, their acquisition is far from immediate or straightforward. Their acquisition takes time, problems arise, children become puzzled, and they have to consider possibilities and alternatives. In written language, for example, since there is no one-to-one correspondence between the marks (alphabetic representations) on the page, and how they are to be pronounced in speech, there is typically a range of alternatives as to how a written letter should be said. But it is in encountering such difficulties, being puzzled, and arriving at resolutions, that children become increasingly aware of the nature of language and thought. And it is this sort of awareness, which involves deliberation and reflection on instances of puzzlement, that allows children to exert increasing control over their mental life, ultimately leading to independence of thought.

In the present volume, where a wide range of topics in children's development is considered, the influence of Margaret Donaldson will be apparent. Nowadays, about a decade after publication of *Children's Minds*, developmentalists write about children with a far better understanding of the importance of paying heed to children's abilities in everyday contexts as well as experimental ones. The need to try to understand situations from the child's point of view is also much better appreciated, as are the difficulties involved in children functioning in disembedded ways. The lessons which Donaldson has been trying to teach us are reflected throughout the following chapters.

The first three chapters are concerned with various aspects of children's ability to understand language. The chapter by Eve Clark focuses on young children's acquisition of word meanings. Here it is proposed that in acquiring the meanings of words, children operate on the basis of two fundamental principles – the Principle of Conventionality, and the Principle of Contrast. The first principle holds that in stable communication, it is conventional to regard the same word as having consistent meaning from one occasion of use to another. The second principle holds that different words will differ in meaning. Following explication and illustration of these principles, Clark notes that earlier work by Donaldson and Balfour (1968) on young children's understanding of the words *more* and *less* appears to provide an exception to the Principle of Contrast. However, Clark argues that this exception is more apparent than real, arising from methodological procedures which essentially precluded scope for contrast.

The next chapter, by Morag Donaldson and Alison Elliot, considers children's understanding of explanations – a topic of interest in itself, and one which has fundamental implications for education. The chapter begins with a critical examination of Piaget's view that young children are severely limited in their understanding of explanations which involve psychological, physical, or logical content. Donaldson and Elliot develop an alternative taxonomy, in terms of empirical, intentional, and deductive modes of explanation. Such modes of explanation are illustrated and distinguished with reference to various experimental studies, which provide an indication of when the different modes of explanation are understood by children. Generally, five-year-olds are held to have 'the basic cognitive and linguistic abilities required for giving and understanding explanations of events and actions'.

The chapter by Peter Lloyd is concerned with the development of children's skills in communication during the early school years. The chapter first provides a critical overview of the standard 'referential communication task', where a child's skills are gauged when required to communicate with another about an array of objects or drawings, while speaker and hearer cannot see one another, being placed behind opaque screens to encourage verbal and preclude non-verbal communication. Lloyd finds this paradigm wanting in various respects, and proceeds to develop an alternative approach in which the non-verbal channel of communication is precluded by asking children to communicate by telephone on a route-finding task. Lloyd draws attention to what he terms a 'communicative support system', which familiar adults use to help young children learn to communicate effectively. During the school years, children must learn to grow away from such a communicative support system, and increase their communicative independence.

The next four chapters are all concerned with some aspect of systems of representation – in reading, writing, computation, and pictorial representation. Jess Reid's chapter undertakes an analysis of children's literature, which involves instances of the written speech and thought of individuals other than the author of the story. Reid illustrates the subtlety of the inferences children must make in order to gain an accurate reading of the texts. In so doing, she reminds us both of the considerable differences between spoken and written language; and of the complexity of the task children face in learning to read and master the written representation of language.

In her chapter of the development of children's ability to write, Miranda Jones describes a longitudinal study she conducted in Edinburgh, which followed children's understanding of writing from the preschool stage, through to how their understanding changed as they learned to write in school. The views of Luria, and the findings of more recent work by Ferreiro on South American children, are not well supported by the outcomes of Jones's Edinburgh study, where the developmental picture that emerges is less neat and tidy than Ferreiro's work would lead one to expect. In conclusion, Jones notes the potential value of explicit instruction on the nature of writing at the preschool level for subsequent success in school.

In the chapter by Martin Hughes on children's uses of computers, both intellectual and social issues are addressed. His basic concerns involve the effects computer-use might have in fostering children's ability to engage in disembedded thinking; and the possibility that girls might not gain so much benefit from computer-use in school as boys. While some aspects of programming are relevant to the process of acquiring disembedded thought, Hughes suggests that much further work remains to be done. For example, a computer pedagogy aimed directly at fostering disembedded thought needs to be devised, as do appropriate evaluation procedures. On the social issue, Hughes notes the recent concern that girls may not benefit so much as boys from using computers. Does this imply that in schools, girls should be introduced to computers in girls-only situations? From the results of a preliminary study, Hughes urges caution, for when girls worked on a computer task with other girls, their performance was found to be noticeably poorer compared to girls who had partnered boys.

In his chapter on children's pictures, Roger Wales considers what is to be made of what children are doing when they produce a picture. Do they draw what they know rather than what they see? One approach to this problem, found in the work of Piaget, and of Goodenough and Harris, assumes that emerging features in children's pictures denote underlying changes in their conceptual development. Another approach, exemplified by Vygotsky and Donaldson, supposes that children's pictures – like all other aspects of their behaviour – must be interpreted in the light of what we know about the context in which the picture is produced and the culture in which the child operates. Through reference to pictures produced by Aboriginal children in Australia, Wales illustrates what can occur when children are exposed to quite different cultural influences. In the same picture, a Walbiri child represents people in quite different ways. Some (white?) people are drawn as 'stick' figures, while

Aboriginal people are drawn as semi-circles. A semi-circle with a smaller semi-circle in it represents an Aboriginal mother and child. Wales notes that great care is needed in making claims about the universality of the forms of children's pictorial representation. There is a need to distinguish between a child's mental representation and the different ways that may be used to realize that mental representation pictorially. In studying children's pictures, a wide variety of cognitive, personal, and cultural factors needs to be taken into account.

In the next two chapters, aspects of children's awareness and perception are considered. In his chapter on children's awareness, Robert Grieve concentrates on children's awareness of language, and focuses attention on what appears to be an elementary question: when do children become aware of language? Two main positions in the literature are described. That of Donaldson emphasizes children's reflective awareness that becomes increasingly apparent around seven years of age when children can consider language independently of its everyday use in social interaction. That of Clark draws attention to the phenomenon of speech repair in two-year-olds, where speech errors are spontaneously corrected, indicating that children must have awareness of language at some level virtually as soon as they begin to talk. Examples of reflective awareness can also be found in two-, three-, and four-year-olds, usually when they are puzzled or teased about how things are said. The answer to the question of when children become aware of language is far from straightforward.

In Lesley Hall's chapter on children's perception, the emphasis is on visual search and how it develops from infancy to childhood and maturity. In reviewing the literature on children's visual search, and through description of some of her own studies on how visual search is affected by the language of instructions, Hall argues that simplistic conclusions about the limitations and inefficiency of search strategies in young children are often inappropriate. If we are to understand visual search and how it develops in children, we need a fuller understanding of the interplay between task characteristics, children's linguistic comprehension of task instructions, and children's appreciation of the economy and efficiency of selective visual search in appropriate contexts. Visual search is held to be multifaceted in nature, involving the growing regulation and interaction of children's visual, linguistic and cognitive systems.

In the final chapter, Robin Campbell and David Olson offer a framework for a theory of children's thinking and its development. Thinking is held to be an effective activity which involves mental 'work'. Such activity is difficult (even repugnant), for it involves struggling with mental symbols which enable the thinker to hold some entity – object, property, proposition, world – in mind. Different forms of thought about such different entities are posited. Unlike recent 'innatist' views of children's intellectual development, Campbell and Olson's framework represents cognitive development as 'the accretion and expansion of representational powers'.

In reading the present volume, it will quickly be evident that while the contributors have been considerably influenced by the views and concerns of Margaret Donaldson, they in no sense follow any 'Donaldsonian line'. Indeed, at various points, the present set of essays will be found to disagree with Margaret Donaldson's views, either at the level of detail, or more fundamentally. The reason for this is simple. One of Margaret Donaldson's outstanding qualities is that she is highly adept at encouraging people not only to think and give rein to the excitement of ideas, but also to think critically, and, above all, to think for themselves. The sort of independence of thought and mind so readily apparent in her own work, she also values in the work of others. If the present set of essays exhibits independence of mind, this is no less than she would wish or expect.

2 Children's Language

Eve V. Clark

Stanford University

Building a vocabulary is fundamental to children's acquisition of language. Words carry meanings, and so do combinations of words. Without words, children could not use language to convey their intentions or attitudes to others. Studies of language development, however, have followed different swings of fashion. After several decades of charting children's vocabulary growth in the first half of the twentieth century, researchers began to focus on children's acquisition of grammar – the rules for combining words into the sequences permissible in a language like English, e.g., *the big boy* but not **the boy big, He brought the book*, but not **He brought*. (Phrases marked with an asterisk indicate that the sequences are not permissible in English.) Since then, researchers in language acquisition have shown that children play an active role in extracting regularities from the language around them. And they apply what they have extracted when they talk themselves (see Maratsos, 1983). Instead of *feet*, for instance, they say *foots*, adding the regular plural *-s* to the stem *foot*; instead of *brought*, they say *bringed*, adding the regular past *-ed* to *bring* (e.g., Berko, 1958; Bybee and Slobin, 1982; Cazden, 1968). Over-regularizations like these provide conclusive evidence that children take an active part in learning their first language.

The starting point is to discover what words mean. Children just beginning on their first language have to solve the problem of how forms map on to meanings. And of course they do not wait until they have mastered a meaning before using each word. Instead, as soon as they have found out something of what a word means, they may make use of it. Early word uses, as well as later ones, provide insight into children's hypotheses about word meanings and the conceptual categories on which the hypotheses appear to be based (e.g., Clark, 1983b; Donaldson and McGarrigle, 1974). In mastering word meanings, children must learn the conventional meanings they carry within the speech community. This often requires analysis of parts of words – the elements in a compound like *dog-sled*, or the added meaning attributable to the suffix *-er* in *opener* compared to the verb *open* – over and above the sense of each word. And it may also demand analysis of the constructions that a word may appear in, for instance, that a verb like *want* can be followed by the term for what is wanted, as in *I want that block*; or by a clause, as in *I want him to come here*. The lexicon therefore offers a critical domain in which to observe the process of language acquisition in children.

In the present chapter, I shall focus on word meaning rather than grammar in lexical development, and look in particular at how children's acquisition of word meanings is governed by two pragmatic principles of language use, *Conventionality* and *Contrast*. I shall then examine an apparent exception to the principle of Contrast, and argue that it is only apparent, and not real.

Two Principles

The first principle, *Conventionality*, is concerned with the maintenance of conventions about how expressions are used within a specific speech community. It states that: 'For certain meanings, there is a conventional form that speakers expect to be used in the language community.' This principle captures the fact that the speakers of languages depend on consistency of denotation from one time to the next in the meaning of a word or expression. In English, the term *tiger* picks out instances of the category 'tiger' today and will still do so tomorrow. Conventionality in a system of communication offers stability, and thereby makes communication feasible from one occasion to the next. Imagine how much time and effort would be required if each speaker had to establish the denotation of each term he produced on each occasion of use. Without Conventionality, communication systems as complex as human language would not be viable.

Conventionality is complemented by the principle of *Contrast*. This principle is concerned with the maintenance of distinctions between linguistic expressions. It states that: 'Every two forms contrast in meaning.' That is, any difference in linguistic *form* in a language signals a difference in meaning. This achieves a critical economy in language, in that it precludes the use of more than one conventional expression to convey a particular meaning. Rather, each conventional expression expresses a different meaning. The differences may be subtle, and therefore pertinent only on certain occasions – e.g., *shut* versus *close*. Notice how this is exploited in a Scottish radio advertisement for an automatic bank system that goes: 'Wouldn't it be helpful to have a bank that wasn't shut just because it's closed?' Differences may reflect subtleties of attitude (e.g., *slim/thin, strong-willed/obstinate*), of register (e.g., *numerous/many, attempt/try, cop/policeman*), and of dialect (e.g., *haystack/hayrick, sack/bag, tap/faucet*), over and above the various kinds of taxonomic differentiations possible among category labels.

Conventionality and Contrast together allow speakers to be consistent from one occasion to the next in their uses of the conventional meanings assigned to linguistic forms, and to maintain the same form-meaning pairings over time. Contrast also grants priority to lexical expressions that conventionally convey a specific meaning. If such an expression is lacking, though, Contrast allows for the construction of new lexical items, or new combinations of expressions, to convey the necessary meaning. The restriction on lexical innovations is that they must contrast in meaning with conventional terms. If they do not, they are pre-empted by the conventional terms since those have priority (e.g., Aronoff, 1976; Clark and Clark, 1979; Hofmann, 1982; Kiparsky, 1983; Zwanenburg, 1981).

When, then, do children begin to observe Conventionality and Contrast? And what consequences do these principles have for children's acquisition of the lexicon?

Conventionality and Contrast Observed

Children appear to observe Conventionality from their very first words. They attempt to adopt adult word forms and use them with increasing consistency from one occasion to the next. And their uses from the start bear some relation to the adult conventions for those words. Although a term like *dog* may be over-extended to pick out cats, sheep, and horses, it is also used to pick out dogs (e.g., Clark, 1973a, 1983b; Leopold, 1949; Pavlovitch, 1920). From around the age of two years, young children also ask for the names of things. Their intensive questioning, in fact, seems to coincide with two other developments in the lexicon. First, as they add new words to their repertoires, they stop over-extending words from the same domain already in their vocabulary (Clark 1973a; Barrett, 1978). Second, they start refusing to name things for which they lack words (Clark, 1974). Further evidence that children are attentive to Conventionality comes from the repairs they make to their own lexical choices. Children repair what they themselves say from as early as one or one-and-a-half years of age. They correct their own pronunciation, e.g., *fwo* to *fwog* (for *frog*); their own morphology, e.g., *the man go* to *the man going* or *the man's going*; and their own lexical choices, e.g., from *ship* to *boat* (for a rowing-boat), or from *shoe* to *sandal* (for a sandal). Repairs to lexical choice, in fact, appear to account for over 40 per cent of the repairs found in the speech of two- and three-year-olds (Clark, 1982b).

Logically, children could start out just as well by assuming that each word carried a different meaning on each occasion. They should then treat each word as if it were a demonstrative like *this* or *that*. To assume the principle of Conventionality, then, is not the only option open to children. Yet the evidence from their earliest word uses, their requests for the names of things, and their repairs to their own utterances, all indicate that they opt for Conventionality as they begin to use their first language.

The evidence that children observe the principle of Contrast is also strong (Clark, 1987, 1988, 1990a). When children add new words to a domain, they typically assume that the words apply at the same level, and so contrast. For example, although they may initially over-extend a word like *dog* to a variety of different four-legged mammals, they cease to apply it to any part of the domain newly taken over with the acquisition of a new word. Once *sheep* is acquired, for instance, the word *dog* is no longer over-extended to sheep, even though it may still be used for other kinds of mammals (Clark, 1973a, 1978; Barrett, 1978). Newly acquired words are treated as if they contrast with ones already known, and so serve to narrow down earlier over-extensions. Adjectives like *big* and *small* are gradually restricted with the addition of pairs like *tall* and *short* for vertical extent, or *long* and *short* for horizontal extent (Donaldson and Wales, 1979). Orientational terms like *top* and *bottom* are narrowed with the addition of *front*, *back*, and *side* (Kuczaj and Maratsos, 1975; Clark, 1980). In each lexical domain, children appear to make the same assumption: newly acquired words contrast with those already known.

Children assign distinct meanings to distinct forms, but the distinctions they make early on do not always coincide exactly with the conventional adult ones. They may contrast deictics like *here* and *there*, for instance, but they may do so by using *here* to signal transfers of possession – 'Here', said as a child hands a toy to a parent; and *there* to signal completion – 'There!' as the last block is placed on a tower (e.g., Clark and Sengul, 1978). They may also impose contrasts on different forms that are orthogonal to the actual adult contrast. Deutsch and Budwig (1983), for example, found that children often used their own names in two-word utterances when they talked about objects currently in their possession, but a pronoun like *me* or *my* when they were claiming something not yet in their hands. Similarly, children may seize on different suffixes or constructions as marking a contrast, but not necessarily hit on the conventional contrast used by adult speakers. Children assume, clearly, that differences in form mark contrasts in meaning.

A Constraint on Acquisition

The principle of Contrast places a strong pragmatic constraint on expressions in the lexicon. If terms that differ in form must differ in meaning, then one should find no true synonyms. Terms may overlap in meaning, but they may not carry identical meanings. This principle, then, makes certain general predictions about acquisition. If children observe the principle of Contrast, they should assume:

a   different words contrast in meaning;
b   priority goes to known, conventional words;
c   new words are to be assigned to gaps in the lexicon;
d   gaps in the lexicon can be filled, when necessary, with new words coined for the purpose.

We have already considered some of the evidence for the first prediction. Children do appear to assume different words contrast with each other in meaning, and they impose contrasts in meaning where there are differences in form. If they also observe the principle of Conventionality, then on those occasions where the meanings of new words would be identical to those of conventional words already known, they should give priority to the conventional words. To what extent do they do this?

Children do give known conventional words priority. Having learned one label for a category, two- and three-year-olds will typically reject a second label. For example, if an adult asks of a two-year-old's toy bear, *Is that your toy?*, a typical response is *No, it's a bear*. That is, children at this age seem to make two further assumptions: (i) all labels belong to a single level, and (ii) they do not overlap. These two assumptions, when combined with Contrast, become equivalent to Markman's (1984) principle of Mutual Exclusivity, and seem to reflect a fundamental factor in the organization of conceptual categories – namely, categories should be organized, at least initially, in non-overlapping fashion at the same level (see also Shipley and Kuhn, 1983, and Clark, in preparation).

The single-level assumption leads children to reject multiple terms for the same category: they already have a label, and that label therefore has priority (e.g., François, 1977; Macnamara, 1982). Of course, once children give up their single-level assumption, they accept the fact that terms at different levels such as *dog* and *animal*, or *bear* and *toy*, may be used to pick out the same object. The single-level assumption appears to be given up somewhere between age two and three years, as children grasp the fact that categories and hence labels for categories may be organized as taxonomies with several levels. Furthermore, once children have acquired the conventional word to express a particular meaning, they tend to use that, and not to coin a new form to use instead. Occasionally, like adults, children may coin a term to fill a momentary gap – e.g., the construction of *cutter* when *scissors* was difficult to retrieve from memory (Clark, 1983a). But, just like adults, children appear to repair such forms as soon as they retrieve the conventional word from memory.

When children acquire more than one language at once, they too begin by acting as if Contrast applied at one level only when they themselves are speaking. In the earliest stages, bilingual children typically produce only one label for a category, despite exposure to the labels from both languages. For instance, for one Spanish/English speaker, the adoption of *leche*, for 'milk', temporarily precluded use of *milk*. And for an English/French speaker, adoption of *bird* for a short time precluded *oiseau*. Once such children realize they are dealing with two languages, however, they begin to use labels from both languages for the same category, both *leche* and *milk*. They start to do this once they themselves can produce about 150–200 words (Taeschner, 1983). One question here is whether bilingual children at the early stage of producing only one label per category in fact *understand* only the label they themselves produce, or whether they understand both labels. If they understand both from other speakers, but produce only one themselves, then Contrast would appear to work separately in comprehension and production. In comprehension, children might already be aware that different speakers used different terms for instances of the same category, *bird* and *oiseau*, say, but they might still be unsure for themselves of the specific conditions under which a speaker used one or other term. In production, therefore, they continue to play safe and so refrain from using one of the terms until they have worked out more fully what difference in meaning (here a difference in language) is associated with the observable differences in form.

Known conventional words have priority, it seems, whenever words new to children appear to be synonymous with what they already know. They reject apparent synonyms within a language until they discover that there is more than one level of categorization to which labels can be applied. And they reject synonyms across languages until they realize that they are dealing with more than one language.

As predicted, children also assume, when they hear unfamiliar words, that these label unfamiliar categories. Golinkoff and her colleagues (1985) showed that children as young as two years made this assumption. The children played with novel objects mixed in with familiar ones, and then heard both familiar and unfamiliar labels. They typically selected novel objects as referents for novel words, and appropriate referents for familiar words. The children also extended the new words to pick out further exemplars from the novel category, and, when given a choice (with the introduction of a second novel word with further novel objects), the two-year-olds assumed that the second novel label must pick out as-yet-unnamed novel objects (Golinkoff *et al.*, 1985). That is, once a familiar or unfamiliar category has been labelled, it is 'taken', so any further unfamiliar words must be labels for yet other unfamiliar categories.

Three- and four-year-olds appear to act on the same assumption. When presented with an unfamiliar colour term in contrast to familiar ones, children assumed that the unfamiliar term picked out a tray of an unfamiliar colour (Carey and Bartlett, 1978). In a series of studies, Dockrell (1981) showed that the immediate context of the contrast influenced the inferences children made in assigning a meaning to an unfamiliar word. In the context of terms of shape, children inferred that an unfamiliar term picked out a shape; in the context of terms of colour, they generally inferred that the unfamiliar term picked out a colour. That is, children relied on Contrast in making their inferences, and where specific 'local' information about the domain pertinent to the contrast was available, they made use of it (see also Clark, 1978a; Heibeck and Markman, 1987). Familiar terms appear to offer children a specific location for the contrasts carried by an unfamiliar word.

This location may vary in specificity with the exact set of hyponyms given. (In hyponymy, the meaning of a specific term, such as *tulip*, is 'included' in the meaning of a more general term, *flower*.) *Blue* and *green*, for instance, would seem to offer a more precise location for the meaning of a colour word like *turquoise* than *red* and *yellow* would. In the former set, *turquoise* is a near neighbour of the two terms, whereas in the latter, the terms are all neighbours primarily in that they are all terms for colours. Presumably, the closer the referents of the familiar terms in a domain are to the potential referent of an unfamiliar word, the more specific are the inferences that children can legitimately make.

Finally, again as predicted, children coin new terms to fill gaps in their vocabularies. Although children begin with a very small vocabulary compared to the adult, they still manage to talk about a large number of things. To do this, they stretch all the resources they have. They extend (and over-extend) the words they can produce; they rely on deictic terms like *that*; and they use general purpose verbs like *do* and *go*. They construct innovative words (Clark, 1978a, 1982a, 1983b). Their spontaneous coinages appear from as young as one-and-a-half to two years of age. They coin nouns to talk about objects, verbs to talk about actions, and adjectives to talk about properties and states (Clark, in prep.). Their coinages are often in explicit contrast to familiar terms or to other innovations. For instance, two-year-olds produce many innovative noun–noun compounds, e.g., *penny-teacher* for a teacher at Sunday School who collected the children's pennies, or *oil-spoon*, for the spoon used for cod-liver oil, versus *egg-spoon*. In a corpus of over 300 such compounds produced by one child between the ages of two years two months and three years two months, over two-thirds marked explicit contrasts, e.g., *tea-sieve* versus *water-sieve* for a small and large strainer respectively, or *car-truck* versus *cow-truck* for pictures of a car-transporter and cattle-lorry (Clark, Gelman and Lane, 1985). And when children are asked to find possible labels for categories that lack conventional terms, they freely coin innovative nouns upon demand (e.g., Clark and Berman, 1984; Clark and Hecht, 1982; Clark, Hecht and Mulford, 1986; Mulford, 1983).

Children coin many words in the early stages of acquisition in order to fill what, for them, are gaps in the lexicon. However, once they learn the conventional term for a specific meaning, they must give up their own coinage and begin instead to use the conventional term. How do they do this? The principle of Contrast itself provides the necessary mechanism. Imagine that a child has expressed some meaning with an innovative term, **a**, and that this meaning is identical to the one expressed by term **b**, the term *conventionally* used for that meaning by adults – e.g., *plant-man* versus *gardener*. Once children discover that, despite the difference in form between **a** and **b**, there is no contrast in meaning between them, they are faced with a violation of the principle of Contrast. At the same time, adults are consistent in using form **b** (*gardener*, let us say), with just the meaning assigned by the child to form **a**, *plant-man*. At that point – and discovering such identity of meaning may take some time – children should give up their form in favour of the conventional one for that meaning (Clark, 1987, 1988).

The principle of Contrast, then, has as a general consequence the elimination of synonyms. A difference in word form signals a difference in meaning, so two different forms cannot carry the selfsame meaning. Children, like adults, appear unwilling to tolerate violations of Contrast (Clark, 1987). But at the same time, several classic developmental studies have reported apparent violations of Contrast: at some stage of language acquisition, children appear to treat certain word pairs as if both terms had the same meaning. Do children really treat such pairs as synonyms and thus violate the principle of Contrast?

An Exception to Contrast?

One major exception to Contrast appears in studies of the terms *more* and *less* (Donaldson and Balfour, 1968; Donaldson and Wales, 1970). These terms have traditionally been studied because of their role in cognitive development. Roughly speaking, children under five or six years often fail to solve problems of comparison containing such terms, while older children evince no such difficulty.

Donaldson and Balfour (1968) showed that when three- and four-year-olds were shown two model apple-trees, with five apples on one, say, and three on the other, they consistently chose the tree with five if asked to judge which had *more*. When asked to judge which tree had *less*, they again chose the tree with the greater number of apples. Similar results were found in a construction task. Shown a pile of apples and two trees, one with three apples and one with none, and asked to make the 'empty' tree so it had *more*, children added apples until there were more on the empty tree. Asked to make the empty tree so it had *less*, children again added apples until there were more on the originally empty tree. These findings were replicated, with both discrete and continuous quantities, by Palermo (1973, 1974). That is, when asked which tree had more or when asked to make a tree so it had more, children responded appropriately: they picked out the tree with the greater number, and they added apples until the target tree had a greater number. But when asked which tree had less, or to make one of two trees have less, children again chose the tree with more, and they added to the target tree until it had a greater amount than the other.

These findings offered important support for theoretical proposals about children's acquisition of the meanings of *more* and *less* as well as of other adjective pairs (e.g., *big/small, tall/short, wide/narrow*), in that they appeared to show that children first learned the meaning of the unmarked term for a dimension (e.g., *big, tall*), and interpreted the marked (negative) member (*small, short*) of the pair as if it had the same meaning as the unmarked (positive) member (see H. Clark, 1970; Clark, 1973a).

However, other studies of unmarked/marked pairs did not offer support for this view. Although children often seemed to understand and produce the unmarked adjective forms more readily than the marked ones, they did not appear to treat *small*, for instance, at any stage as if its meaning was identical to that of *big* (see Bartlett, 1978; Clark, 1972; Eilers, Oller and Ellington, 1974). Rather, children seemed to grasp the fact that some terms pick out the positive end of a dimension, and others the negative end, before they necessarily identify which terms belong together as pairs.

Other researchers failed to find the '*less* is more' effect. Typically, such researchers used both *more* and *less* in their questions. Weiner (1974), for example, added or subtracted counters from rows as two- and three-year-olds watched, and then had the children choose the row with *more* or with *less*. Errors on *less* reflected chance performance rather than choices of the greater amount. She suggested that the non-linguistic context might affect the kinds of responses children offered at a stage when they have an imperfect grasp of the meanings of one or both terms. Where the only possible error consists of choosing the item with the greater amount, children may simply appear to treat *less* as 'more'. In fact, in situations that allow more than two choices, and use both terms, young children seldom make errors at all. For instance, when shown arrays of beads on wire columns, of three different heights, children's choices for *less* were nearly always correct (Wannemacher and Ryan, 1978). Also, when presented with questions like 'What eats less, a horse or a bunny?', or a practical situation like 'Pretend you had to carry a bucket full of dirt and it was really heavy. What could you do to make it so there was less dirt in your bucket?', children were nearly always correct. If they did not reply correctly, they either failed to say anything, or answered with 'I don't know' (Wannemacher and Ryan, 1978; see also Grieve and Stanley, 1984; Kavanaugh, 1976; Trehub and Abramovitch, 1978).

Why then did children choose the greater of two amounts in Donaldson and Balfour's original study, and in Palermo's replications? Part of the answer may hinge on children's reliance on non-linguistic strategies in the absence of lexical knowledge. Klatzky, Clark and Macken (1973) found that children learned nonsense words for the positive, extended, ends of dimensions before they learned their negative counterparts. They attributed this to a conceptual bias favouring greater extent over lesser extent, a bias that should allow positive, unmarked terms to be 'mapped' earlier than negative, marked ones. However, this study looked only at physical dimensions such as size, height, and width. Trehub and Abramovitch (1978) showed that three- and four-year-olds exhibited a similar preference when simply asked to choose between two piles of different sizes: they preferred the larger one. This preference showed up in 91 per cent of the children who, in another task, made errors on *less*. It also showed up in 69 per cent of the children who interpreted both *more* and *less* correctly. Errors on *less*, in other words, are probably attributable, in part or even entirely, to a non-linguistic strategy of choosing the greater amount, a strategy typically invoked when children are unsure of the response required.

But while a non-linguistic preference or bias might explain why the meaning of *more* appears to be acquired before that of *less*, there still appears to be some violation of the principle of Contrast when children respond to *more* and *less* as if their meanings were identical.

But did children really do this? The answer, I argue, is 'no'. In fact, Donaldson and Balfour, and nearly all the researchers who followed them, gave children questions with *more* on one occasion, and questions with *less* on another, so the two terms never appeared in the same session or the same block.

When children hear both terms in the same instruction or in the same condition, they do not treat *more* and *less* as synonymous. While Palermo (1973), for example, found that four- to five-year-olds responded appropriately to *more* nearly all the time, but to *less* only 39 per cent of the time, an earlier study by Griffiths, Shantz and Sigel (1967) reported that children of that age understood both *more* and *less* almost equally well (70 per cent and 65 per cent). What was the difference? Palermo (1974) attributed it to 'much more syntactic context . . . which may have aided performance', but an alternative interpretation is that, because children heard both *more* and *less* in each question in the study by Griffiths *et al.*, they had to take Contrast into account. Instead of hearing blocks of questions that used only *more*, or only *less*, they had to respond to such questions as 'Does this set of lollipops have more lollipops, less lollipops, or the same number of lollipops as this set?' Similarly, when Wannemacher and Ryan (1978) in one condition asked three- to five-year-olds to identify rods with either *more* or *less* beads than a standard, the children did well on both *more* and *less*: 98 per cent and 95 per cent correct. (Children saw three, five, or six rods at a time, with different numbers of beads on each. The standard chosen was always a rod with a middle-sized number of beads.) In this and a variety of other tasks, Wannemacher and Ryan were able to distinguish 'incorrect' from 'opposite' responses. Indeed, where no obvious alternative response was available in some of their tasks, children who did not know the meaning of *less* typically opted for no response, or 'Don't know.' (As in previous studies, most three-year-olds did not understand *less*, and most five-year-olds did.)

Overall, Wannemacher and Ryan attributed their children's success to two factors: the presence of a standard for comparison (the rod with the middle number of beads), and use of both words, *more* and *less*, in the same trial. As they pointed out, studies where children appeared to treat *less* as 'more' gave the two terms in separate sessions on different days (Donaldson and Balfour, 1968), or in different blocks (Palermo, 1973), or gave only one term, *less*, in all the questions (Palermo, 1974). In other words, in those studies where children heard both *more* and *less* in the same trials or same sessions, and where there were more than two responses possible, they showed no evidence of treating *less* as if it meant *more*. If they did not know the word *less*, their responses followed a pattern of chance responding; if they did know it, they got it right nearly all the time. In addition, four- and five-year-olds often said explicitly that they did not know *less*, or even asked what it meant.

Further evidence in support of this comes from studies that introduced a third term, in the form of a nonsense word, in contrast to *more* and *less*. Children who know the meaning of *more* or of both *more* and *less* are careful to distinguish them from each other and from nonsense words introduced in the same setting. When asked to make one of two equal piles of pennies *tiv*, after having made one pile *more* or *less* than the other, three- to five-year-olds will do one of several things. They may refuse to respond, on the grounds that they do not know what *tiv* means (see Carey, 1978); they may ask what *tiv* means, and having been told to guess, offer a response; or they may select a response without querying *tiv*.

When children who knew *more* and *less* did respond, they were consistent in differentiating their response from what they had done for *more* and for *less*. One five-year-old, for instance, when asked to make one pile so it was *tiv*, picked up one coin from it, placed it between the two piles, and announced that it was *tiv*. Another stirred one of two glasses of beans with his finger for *tiv* (he had added and subtracted appropriately in response to *more* and *less*). Another decided that *tiv* must mean 'just a tiny bit' and so added a teaspoon of water, compared to half a glass for *more*, and so on (Clark, unpublished data). Children who were presented with a nonsense syllable alongside *more* and *less* in a variety of contexts made it contrast with *more* and *less* by adding or subtracting much smaller amounts; by adding or subtracting everything; by introducing some quite different manipulation (stirring, flicking, rolling, tossing up and down, mixing both piles together), and so on. Two- and three-year-olds, who did not yet know *less*, were not as consistent, and their responses to *less* and *tiv* – and possibly to *more* as well – suggested that, in the absence of lexical knowledge, they were probably relying on a non-linguistic strategy of choosing the greater amount (Trehub and Abramovitch, 1978). When a second nonsense syllable was given following two instances of *tiv*, mixed in with several instructions containing *more* and *less*, the same children typically queried its meaning or responded with 'Don't know.' They did not treat it as equivalent to either the other nonsense word or to *more* or *less*. These data, along with the findings from Griffiths *et al.* (1967) and Wannemacher and Ryan (1978), offer further support for children's observance of Contrast in their acquisition of *more* and *less*.

In summary, the questions in studies of *more* and *less* have revolved around three issues: (a) whether children have full or only partial lexical knowledge about the pertinent word meanings; (b) the extent to which children rely on non-linguistic strategies in the absence of lexical information (clearly children know none of the pertinent meanings at first for a domain, and several studies have documented the kinds of non-linguistic strategies they then rely on in responding to instructions – see Clark, 1973b, 1979, 1980; Donaldson and McGarrigle, 1974); and (c) whether children observe the principle of Contrast. Most studies of *more* and *less* have focused on lexical knowledge of the pertinent terms. These studies gave rise to the view that children went through a stage of treating *less* as if it was synonymous with *more*. But these findings turn out to be artefactual. Children were constrained in the kinds of response possible and so appeared to treat *less* as *more*; the younger children probably relied on a non-linguistic strategy of choosing the greater of two amounts, and this would account for responses to both *more* (apparently correct) and *less* (apparently wrong) when combined with partial or even no lexical knowledge; and lastly, children were not given instructions with both *more* and *less* on the same occasion. Once these conditions were altered, children clearly contrasted the meanings of *more* and *less* even when their lexical knowledge was still imperfect. Equally clearly, they relied on non-linguistic strategies for deciding how their addressees wished them to act in the absence of adult-like understanding of an instruction. Finally, they adhered to the principle of Contrast in distinguishing *less* from *more*.

Conclusion

Lexical development offers critical insights into the process of language acquisition. What strategies do children rely on when they do not understand what is said, or only partially understand? Where do children's hypotheses about word-meanings come from? What stages do they go through as they acquire new words? How do they organize and represent lexical knowledge? What pragmatic principles govern lexical acquisition? What principles do children rely on as they analyse the structure of words and make use of their knowledge? To what extent can children be said to apply 'rules' in word-formation? And when children over-regularize their systems, how can they eventually get rid of the over-regularizations? These questions characterize some of the issues that research on lexical development has attempted to answer.

The focus here has been on Conventionality and Contrast, two pragmatic principles that together govern the lexicon. They also, of course, govern linguistic units larger than words – idioms, phrases, and larger constructions. These principles play a central role in how children make use of terms in the conventional lexicon, as well as when they go beyond those to coin new words. These pragmatic principles offer a source of regulation for conventional forms taking priority over innovative ones, and for setting conditions on when innovation is allowed.

More importantly still, Conventionality and Contrast together offer a mechanism whereby children can eliminate their over-regularizations. Since each difference in form must signal a difference in meaning, children must make certain choices among forms when they find themselves faced with two different forms with apparently the same meaning – e.g., *bringed* and *brought*, or *cooker* and *cook*. If children can find no difference in meaning between such pairs, and yet wish to maintain the principle of Contrast, they must eliminate one member of the pair. Which one? Here Conventionality takes a role: the term to be retained should be the conventional one, the one used by adults in the speech community, and the term eliminated must be the innovative one introduced (as a regularization) by the child.

To discover that there is no difference in meaning between two forms may, of course, take children a long time. The time it takes should vary from child to child, and from expression to expression. The propensity children have for imposing meaning distinctions of their own in their adherence to Contrast may delay their discovery of the absence of a difference between an adult form and a child innovation. Children may 'decide' that the adult past *brought*, for instance, indicates distant past, while the child's *bringed* is retained to indicate more recent past. (I am indebted to Jill de Villiers for this example.) *Cooker* and *cook* may be distinguished on the basis of sex (male, female), or location (home, restaurant), and so on. Even variant pronunciations of the same word may on occasion be assigned contrasting meanings. For instance, US *vase* pronounced [va:z] was identified by one child as a smallish flower vase, while [veiz] was taken to be a really large kind. (Both pronunciations are found, though typically not in the same speaker.) To rectify such mistakes may take extensive exposure to different usage from other speakers around them, before children find out that they have a real case of no *difference* in meaning (Clark, 1987, 1988).

Finally, contrast in meaning is a matter of *sense*, not simply of *reference*. Children evidently realize this quite early in the process of language acquisition, and accept the fact that different words may *refer* to the same entity – e.g., *our dog, Fred, that wretched animal*, and so on. They take for granted that they themselves have a name they may be called by, as well as nicknames and endearments, alongside such designations as *the kid, the boy*, and so on. They can formulate hypotheses about reference on the basis of the contexts in which they hear new words, and, with the help of Contrast, they also start out with a strong guiding principle about relations among word senses. Namely, wherever there is a difference in *form*, they should expect to find some difference in *meaning*. This assumption appears to be one that children take to heart very early, and rely on extensively as they acquire the meanings of their first language.

Preparation of this chapter was supported in part by a grant from the National Institute of Child Health & Human Development (5 R01 HD18908), and in part by the Sloan Foundation.

3 Children's Explanations

Morag L. Donaldson and Alison Elliot

University of Edinburgh

Adults have fairly low expectations about children's ability to explain things. They are agreeably surprised if a child shows a grasp of a phenomenon, such as how a machine works, which they themselves have only recently mastered. More often, they are indulgently amused by the cute tangles children get themselves into when they try to explain something, or to define abstract notions or emotionally laden terms. This can become highly marketable entertainment, as demonstrated by the success of anthologies of children's letters to God or television comedy like 'Child's Play'. Furthermore, psychologists have added to the mistrust of children's ability to explain by publishing studies which show that their explanations are often inappropriate to the phenomenon in question (e.g., Piaget, 1929, 1930).

The ability to give and understand explanations is naturally of considerable educational importance. Explanation extends our understanding of the world, by moving beyond simple observation of events to the causal links underpinning them. Understanding a teacher's explanations, and also being able to have one's own attempts at explanation evaluated and discussed, are crucial processes in education. Consequently, if young children really do lack the ability to handle explanations, their capacity to benefit from the early years of schooling will be severely restricted.

In this chapter, we will look at what is known about children's use and understanding of explanations. As we will see, the ability to explain consists of both cognitive and linguistic components: the ability to understand a phenomenon; and the ability to communicate this understanding to others, usually, but not always, by using terms such as *because* and *so*. In the same way, understanding other people's explanations has both cognitive and linguistic components. Thus the study of children's explanations is not only an important topic in its own right; it also bears on more fundamental questions concerning the relationship between cognitive and linguistic development.

Piaget's Studies of Explanation

Piaget argues that a major advance in children's ability to explain occurs around the age of seven years, and he views this advance as being attributable to the decrease in egocentrism which marks the advent of operational thought. The picture which Piaget paints of young children's ability to explain is essentially a negative one. He claims that until the age of seven years 'causality and the faculty for explanation are still unexpressed' (Piaget, 1926: 49).

In support of this claim, Piaget presents evidence from several studies. We shall consider the two studies which he reports in most detail, and which were most systematically carried out: a sentence completion study (Piaget, 1928), and a series of studies in which an adult interviewed children about causal phenomena (Piaget, 1929, 1930). In addition, Piaget (1926) carried out an observational study of children's spontaneous speech, and a study in which children had to listen to a spoken explanation and then relay it to another person.

Piaget's sentence completion study involved asking seven- to nine-year-olds to write completions for each of the following written sentence fragments:

1   *I shan't go to school tomorrow, because. . . .*
2   *That man fell off his bicycle, because. . . .*
3   *Paul says he saw a little cat swallowing a big dog. His friend says that is impossible (or silly), because. . . .*
4   *Half nine is not four, because. . . .*

These items were designed to assess children's ability to handle explanations involving three different types of content: psychological (item 1), physical (item 2), and logical (items 3 and 4). Piaget defines psychological content as being concerned with actions, motives and intentions. Explanations with physical content draw on the laws of physical causality. Logical content involves rules, customs, or the classification of ideas. Piaget argues that the ability to handle psychological content develops before the ability to handle physical content, which in turn develops before the ablility to handle logical content. The findings from the sentence completion study seem to support this argument, in that performance was better on item (1) than on item (2), and performance on item (2) was better than on (3) and (4). However, the generalizability of these findings is questionable due to the very small number of items in each category. Indeed, the fact that performance varied between the two logical items suggests that factors other than the physical/psychological/logical distinction may be responsible for the variations in performance.

Piaget describes two types of error which children made in the sentence completion task. One type of error was to complete the sentence by referring to an effect instead of a cause, for example:

5   *That man fell off his bicycle, because he broke his leg.*

(We shall use asterisks to indicate incorrect sentences.)
Such errors are known as cause–effect inversions. Piaget views these inversions as evidence that children younger than seven years are confused about the meaning of *because*, and about the distinction between cause and effect: they do not know that *because* should introduce a cause rather than an effect. However, in drawing this conclusion, Piaget is giving undue emphasis to the more negative aspects of his results. In particular, he fails to comment on the fact that eighty-five per cent of the seven-year-olds passed item (1) – a fact which suggests that even younger children might have been capable of passing this item, especially if it had been presented in an oral rather than a written form. (Piaget did carry out an oral version of the task, but he does not report details of the results.)

The second error involves completing the sentence fragment with an inappropriate type of content. In particular, Piaget claims that young children tend to give psychological explanations – known as psychologizing – for physical and logical phenomena, such as:

6   *Half nine is not four, because he can't count.*

Further evidence of young children's tendency to psychologize comes from a series of studies in which Piaget (1929, 1930) interviewed children about the causes of various phenomena, such as dreams, the origin of the sun and the moon, the weather, the nature of air, the movement of the clouds, the floating of boats, and the workings of a steam-engine. As one would expect, young children do not give explanations of these phenomena which are correct from the point of view of modern scientific knowledge. However, Piaget claims that the children's explanations were not simply incorrect but were of the wrong type, in that the children tended to give psychological explanations for physical phenomena. Unfortunately, Piaget's accounts of these studies are rather lacking in frequency data so the extent to which the children psychologized is not clear. Also, the causes of the phenomena which Piaget asked the children to explain were not directly available to them. Thus it could be argued that children only psychologize as a last resort when they do not have ready access to information about plausible causal mechanisms. Several studies (Berzonsky, 1971; Morag Donaldson, 1986; Huang, 1943) have provided empirical support for this argument, and in doing so have produced a much more optimistic picture of young children's ability to explain.

A further point is that although Piaget implies that explanations which combine two types of content are always inappropriate, this is not in fact the case. For example, although item (2) in Piaget's sentence completion task is classed as a physical item, it could be appropriately completed with psychological content:

7   *That man fell of his bicycle, because he wanted to attract attention to himself.*

It appears that the content categories are actually rather more complex than Piaget proposed. We shall explore this issue more fully in the next section.

A Taxonomy of Explanations

Imagine that John throws a ball at a window and the window breaks. This sequence of events can give rise to several explanations depending on how we view the phenomenon. Consider the following:

8   *The window broke because John threw a ball at it.*
9   *John threw the ball because he wanted to break the window.*
10 *We know that the window broke because there is glass on the ground.*

In these examples, the speaker is aiming to answer different kinds of questions about the phenomenon. We shall categorize the explanations which result as being in different *modes*. In this chapter we will concentrate on three different modes of explanation, of which the above are examples; namely, the *empirical mode*, the *intentional mode* and the *deductive mode*.

The explanation in (8) is in the empirical mode. The speaker views the phenomenon as an event or state which can be explained in terms of another, temporally prior, event or state. This type of explanation would be an appropriate answer to a *why?* question (e.g., *Why did the window break?*) where *why?* is interpreted as meaning 'what happened to cause?'

Explanations in the intentional mode are also responses to *why?* questions, but in this case *why?* is interpreted as 'for what purpose?' Sentence (9) is an example of an intentional mode explanation. The speaker is viewing the phenomenon as an action (John throwing the ball) which can be explained in terms of the agent's intention to achieve a particular result (the window breaking).

Deductive mode explanations occur when the speaker views the phenomenon as a 'mental act' such as an idea, judgement or conclusion. The mental act is explained by referring to another mental act, or a rule, or a piece of evidence, as in (10). In giving an explanation in the deductive mode, the speaker is aiming to answer a *How do you know?* question (e.g., *How do you know the window broke?*).

The explanations in (8), (9) and (10) are concerned with physical events, but psychological phenomena can also give rise to explanations in different modes, as in (11), (12) and (13):

11   *John is happy because Mary has invited him to her party.* (Empirical mode)
12   *Mary invited John to her party because she wanted to cheer him up.* (Intentional mode)
13   *We know that John is happy because he is smiling.* (Deductive mode)

We noted earlier that Piaget distinguishes three types of causal relations: physical, psychological, and logical. However, it is not clear whether this distinction applies to the type of phenomenon or the way in which it is being explained. In this chapter, we shall describe the phenomenon being explained as either *physical* (as in (8), (9), (10)); *psychological* (as in (11), (12), (13)); or *logical*. And we shall describe the explanation itself as being in the *empirical* ((8), (11)), the *intentional* ((9), (12)) or the *deductive* ((10), (13)) mode.

We will now review evidence on children's ability to handle explanations in each mode.

Empirical Mode Explanations

We said earlier that the ability to distinguish between cause and effect is a fundamental component of the ability to explain. In the empirical mode, both the cause and the effect are events/states. Also, the event/state which is the cause occurs before the event/state which is the effect. This is known as *the principle of temporal priority* (or temporal precedence). These characteristics of the empirical mode raise two issues which have been explored in studies concentrating on the cognitive abilities underpinning this mode, namely:

a At what age are children able to distinguish between causes and effects?
b How is children's understanding of the cause/effect distinction related to their understanding of the temporal priority principle?

There is now considerable evidence that children are able to distinguish between causes and effects at a much earlier age than Piaget originally proposed – see the reviews by Bullock *et al.*, 1982; Sedlak and Kurtz, 1981; Shultz and Kestenbaum, 1985. For example, Bullock and Gelman (1979) found that even three-year-olds are able to distinguish between causes and effects. In their study, three- to five-year-old children observed causal sequences involving a Jack-in-the-box with two runways into the box. The causal sequences consisted of three events: a puppet dropped a marble down one runway, then Jack jumped, and then another puppet dropped a marble down the other runway. (Notice here that the 'causal relation' between the events is artificially contrived, and indeed the only basis for attributing causal status to the events is their temporal relation.) The children were asked to carry out various tasks, such as choosing the marble which made Jack jump and explaining their choices. The results indicated that even three-year-olds consistently selected the first event as the cause. However, temporal order was only rarely mentioned in the children's explanations of their judgements, indicating that children may not be particularly aware of the temporal order information on which they base their judgements.

Bullock and Gelman also included a condition in which temporal priority conflicted with spatial proximity as a basis for judging which event was the cause. They found that three-, four-, and five-year-olds based their judgements on temporal priority rather than spatial proximity. However, Sophian and Huber (1984) found that when the causal task involved a larger number of conflicting cues, three-year-olds did not consistently rely on temporal priority cues, whereas five-year-olds did.

When empirical mode explanations are given for naturally occurring causal sequences, causes do precede their effects, as was the case in the artificial experimental sequences. However, it can be questioned just how central this principle of temporal priority is to children's understanding of natural causal relations. Shultz and his colleagues (Shultz, 1982; Shultz and Kestenbaum, 1985; Shultz *et al.*, 1986) argue that rather than temporal priority, the most important principle in causal reasoning is that of generative transmission. They argue that causation involves one event (the cause) generating or producing another event (the effect), and that we can obtain direct knowledge about this causal generation: we do not have to infer causality on the basis of temporal priority. The generation of an effect by a cause occurs through some form of transmission (for example, of physical energy) between cause and effect. Shultz argues that our understanding of causality is based primarily on knowledge about the ways in which generative transmission occurs. In other words, we identify a particular event as the cause because we know how it could have made the effect happen, not because we know it happened before the effect. Consequently, Shultz *et al.* (1986) predict that children will be able to distinguish between causes and effects on the basis of information about generative transmission before they can do so on the basis of information about temporal priority.

In order to test this prediction, Shultz *et al.* carried out an experiment in which four-, eight-, and twelve-year-olds were asked to indicate which member of a pair of blocks had made the other block move. In the temporal priority condition, one of the blocks moved before the other block, but the string which connected the two blocks was screened from the children's view. Thus the children were provided with information about temporal priority but not about generative transmission. The converse situation applied in the generative transmission condition: the two blocks moved simultaneously (so there was no information about temporal priority) but the children could see the string connecting the two blocks (so there was information about how the cause generated the effect). Children in all the age groups systematically made correct use of generative transmission information, whereas only the eight- and twelve-year-olds showed the ability to make use of temporal priority information. Furthermore, Shultz *et al.* found that when eight-year-olds were asked to justify their judgements, they showed a strong tendency to refer to information about generative transmission, even in conditions where they were supplied only with information about temporal order.

When we turn to the linguistic abilities which are required to give empirical mode explanations, we find that the role of the temporal priority principle is again a matter of debate. In the empirical mode, the clause which immediately follows *because* describes a cause, whereas the clause which immediately follows *so* describes an effect. Moreover, the event described in the clause following *because* will have happened before that described in the main clause, whereas the event described in the clause following *so* will have happened after that described in the main clause. These points are illustrated in the following sentences:

14   *The cup broke because it fell off the table.*

15   *Because the cup fell off the table, it broke.*
16   *The cup fell off the table so it broke.*

If children do not understand this distinction between *because* and *so*, then they will be likely to produce errors, known as cause–effect inversions, such as:

17   **The cup fell off the table because it broke.*

Similarly, children who do not understand the meaning of the causal connectives will be likely to confuse cause and effect in their comprehension of other people's causal explanations.

As we saw earlier, Piaget argued that children do not understand the directional component of the causal connectives' meaning until the age of about seven years (i.e., they do not understand that *B because A* and *A because B* mean different things). Several more recent studies have provided support for Piaget's argument (Bebout *et al.*, 1980; Corrigan, 1975; Emerson, 1979; Emerson and Gekoski, 1980; Epstein, 1972; Kuhn and Phelps, 1976). However, other studies have challenged Piaget's argument by showing that even three-year-olds are able to use causal connectives correctly and rarely produce cause–effect inversions (Hood, 1977; McCabe and Peterson, 1985; French and Nelson, 1985; Morag Donaldson, 1986). This discrepancy in results coincides with methodological differences between the two groups of studies. The studies which support Piaget's argument fall into two main categories: metalinguistic tasks and comprehension experiments. In contrast, most of the studies which challenge Piaget's argument are observational studies of children's production.

This discrepancy between good performance in spontaneous speech and poor performance in metalinguistic tasks and comprehension experiments is not without precedent in the child language literature (e.g. Bloom, 1974; Chapman and Miller, 1975; Margaret Donaldson, 1978; Morag Donaldson, 1980; Hoenigmann-Stovall, 1982; Tunmer and Grieve, 1984). There are several possible explanations for such discrepancies. (For an extended discussion, see Morag Donaldson, 1986.) For example, the linguistic representations guiding comprehension might be distinct from those guiding production and those guiding metalinguistic judgements. Alternatively, the discrepancies might be due to characteristics of the tasks used to assess the different types of linguistic ability. In particular, most metalinguistic and comprehension tasks are examples of what Margaret Donaldson (1978) refers to as 'disembedded tasks', and as such are likely to prove difficult for young children. Success on such tasks is dependent on children's ability to accept the task as defined by the adult. They have to be able to set aside their own intentions, purposes, experiences, and expectations. They have to consider the task in its own right. In the case of metalinguistic and comprehension tasks, the disembedded quality of the tasks is often related to the requirement that children think about particular words or phrases in isolation from their linguistic and non-linguistic contexts, and in isolation from their usual communicative functions. Furthermore, the design of a comprehension experiment reflects the experimenter's assumptions about the type of knowledge which is required in order to 'understand' a particular word. Thus children may fail the task because their knowledge does not match the adult's assumptions. We shall argue that, in the case of causal connectives, most comprehension experiments have assessed children's understanding of temporal order rather than causal direction. To see how this argument applies, let us consider an example of a comprehension experiment in some detail.

Emerson (1979) presented six- to eleven-year-olds with a picture-sequence task. For each item, the children heard a causal sentence (e.g., *The snowman started to melt because the sun started to shine*), and were shown two picture-strips. Each picture-strip depicted both of the events referred to by the sentence, and the two strips differed only with respect to the order in which the events were depicted. For example, in one strip the picture of the sun shining came first (i.e., on the left), and the picture of the snowman melting came second, whereas in the other strip the pictures were arranged in the opposite order. Half of the sentences were of the form *B because A* (as in the above example), and half were of the form *Because A, B* (e.g., *Because the sun started to shine, the snowman started to melt*). The children's task was to choose the picture-strip which 'goes with the sentence'. Emerson found that the youngest group of subjects (5;8 to 6;7) did not succeed on this task, but that the older groups of subjects (7;6 to 8;6 and 9;7 to 10;11) did. On the basis of these results, Emerson argued that children do not understand the directional component of the causal connectives' meaning until the age of about seven or eight years.

What Emerson demonstrated was that her younger children had difficulty in using the causal connective as a clue to the temporal order of the events described. In the examples she used, which were all in the empirical mode, it was the case that the event following *because* was the one which happened first. However, as we shall see, in other modes, *because* does not necessarily introduce the first event. The relationship between the causal connective and the temporal order of the events is therefore complex, and depends on the mode of explanation. On the other hand, it is always the case that the clause following *because* will refer to the cause of the phenomenon of interest. Young children may well appreciate this before they have sorted out the relation between connective, mode, and temporal order.

This leads us to propose the 'causal direction hypothesis': children learn about the role of causal connectives as indicators of which event is cause and which effect before they learn about their role as indicators of which event happened first. They learn that *because* introduces the cause, rather than the effect, before they learn that in certain circumstances, *because* introduces the event which happened first. Thus it is proposed that they will understand the directional component of the meaning of *because* in connection with the distinction between cause and effect (viz. the causal direction), before they understand the directional component of its meaning in connection with temporal order.

This hypothesis predicts that children will perform worse on tasks which require them to make use of information about temporal order than on tasks which allow them to make use of information about causal direction. It also raises the possibility that the younger children in Emerson's task may indeed have understood that there is a directional component to the meaning of *because*, but that this was based on a grasp of causal direction and not the temporal priority for which Emerson was testing. In other words, this may be a case in which the children fail the task because their knowledge about a word's meaning does not match the experimenter's assumptions about it.

According to the causal direction hypothesis, Emerson's task is disembedded in that it requires children to consider causal connectives in a way which differs from their usual communicative function. When a speaker uses *because* in normal conversation, it is likely that her intention is to communicate information about causal direction – she wants to inform the hearer that the event mentioned after *because* is the cause. If the speaker's main intention was to communicate information about temporal order, she would be more likely to use a temporal connective such as *before*, *after* or *then* than to use a causal connective. In other words, the primary communicative function of causal connectives is to signal causal direction. Emerson's task requires children to respond on the basis of the causal connectives' secondary function of conveying information about temporal order. Thus, it is difficult for children to relate the task to their own communicative intentions. Furthermore, the causal direction hypothesis is consistent with the argument of Shultz *et al.* (1986) that, as far as causal reasoning is concerned, the generative transmission principle is more fundamental than the temporal priority principle.

In order to test the causal direction hypothesis, Morag Donaldson (1986) carried out an experiment with five-, eight- and ten-year-olds. The children received either a task which required them to make use of temporal order information (the temporal task), or a task which allowed them to make use of causal direction information (the causal task). The causal direction hypothesis predicts that performance will be better on the causal task than on the temporal task.

The items for both tasks were based on sequences of three events, A, B, and C, which were chosen so that A caused B, and B caused C (e.g., Coco pushes a cup; the cup falls; the cup breaks). The same sequences were used for each task and video-tapes were made of each sequence. For the causal task, the child was shown a video sequence (ABC). Then the child heard a sentence fragment of the form *B because* ... (e.g., *The cup falls because* ...) and presented with two single pictures of A and C. The child's task was to choose the appropriate picture and complete the sentence. In the temporal task, the child was given a sentence of the form *B because A* (e.g., *The cup falls because Coco pushes it*), and shown two static picture-strips with a picture of event A either to the right or to the left of a picture of event B (the order BA, or the order AB). As in Emerson's study, the child's task was to choose the picture-strip which matched the sentence.

In both the causal task and the temporal task the children were also given items using *so* instead of *because*. The main difference between the two tasks was that the causal task required a choice between two different events (the cause and the effect of B), whereas the temporal task required a choice between two different event-orders.

Table 3.1 shows the mean number of correct responses given by each age group. These results support the causal direction hypothesis, since performance is significantly better on the causal task than on the temporal task for each age group. Also, the findings for the causal task indicate that even five-year-olds have some knowledge of the directional component of the causal connectives' meaning, in that their mean score is considerably higher than the score (of 8) which one would expect if they were simply responding at chance level. Their performance on *because* items was particularly good. (For further details, see Morag Donaldson, 1986.)

In summary, the evidence from causal connective studies indicates that from the age of three years children have some understanding of the directional component of the causal connectives' meaning. They appreciate that *B because A* and *A because B* are different in meaning, and this understanding is probably based on causal direction rather than temporal order. There is therefore not a large discrepancy

Table 3.1. *Mean number of correct responses for each age group (maximum 16).*

Age (years)	Causal task	Temporal task	Difference*
5	12.12	7.38	$p < 0.001$
8	13.12	8.19	$p < 0.001$
10	14.81	10.94	$p < 0.001$

* The significance levels are based on 1-tailed Mann–Whitney U tests.

between studies of children's linguistic abilities in this area, and studies of their cognitive abilities which show that three-year-olds are able to distinguish between causes and effects.

Intentional Mode Explanations

Here we need to consider sequences consisting of three elements:

reason (e.g., *John wants the car to go*)

action (e.g., *John winds up the car*)

result (e.g., *The car goes*).

Explanations in the intentional mode express the relation between the action and the reason (e.g., *John wound up the car because he wanted it to go*). However, since the reason corresponds to the agent's intention to achieve the result, intentional explanations include a reference to the result of the action. This gives intentional explanations a forward-looking quality which contrasts with the backward-looking quality of empirical explanations. Consequently, in the intentional mode, there is a complex relationship between causal direction and temporal order.

The task of dealing with explanations in the intentional mode imposes both cognitive and linguistic demands on the child. It is cognitively demanding in that the child has to distinguish between the reason and the result, despite the fact that they are interdependent. Indeed, in some situations, the child may have to exploit this interdependence to infer the reason on the basis of information about the result, while continuing to maintain the reason/result distinction. To do this, the child requires considerable cognitive flexibility and a good understanding of the concept of intention. The task of dealing with intentional explanations is also linguistically demanding in that children have to show that they have maintained the reason/result distinction by using a linguistic construction which is appropriate to the intentional mode, such as:

18   *John wound up the toy car to make it go.*
19   *John wound up the toy car because he wanted it to go.*
20   *John wound up the toy car so (that) it would go.*

Despite these cognitive and linguistic demands, there are grounds for predicting that young children will be able to handle intentional explanations. In particular, Margaret Donaldson (1978) argues that young children's cognitive and linguistic abilities are at their best in tasks involving intentions, motives or purposes, since such tasks make 'human sense'. Piaget would have agreed that intentions are particularly salient to the young child. However, he devalued the ability to reason about intentions as he regarded it as an immature form of causal reasoning. Yet the above analysis implies that intentional mode explanations are, if anything, more complex cognitively and linguistically than empirical mode explanations.

Shultz and his associates carried out a series of studies to investigate children's understanding of intentions. They found that from the age of three years, children were able to distinguish correctly between intended actions and mistakes (Shultz, 1980). In addition, five-year-olds were able to distinguish intended actions from reflexes and passive behaviours (Shultz, 1980); to distinguish between intending to carry out an act and intending to achieve a consequence (Shultz and Shamash, 1981); and to disguise their intentions deliberately from other people (Shultz and Cloghesy, 1981).

Thus by the age of five years, children have a good grasp of the concept of intention. But the question still remains – do young children actually view intentions as causes of actions? Shultz (1982) argues that they do. Specifically, he argues that intentions are a form of generative transmission, and that children's causal reasoning about actions (like their causal reasoning about events) is based on knowledge of generative transmission. Shultz supports this argument with evidence that children use certain rules in deciding whether or not behaviour is intentional (Shultz and Wells, 1985; Shultz et al., 1980). In particular, Shultz and Wells (1985) propose a matching rule which specifies that if the result matches the intention, then the result was intended. They found that even three-year-olds were able to use the matching rule in a task which involved judging whether an agent had meant to achieve a particular result. Moreover, children gave precedence to the matching rule in situations where it conflicted with another rule.

In making use of the matching rule, children are comparing the intention with the result, and so they are showing the ability to coordinate these two components of a behavioural sequence. Further evidence that three-year-olds are able to integrate intention and outcome information is provided by Yuill (1984), who asked children to make judgements about a story character's degree of satisfaction with various outcomes. She found that even three-year-olds judged a character to be more pleased when the result of his action matched his intention than when there was a mismatch between the intention and the result. Moreover, the findings from Stein and Trabasso's (1982) study of children's understanding of stories suggest that five-year-olds are able to use the matching rule to infer an intention from information about a result.

We have seen that young children have considerable understanding of intentions, and of the relationships between intentions, actions and results. Such understanding is an important component of the ability to give and understand explanations in the intentional mode, but it is not sufficient in itself. Linguistic abilities are also required.

A study by Astington (1986) explored children's understanding of linguistic expressions of intention, such as *means to, is going to, wants to,* and *intended to.* Astington found that it was not until the age of nine years that the majority of children gave consistently correct responses. However, in her experiment, the children's task was to match the linguistic expressions of intention with pictures which were designed to depict intentions. As Astington herself acknowledges, intentions cannot be readily depicted. It may well be that children younger than nine years have difficulty picking up information about intentions from pictures.

Let us now look in detail at the linguistic abilities required to handle intentional mode explanations. Sentences in the intentional mode (such as (18), (19), and (20)) express a reason–action relation, and the verb which is used to refer to the result of the action occurs in its non-finite form (e.g., *go*). This contrasts with sentences in the empirical mode which express an action–result relation, and in which a finite verb form (*went*) is used to refer to the result of the action:

21 *The toy car went because John wound it up.*
22 *John wound up the toy car so it went.*

If children fail to observe this distinction between the empirical and intentional modes, then they will tend to produce cause–effect inversions, such as:

23   *John wound up the toy car because it went.*

A further linguistic demand is that children have to distinguish between *because* and *so* constructions within the intentional mode. In a *because* sentence, the reason is expressed by using a phrase which refers to the agent's desire or aim (e.g., *wanted to*), whereas in a *so* sentence the reason is expressed by using a modal construction (e.g., *would*), which refers to the predicted result of the action. Again, failure to observe this distinction will result in cause–effect inversions:

24   *John wound up the toy car so he wanted it to go.*
25   *John wound up the toy car because it would go.*

(It should be noted that the distinction between correct and inverted sentences is complex, and related to the mode of explanation. In particular, inversions such as (24) can sometimes become acceptable if they are interpreted as being in a different mode, such as the deductive mode.)

Studies of children's comprehension of causal connectives have tended to concentrate on the empirical mode. On the other hand, studies of children's spontaneous production have revealed that most of the causal sentences which children produce refer to intentions (Hood, 1977; McCabe and Peterson, 1985). This suggests, once again, that comprehension experiments may have been looking in the wrong place for evidence of young children's linguistic competence.

Morag Donaldson (1986) carried out a study which assessed five- and eight-year-old children's ability to handle intentional mode explanations in an experimental setting. The subjects received two tasks (on different days): a questions task and a sentence completion task. For each item in both tasks, the child was presented with two pictures and was told a story about the pictures. The top picture depicted an action (e.g., John winding up the toy car), and the lower picture depicted a result of the action (e.g., the car going). In the questions task, the child was required to answer a *why?* question about the action (*Why did John wind up the car?*). In the sentence completion task, the child was asked to complete a sentence fragment which described the action and which ended in *because* or *so* (*John wound up the car because/so . . .*). The agent's intention was not explicitly mentioned in the story, nor was there any attempt to depict it (e.g., by making the agent look excessively pleased in the second picture). Thus the task required the children to infer the intention, on the basis of knowledge of the result and of the action–result relation, while at the same time maintaining the distinction between the intention and the result. In addition, the children had to show that they had maintained the intention/result distinction by using a linguistic construction appropriate to the intentional mode.

The results indicate that five- and eight-year-olds are able to cope with all of these cognitive and linguistic demands. In the questions task, eighty-one per cent of the five-year-olds' responses, and eighty-two per cent of the eight-year-olds' responses, were well-formed intentional explanations. The corresponding results for the sentence completion task were sixty-five per cent and eighty-three per cent. In the questions task, both age groups showed a strong preference for expressing intentional explanations by means of the infinitive construction (e.g., *John wound up the toy car to make it go*). Nevertheless, the children also demonstrated an ability to use *because* and *so* constructions appropriately. As Table 3.2 shows, the children produced more well-formed *because* and *so* sentences in the intentional mode than inversions. Although the inversion rate was low for both age groups, it was significantly lower for the eight-year-olds than for the five-year-olds.

Table 3.2. *Comparison between mean of inversions and well-formed intentional sentences using 'because' or 'so' (maximum 12).*

	Inversions	Intentional sentences
Questions		
5 years	0.75	3.42
8 years	0.21	4.79
Sentence completion		
5 years	1.40	6.80
8 years	0.65	8.10

These results confirm previous findings which indicate that young children have a good understanding of the concept of intention, and are able to reason about intentions and results simultaneously. But Donaldson's results extend these previous findings by showing that young children also have considerable linguistic abilities. The five-year-olds in her experiment showed not only the ability to use causal connectives in the intentional mode, but also the ability to use linguistic expressions which refer to intentions, such as *wanted to* and *was going to*. Thus young children have both the cognitive and the linguistic ability to explain actions in terms of intentions.

Deductive Mode Explanations

An explanation in the deductive mode is an explanation of a 'mental act' (idea/judgement/conclusion) in terms of another mental act, or a rule, or a piece of evidence. The contrast between the empirical and deductive modes is illustrated by the following sentences:

26   *The window broke because a ball hit it.* (Empirical)
27   *We can tell that the window broke because there is glass on the ground.*
     (Deductive)

In the empirical mode sentence, (26), one event (the window breaking) is explained in terms of another event (the ball hitting the window). In the deductive mode sentence, (27), a conclusion (that the window broke) is explained in terms of a piece of observable evidence (there is glass on the ground). As these examples show, a particular phenomenon (e.g., the window breaking) can be regarded either as an event, or as the subject-matter of a conclusion. Similarly, the phenomenon which is treated as evidence in the deductive explanation (e.g., there is glass on the ground) can also be treated as an effect in an empirical explanation:

28   *The window broke so there is glass on the ground.*

Indeed, the speaker's knowledge of the cause–effect relation described in (28) forms the basis for the inference described in (27). The deductive mode (like the intentional mode) is both dependent on and distinct from the empirical mode.

Sentences in the deductive mode sometimes contain deductive markers, such as *we can tell that, know that, think, must, might,* or *perhaps.* Deductive markers provide a linguistic means of signalling the deductive/empirical distinction: they signal that what follows should be interpreted as a conclusion rather than as a description of an event/state. However, it seems that deductive markers are optional and can sometimes be omitted from deductive explanations, as in:

29   *The window broke because there is glass on the ground.*

This sentence could be regarded as an elliptical version of the deductive explanation given in (27). Alternatively, sentence (29) could be regarded as an incorrect empirical explanation. In other words, such sentences are potentially ambiguous. It is likely that in normal discourse, the context of the sentences will help to resolve these potential ambiguities.

In order to handle deductive mode explanations, children require various cognitive and linguistic abilities. They have to be able to distinguish between the empirical and deductive modes. This involves understanding the distinction between cause–effect relations and evidence–conclusion relations. It also involves understanding the linguistic cues (deductive markers) which can be used to signal the empirical/deductive distinction. Within the deductive mode, children have to be able to distinguish between conclusions and evidence, and they have to know that *so* introduces the conclusion whereas *because* introduces the evidence.

Morag Donaldson (1986) carried out two experiments to explore the extent to which five-, eight-, and ten-year-old children possess these cognitive and linguistic abilities. The deductive/empirical experiment assessed children's ability to distinguish between the deductive and empirical modes on the basis of linguistic cues provided by the adult. The deductive marking experiment investigated the extent to which children take account of the deductive/empirical distinction in their use of language when they are cued into the deductive mode by the context.

In the deductive/empirical experiment, each child received either a questions task or a sentence completion task. The items for both tasks were based on sequences consisting of three elements, such as:

A = Mary hit John with the pillow.

B = The pillow burst.

C = Mary is covered in feathers.

In each sequence, A is the cause of B, and C is evidence that B occurred (and is also the effect of B). The children were presented with two coloured pictures depicting A and C. In the questions task, children were asked deductive questions of the form:

The pillow burst, didn't it? How do you know the pillow burst?

(Expected answer: *Because Mary is covered in feathers*);

and empirical questions of the form:

The pillow burst, didn't it? Why did the pillow burst?

(Expected answer: *Because Mary hit John with the pillow*).

In the sentence completion task, children were asked to complete sentence fragments which, for deductive items, were of the form:

>   *We can tell that the pillow burst because . . .*
>
>   (Expected answer: *Mary is covered in feathers*),

and, for empirical items, were of the form:

>   *The pillow burst because . . .*
>
>   (Expected answer: *Mary hit John with the pillow*).

Both tasks were designed to assess children's ability to respond to some of the linguistic cues which can be used to signal the deductive/empirical distinction. The results presented in Table 3.3 show that, on the whole, the children performed very well on the empirical items. There were no significant age effects for these items in either task. This is consistent with the results we reported earlier showing good performance on the causal task (see Table 3.1).

However, on the deductive items, the children had more difficulty. There were significant age effects in both tasks on these items, and many of the children in the two younger age groups failed to distinguish between deductive and empirical items and treated them all as if they were empirical items. Similar results were obtained by Trabasso *et al.* (1981). They found that five-year-olds and nine-year-olds showed a tendency to respond to *How can you tell that?* questions by referring to a cause rather than to evidence, though this tendency was less strong for their nine-year-olds than for their five-year-olds.

From these results, it would appear that the younger children were not able to pick up the linguistic cues to the deductive/empirical distinction contained in the experimenter's questions. Would they make these distinctions in their own speech when given the oppor-

Table 3.3. *Mean number of correct items for each age group in the deductive/empirical experiment (maximum 16).*

	Empirical	Deductive items
Questions		
5 years	15.25	3.50
8 years	15.38	8.12
10 years	15.19	10.31
Sentence completion		
5 years	13.50	7.19
8 years	13.38	8.06
10 years	14.19	11.75

tunity to do so? The deductive marking experiment was designed to answer this question.

A different group of five-, eight- and ten-year-old children took part in the deductive marking experiment. It was presented to them as a detective game in which they were encouraged to help the Pink Panther to solve some mysteries. For example, the children were shown four pictures in each of which a cloaked and hooded figure was committing a 'crime', namely, stealing flowers out of a garden, eating a cake, breaking into a jeweller's shop, and painting red spots on a fence. The children were introduced to a toy Pink Panther who, they were told, had caught the culprits but did not know who had committed which crime. The children were then to be given clues to help them solve the mysteries and they were to tell the Pink Panther (who was not privy to this information) who had committed which crime. The clues consisted of four pictures: Snoopy with cream on his face, Charlie Brown with red paint on his hands, Donald Duck with muddy feet, and Mickey Mouse with a necklace sticking out of his pocket. For each item, the children either had to complete a sentence, such as

Snoopy has cream on his face so . . . ,

or they were given a description of the clue, such as

The clue is that Snoopy has cream on his face,

and were asked to tell the Pink Panther about the clue and what they had worked out. These were referred to as the *sentence completion condition* and the *open-ended condition* respectively. (Other similar tasks were given to the children and these are described in Morag Donaldson, 1986.)

The question of interest was whether the children would use deductive markers and causal connectives appropriately in these circumstances. It was also important to establish whether adults would use deductive markers in these contexts, and so a written version of the tasks was given to a group of undergraduates.

The results for both tasks indicated that deductive markers were frequently omitted by all age groups, including the adults. Fewer than half the responses from each group contained deductive markers, and in the open-ended task fewer than half the responses in each group contained causal connectives. The five-year-olds were less prolific than the other groups in producing either deductive markers or causal connectives. When the eight- and ten-year-olds did produce causal connectives, they used them in a way appropriate to the deductive mode, by using *because* to introduce evidence and *so* to introduce a conclusion.

It would appear from these results that children's grasp of the deductive mode is less secure than their grasp of the empirical and intentional modes. Five-year-olds did not show much understanding of the deductive/empirical distinction at all, even in the deductive marking experiment. Eight-year-olds were beginning to acknowledge the distinction, in that when they used the causal connectives in the deductive mode they appropriately followed *because* with evidence and *so* with a conclusion. However, even the ten-year-olds were still having difficulty in responding to the linguistic cues to the deductive mode, as was shown by the deductive/empirical experiment. This difficulty may be related to the fact that deductive markers are optional – they were frequently omitted by both children and adults in the deductive marking experiment. Thus it may be that children are not accustomed to relying on purely linguistic cues to the deductive mode.

Explanation in School

As we noted earlier, explanation plays a central role in education. Teachers spend a substantial amount of time giving explanations. Flanders (1970) found that, on average, two-thirds of classroom time is taken up with the teacher talking, and two-thirds of this talk consists of lecturing or explaining. Furthermore, there is evidence that pupils regard the ability to give clear explanations as being the most important quality of the 'ideal teacher' (Wragg and Wood, 1984), and that the clarity of a teacher's explanations is indeed positively associated with her pupils' educational achievement (Good and Grouws, 1977). (For a review of such evidence, see Brown and Atkins, 1986.) In addition to giving explanations, teachers try to elicit explanations from their pupils by asking questions. Like explanations, questions figure prominently in classroom interactions. One of the most typical structures in classroom dialogue is the teacher asking a question, a pupil responding, and the teacher evaluating the pupil's response (Sinclair and Coulthard, 1974; Stubbs, 1976).

In view of the educational importance of explanation, it is surprising that so little research has focused directly on the development of children's ability to give and understand explanations; or on how children actually cope with explanations in the classroom. So far, we have discussed evidence which is particularly relevant to the first of these issues, but which also has implications for the second. We have seen that by the time children start school they have developed the basic cognitive and linguistic abilities required for handling explanations in the empirical and intentional modes. While this evidence does not necessarily imply that children will always cope with empirical and intentional explanations in the classroom, it does imply that failure to do so is likely to be due to factors other than children lacking an understanding of causality, of intentionality, or of the causal connectives.

The nature of classroom interaction is one factor which may affect children's ability to cope with explanations in the classroom. It has frequently been observed that many classroom interactions do not conform to the rules of normal conversation, and this applies particularly to teachers' use of questions (e.g., Barnes, 1969; Stubbs, 1976; Edwards, 1980). Typically, teachers ask questions not because they do not know the answers, but because they want to test their pupils' knowledge. Furthermore, the teacher will often have a specific 'correct' answer in mind. The pupils perceive their task as being to figure out what the teacher is 'getting at', and so classroom interactions can become elaborate guessing games. In everyday conversation, speakers usually ask questions in order to extend their knowledge. Questions are asked by people who lack a particular piece of knowledge, and questions are addressed to people who are assumed to be more knowledgeable about that topic. But in the classroom, the roles are often reversed: the person who asks the questions is the one who is assumed to be more knowledgeable.

Research into classroom interaction has not focused directly on children's explanations. However, since explanations can be regarded as responses to explicit or implicit questions, the research into the pragmatics of questioning in the classroom provides hints about the pragmatics of explanation in the classroom. In particular, it suggests that many of the explanations which children produce at school will be produced in response to the teacher's test questions, and so will serve to display rather than transmit knowledge. Again, there is likely to be a mismatch between the function of explanations in the classroom and the function of explanations in everyday conversation.

Explanations can serve a variety of functions. Two functions of particular interest are: 'sharing' and 'displaying'. These functions relate to the speaker's reasons for making public his understanding. An explanation has a sharing function if the speaker is producing it in order to share his knowledge with other people, and so extend their understanding. Explanations which are produced in order to demonstrate that the speaker possesses a particular piece of knowledge have a displaying function.

It can be argued that the central function of explanations is the sharing function. There is an obvious social motive behind explanations with a sharing function. In Margaret Donaldson's terms, such explanations are produced for reasons which make 'human sense'. Explanations which are produced in normal conversation are likely to have a sharing function. In contrast, many of the explanations which are produced in the classroom have a displaying function. Such explanations tend to emphasize the possession of knowledge for its own sake.

Explanations in each of the three modes (empirical, intentional, and deductive) can serve either a sharing or a displaying function. However, there seems to be a particularly close relationship between the displaying function and the deductive mode, in that both turn the spotlight on to the speaker's knowledge, and so have a more 'reflexive' quality than the other explanations. An explanation in any mode will have a displaying function if it is produced to demonstrate what the speaker knows. Deductive mode explanations are explanations of this knowledge. Thus deductive mode explanations which have a displaying function are being used to demonstrate knowledge about knowledge. In other words, they demonstrate not only that you know, but that you know how you know! Such explanations are highly disembedded, and, like other aspects of disembedded thinking, they are of considerable educational significance, since they provide a means of checking that pupils actually understand what they are doing, and not just giving correct answers through chance, imitation, or rote learning.

Earlier, we saw that children have more difficulty with deductive explanations than with empirical or intentional explanations. Given the educational importance of deductive explanations, it is important to consider some possible reasons for the children's difficulty. One possibility would be that the children lacked the ability to think about epistemic states, such as knowing, thinking and believing. However, several recent studies have shown that the ability to reason about and talk about epistemic states develops before the age of five years (Abbeduto and Rosenberg, 1985; Perner and Leekam, 1986; Shatz *et al.*, 1983). On the other hand, there is an interesting parallel between the five-year-olds' poor performance in the deductive mode experiments and Wimmer and Perner's (1983) finding that the ability to reason about another person's false belief develops between the ages of four and six years. Wimmer and Perner argue that this ability

involves the ability to represent the relationship between two conflicting beliefs. Since deductive explanations are most natural in
situations where speakers encounter (or anticipate) a conflict between
their own and someone else's beliefs, it may well be that the ability to
represent the relationship between two conflicting beliefs helps
children appreciate the need for deductive explanations.

This brings us back to the importance of considering the functions
which explanations serve in particular contexts. In the deductive
marking experiment there was not a conflict of beliefs, so the
five-year-olds' performance might have been due to the fact that the
context did not highlight the need for a deductive explanation. On the
other hand, the context created in the deductive marking experiment
did involve the child having knowledge which the addressee (the
Pink Panther) lacked, and so it was probably more conducive to the
production of deductive explanations than many of the contexts
children encounter in school.

It is being argued that children's explanations will be at their best in
situations which conform to the normal rules of discourse. In a school
setting, it may be possible to approximate to such situations by
encouraging peer learning groups and discussions in which the
teacher assumes a facilitatory role rather than a didactic role. Future
research could profitably explore the nature of children's explanations in a range of classroom contexts.

Concluding Comments

The material presented in this chapter echoes some of the themes
developed by Margaret Donaldson in *Children's Minds* (1978). One of
these themes is that Piaget seriously over-estimated the extent to
which young children are egocentric. As we saw earlier, Piaget
argued that children younger than seven years lack the ability to
explain, and he sees this as yet another symptom of their egocentrism. However, the more recent evidence reviewed in this chapter
clearly indicates that children are able to give and understand
explanations well before the age of seven years. This evidence, like
the evidence discussed in *Children's Minds*, provides support for the
argument that young children are not nearly as egocentric as Piaget
claimed.

A related theme in *Children's Minds* is that young children often
perform less well on experimental tasks than in more natural situations. This theme is echoed by the discrepancy in results between

experimental and observational studies of children's knowledge of causal connectives.

The theme of 'human sense' is particularly central to Margaret Donaldson's argument. She argues that young children's cognitive and linguistic abilities can be seen at their best in situations involving intentions, motives, or purposes – situations which make human sense. As this argument would lead one to expect, children showed considerable cognitive and linguistic abilities in handling intentional mode explanations, despite their complexity.

The converse of the 'human sense' theme is the 'disembedded task' theme: young children are likely to have difficulty with tasks which are divorced from human sense. Yet, as Margaret Donaldson points out, the ability to cope with disembedded tasks is crucial to educational success. In other words, young children's area of weakness coincides with an area of considerable educational importance. Again, a similar picture emerges regarding children's explanations. Children are less competent at handling explanations in the deductive mode than in the empirical or intentional modes, yet deductive explanations are likely to be particularly important in educational contexts.

Although studies of children's explanations have identified some weaknesses, the overall picture, as with many other aspects of cognitive and linguistic development, is of an extremely competent five-year-old who has the basic cognitive and linguistic abilities for giving and understanding explanations of events and actions.

4 Children's Communication

Peter Lloyd
University of Manchester

This chapter will focus on the capacity of children to use language as a vehicle for communication once they reach school age. Like most previously published research in this area, attention will be confined to primary school children aged between five and ten years.

Before outlining the scope of the chapter, a word is in order about the term 'communication'. When people communicate, they are not, of course, restricted to verbal language. Moreover, it has been argued that whenever two or more people are together it is impossible not to communicate. Silence itself is a form of communication, and the many ways in which human beings can send 'messages' by way of gesture, facial expressions, and non-linguistic sounds (the deep sigh much favoured by the late British comedian, Tony Hancock, is a good example) have been well documented. Furthermore, verbal communication, the prime way of exchanging meaning between human beings who have acquired spoken language, is almost invariably accompanied by communication in non-verbal channels. Recognition of this fact will emerge in some of the criticism to be offered of much work in this field. Nevertheless, the focus of the chapter will be on verbal communication, since this is an area in which interesting and important developments appear to be taking place during the primary school years.

I start by reviewing research in the field known as referential communication, in which children are required to use language to help each other identify particular items, and then go on to outline some limitations in the standard experimental approach used in this area, drawing heavily on the work of Margaret Donaldson. It will be argued that if studies of communication are to be artificially restricted to the verbal channel, then a medium that does this 'naturally' like the telephone should be used. A further case will be made that the standard speaker and listener measures used in referential communication research neglect a host of linguistic and pragmatic features which contribute centrally to the negotiation of verbal meaning. Some work of my own which uses the telephone and takes advantage of recent advances in discourse analysis will be presented, and the idea of a communicative support system will be put forward as a possible explanation of the findings obtained. This idea links closely both to Donaldson's notion of embedded and disembedded thought and to Vygotsky's demand that we look at the total context in which information is exchanged and understood. It also helps create links between the additional context of the experiment and the real-life world of the classroom.

Studies of Referential Communication

Historically, work on verbal communication between children has taken place in two traditions, naturalistic and experimental. Both of these found expression in an early landmark in the area, Piaget's *Language and Thought of the Child* (1926/1959). Piaget's experimental studies required children to recount a story they had heard, or explain the working of an instrument such as a tap. His results showed that children below the age of seven years did not structure their stories or explanations coherently, nor did they keep in mind the extent of the listener's ignorance. This basic defect, also found in his naturalistic study of spontaneous dialogue among kindergarten children, was called 'egocentrism' by Piaget. Egocentrism manifests itself in communicative terms as an inability to take account of another's point of view; instead, the world is seen rigidly from the standpoint of the self. Since effective communication is to be regarded as an essentially cooperative enterprise (Grice, 1975), egocentrism would be an overwhelming handicap. If children were egocentric, the capacity to sustain an effective dialogue would be impossible, for this requires the ability to switch speaker and listener roles constantly, to monitor the effects of one's messages, and to modify them according to feedback received from the listener. Listeners have to recognize that for them, too, communication is an active process, requiring them to relate the utterance to the context obtaining and to signal any inadequacy or comprehension failure when it occurs.

There has been a wealth of research charting the development of these skills. The area is known as referential communication, as the role of the speaker is to describe verbally a given object (or, more rarely, an action or relationship), so that the listener, relying entirely on the language received, can work out what the message refers to. In the standard paradigm the two communicators are seated at a table opposite one another but separated by a screen so as to restrict communication to the verbal channel. The task is for the speaker to select and describe one of a series of items so that the listener is able to identify the chosen item from an identical set. No limits are placed on what the participants can say, and the experimenter is able to control the complexity of the stimulus array in terms of the size and number of varying attributes. This paradigm can be used to study child–child communication, but it can also be used in a more controlled fashion, in which the experimenter takes the role of one participant in order to control more precisely one side of the communication process.

Early studies in this area focused on the child's ability to enact speaker and listener roles. The initial emphasis was on speakers and their ability to encode messages sufficiently clearly to enable listeners to identify the target object. It was recognized that accurate message construction presupposed the capacity to identify the critical features of an item – that is, those features that uniquely identified the target. Speakers who were unaware of or unable to select and then transmit these differentiating features were clearly going to be ineffective communicators. It was further noted that when asked, either directly or indirectly, to provide further information, young school-aged children proved poor at responding. Their standard reaction was to repeat the initial description without modification. However, it has been shown (Lloyd and Beveridge, 1981) that when the task is within the child's realm of experience (familiar objects varying on comprehensible features such as size, form, and colour), and when paired with adult listeners who provide optimal feedback, even the preschool child is capable of repairing inadequate messages, leading ultimately to successful communication. A similar finding has been reported with the child in the listener mode (Lloyd and Beveridge, 1981). When presented with adequate messages, even though they may contain only the minimal information necessary to locate the target, young children are capable of the necessary perceptual discrimination and message decoding to perform effectively as listeners.

Following the demonstration that children could achieve various levels of skill in referential communication tasks, attention became increasingly directed at the reasons for the relatively limited success of preschool and early primary school children at these tasks. There was mounting dissatisfaction with the concept of egocentrism as an explanatory construct (see Donaldson, 1978; Lloyd and Beveridge, 1981, for a fuller account of this argument). The research focus shifted to the role of the message in referential communication, and also to listeners who had hitherto been regarded as a somewhat passive element. One of the problems which Lloyd and Beveridge (1981) identified as giving rise to poor performance on the part of young receivers of messages was the phenomenon they referred to as 'premature selection'. This was the strong tendency to select a referent before completion of the speaker's message, and, at times, before even the start of it. Here, listeners were acting in a highly focused, not to say impulsive, fashion, and they were not carrying out analysis of the message at a level that would produce success.

In a series of studies in the late 1970s and early 1980s, Robinson and Robinson (e.g., 1983) drew attention to the critical connection between the message and the listener's perception of it. They used a 'Whose fault?' technique, in which children were asked who was to blame for an unsuccessful piece of communication – e.g., where the listener's choice of referent did not match that of the speaker. Robinson and Robinson found that children up to the age of seven years typically blamed the listener for failure, and seemed unaware that the message provided by the speaker might be inadequate. Robinson and Robinson showed that a shift from listener-blaming to speaker-blaming, and a consequent recognition of the role of the message in referential communication, occurred during the early school years.

The attention given to the listener, however, did not result in a truly interactive analysis of peer communication. Instead, studies were carried out with the focus now on the listener rather than the speaker. Listeners were fed a mixture of adequate and inadequate messages, usually by an adult, and their reactions noted. A series of studies by Patterson and her colleagues (e.g., Patterson and Kister, 1981) hypothesized that if children knew that they should ask questions when they were uncertain of a message's adequacy, then they would have a procedure for resolving communication failure. Patterson trained her subjects to ask questions when they found that they could not choose between competing referents. This resulted in more overt recognition of message ambiguity and subsequent discrimination.

A model was now starting to emerge which indicated that a number of stages were involved in the business of assessing the role of the message in communication (Ackerman, 1983). The first stage was to detect ambiguity in a message – that is, to be aware that the information currently available did not allow an unequivocal choice.

The next stage was to carry out a proper evaluation of the message, in an attempt to determine what was giving rise to the ambiguity (i.e., what was missing from the message). The final stage was to resolve the ambiguity, by formulating and asking appropriate questions in order to secure the missing information.

A complementary body of work was carried out at this time by Flavell and his colleagues (1981). This also examined children's reactions to a variety of inadequate messages, and proposed a metacognitive explanation of the inability to recognize message defects (see also Shatz, 1978; Markman, 1981; Lloyd and Beveridge, 1981). Essentially, the argument is that the information-handling resources which a young child brings to the communication task are limited. They may be fully stretched by the cognitive demands – attending to input; accessing the lexicon and syntactic knowledge; discriminating differences in the referent array; relating verbal input to the visual array; making a selection; and so on. The more effort that has to be put into these component skills, the less processing space there is for monitoring the procedure – i.e., taking the message as a cognitive object and scrutinizing it for possible inconsistencies.

There is indeed some evidence to suggest that children recognize ambiguity in messages at a threshold 'below' the level of language. In a study in which children's eye movements were recorded while they scanned an array and listened to messages to focus on items in the array (Lloyd, 1983), it was found that the number of shifts between the items in the referent array varied significantly as a function of message adequacy. When a message allowed unambiguous identification of the requested target, children directed their gaze back and forwards across the array relatively infrequently. However, when the message did not allow unambiguous identification but instead could have referred to one of two items in the array, the number of shifts almost doubled in number. This finding suggests that children were signalling their recognition of ambiguity in the message by engaging in an increased amount of comparison activity. However they were not, in the main, demonstrating this recognition verbally. Indeed, they generally assured the speaker that they had found the target item.

Referential Communication: A New Approach

The standard referential communication approach suffers from a number of shortcomings. These will now be briefly examined under the four headings of Task, Medium, Subjects and Data Analysis. As we do so an alternative approach will be offered which seems closer to communication in everyday situations.

Task

In the standard referential communication task the speaker describes one of a restricted set of items so that the listener is able to identify the target. What this task lacks is a clear goal for the participants. However carefully worded the adult's instructions, the task seems to be arbitrary, the interdependent nature of the enterprise not being clearly apparent. Since communication is, first and foremost, a collaborative undertaking, a task where such behaviour is encouraged or even naturally elicited would represent the ideal at which to aim.

A task which fulfils these requirements is the exchange of route directions with the aid of a map. One participant has to describe a route traced out on the map so that both speaker and listener follow the identical route. Both participants are aware of the starting point, and that a final goal has to be achieved at the other side of the map, stopping at various intermediate points on the way (see Figure 4.1).

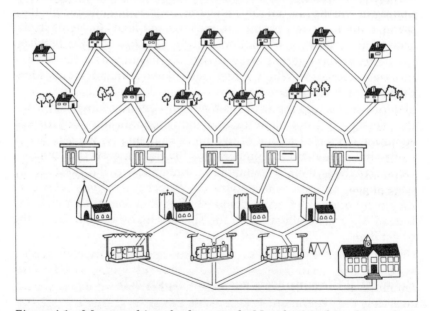

Figure 4.1   Map used in telephone task. Not depicted are key colour cues including *blue* flags on the garages, *yellow* strips on the row of 'shops' and *orange* roofs on the top row of houses.

This means that despite the precise route being available to only one of the interlocutors, the shared knowledge and context, especially in terms of the goal to be achieved, allows the sort of negotiation that takes place in everyday communication. The task therefore observes the principal of human sense which Donaldson (1978) has so clearly brought to our attention. This is not to say that children have necessarily experienced the precise task that is being used. However, the idea and goal of the game will be clear by its very nature.

Medium

In the standard paradigm the interlocutors are separated by a screen to ensure that communication is restricted to the verbal channel. Another common procedure is for the subjects to sit back to back. The artificial nature of such methods has often been criticized (e.g., Frederickson, 1981), and the benefits of face-to-face communication, where gestures can play their full part, demonstrated (Evans and Rubin, 1979). Given that we do want to study children's capacities in a purely verbal medium we therefore need a medium which is essentially verbal but without artificial restrictions.

There is in fact a ubiquitous medium available for this purpose – the telephone. Its incorporation into referential communication tasks obviates the need to prevent non-verbal communication artificially, with the degree of distortion to the communication process that this entails. Moreover, children are attracted to telephones which 'demand' to be picked up and spoken into, and the prohibitions which adults usually place on children's use of these instruments serves only to enhance their attractiveness. This supposition has certainly been borne out in our own research. It quickly became evident that the telephone releases many of the inhibitions that are present in the standard referential research approach, and we have recorded long, frequently sophisticated, dialogues with children as young as seven years of age.

Subjects

The experimental study of peer communication has steadily diminished so that most studies of the ability of young children to communicate verbally place the child together with an adult, almost invariably the experimenter. Ostensibly this gives greater control, but at considerable cost. The issue centres mainly around the question of power.

The influence of the adult experimenter on the child's performance is one that has concerned Donaldson, who has shown convincingly that the child does not always interpret adult meanings as intended (McGarrigle and Donaldson, 1975). It has also been shown that more sensitive judgements can be obtained from children when the power figure – so often represented by the adult – is removed (Lloyd and Donaldson, 1976). It is clearly ridiculous to suggest that effective research can be carried out only in the absence of an adult experimenter. There is a case, however, for putting more emphasis on studies where the participating subjects have the destiny of the task performance in their own hands rather than sharing it, in some little-understood manner, with an unfamiliar adult. A comparable area of research has been that by Genevan workers with a concern for environmental processes such as Doise and Mugney (1984) and Perret-Clermont (1980), who have claimed significant advances in cognitive development when children work in pairs on Piagetian tasks. In our task situation, the children were left entirely alone in separate rooms, but in touch with one another by telephone. The outcome was uninhibited dialogue with many examples of communication failures being followed by successful repair procedures.

Data analysis

The measures taken in referential communication research focus on the performance of speakers and listeners. Speaker skills comprise such things as the ability to provide critical information, and the number of trials or messages to identify the target. Listener measures have ranged from the simple identification of the target, where binary scores are noted (correct or incorrect), to the ability to recognize and act on ambiguity. What has been noticeably lacking is any attempt to treat communication for what it is – an interpersonal, dynamic activity.

The sociolinguistic approach to peer communication records naturalistic dialogue and looks at the structure of conversation in terms of maintaining discourse effectively (Garvey, 1984; McTear, 1985). In the telephone route-following task an attempt to combine the strengths of the experimental and naturalistic approaches has been made by using methods of discourse analysis to illuminate the communication success and failure of our child subjects. A proper account of referential communication must grapple with the intrinsically reciprocal nature of conversation, not merely to satisfy the objections of sociolinguists but also to discover if a deeper analysis of discourse clarifies the procedures by which children use and make sense of verbal information. Many possible measures might be used (Brown and Yule, 1983), but following Garvey's lead with younger children (Garvey, 1979), the distribution and pattern of clarification requests has been used as a starting point.

Communicating Information by Telephone

The telephone route-following task has now been carried out with pairs of seven-year-olds, ten-year-olds, and adults. It is clear that the task has achieved its aim of getting children to collaborate productively. Even the youngest children worked assiduously to achieve the goal of a correct and mutually agreed route and destination.

When measuring success and failure, the standard referential communication approach to the problem is to carry out a task analysis to determine which critical features need to be communicated for a successful outcome. The implication is that there is only one right way of doing the task. It turned out, however, that it was possible to succeed on the present task by using one of several strategies.

Table 4.1 shows that the preferred strategy varies as a function of age. The unsuccessful *minimal* strategy (in which no critical information is supplied) is most evident among the younger children, while the sophisticated *directional* strategy (which makes use of instructions involving 'left', 'right', etc.) is used with any frequency only by adults. The older children prefer a *components* strategy (in which features of the relevant buildings are described) while the younger ones prefer a *numbering* strategy (in which items are counted off – e.g., 'the third one', etc.).

Even though identifying the range of strategies marks an advance over standard referential communication measures, information about the success or otherwise of these strategies is required as well as the form in which they were used. Not surprisingly adults were the most successful subjects, with speakers and listeners achieving the correct route on 92 per cent of occasions. However, ten-year-olds

Table 4.1. *Strategies used in route-finding task (proportions).*

	7 years	10 years	Adults
Components	0.28	0.57	0.21
Directional	0.05	0.08	0.46
Numbering	0.38	0.21	0.26
Minimal	0.16	0.07	0.04
Other	0.13	0.07	0.03

were not significantly different from the adults, with an overall success rate of 86 per cent, though the seven-year-olds were significantly poorer with a mean of 57 per cent.

When we looked more closely at what adult speakers were doing, it seemed that the majority achieved greater efficiency by using a combination of strategies in their descriptions. In (1), a combination of directional and components strategies is being used and this is clearly an effective procedure.

1 *Speaker:*   Carry on from there, still going to the building with the yellow flash under the window.
   Listener: Yeah.
   Speaker: Up from there bearing left to the house with two trees on either side and the door at the end. Go up from there, bearing right, to the house at the top with the two windows above each other.
   Listener: Right. Got it.

Combination strategies of this kind were extremely rare among the ten-year-olds, only one of the 24 subjects typically using this approach. But a closer look at the data revealed many examples of different kinds of combinations strategy which were constructed jointly within the pair.

2 *Speaker:*   You go to the left.
   Listener: Left, yeah. With the yellow at the bottom?
   Speaker: Yeah.

3 *Speaker:*   Go up to the second garage, next to it.
   Listener: The one with the three dots on the top?
   Speaker: No, the other one, next to the school.

In (2) the listener is confirming a correct directional message with a components description. In (3), an accurate numbering strategy is rescued by the listener enquiring about the components involved, causing the speaker to modify the description. Clear examples of joint combinations were less common among the seven-year-olds. However, these children did demonstrate the ability to shift or switch strategies if the one in force did not appear to be working – e.g., (4):

4 *Speaker:*   Now you see those houses, the black ones.
   Listener: Yeah.
   Speaker: Well it's got ... um ... a black roof, a chimney, a black door.

> Listener: Wha ... just first, second, third. Do I go to the third or fourth?
>
> Speaker: Yeah, you go to the fourth one.

Among the ten-year-olds, the protocols revealed the care and sensitivity with which 'instructors' responded to the needs of their 'pupils'. In (5) the speaker uses a 'setting up premises' procedure. This is illustrated in (5)a.

5   a   *Speaker:*   Right, then is a house, two houses, right?
    b   *Listener:*   Yeah.
    c   *Speaker:*   On each side, now there's one with a, er, aerial *in't* there?
    d   *Listener:*   Right, where?
    e   *Speaker:*   On the chimney.
    f   *Listener:*   Yeah.
    g   *Speaker:*   An' there's one without one.
    h   *Listener:*   Yeah.
    i   *Speaker:*   Well, then you go to the one without a chimney, I mean without without a, the ... without an aerial.
    j   *Listener:*   Right, Philip.

The speaker establishes that the listener is at a decision point where the route will go *via* one of two houses (on the left in Figure 4.1). In (5)c the speaker elaborates on the premise by setting out one choice option followed later by the other ((5)g). There is a 'loop' ((5)d–(5)f) while the listener establishes the siting of the aerial but having established the options the speaker then goes on to indicate the next step of the route – ((5)i). What is impressive about this piece of route-giving is the way in which the speaker provides information in manageable chunks and waits for an acknowledgement after each bit. In this way he 'carries' the listener with him.

Since the route-finding task took place within a discourse framework, unlike the conventional referential communication task where the activity seems to be virtually disembedded from natural dialogue, it was appropriate to use methods of discourse analysis to throw further light on the communication process. Accordingly, two entire trials for each pairing were subjected to detailed analysis. The focus was on the child as listener, since a classificatory scheme was available for this purpose – the system of clarification requests developed by Garvey (1979).

Garvey's clarification requests depend on a contingency pair analysis in which the second speaker comments on the utterance of the first speaker by asking for a measure of clarification. There are three main types: non-specific, specific, and potential. Non-specific requests are of a very general kind, such as 'What?' and 'Pardon?' Specific requests refer to a particular aspect of clarification, either a request for repetition, confirmation, or specification. Potential requests 'focus on an element which is missing from the surface form of the prior utterance but which is "potentially available"' (McTear, 1985: 165). They therefore demand more work on the part of the listener.

McTear's version of Garvey's system has been adapted for this

---

Table 4.2. *Categories of clarification requests used in route-finding task.*

Non-specific request for repetition (NRR)
Speaker:	I mean the fourth (?) from the bottom.
Listener:	What?
Speaker:	On the fourth from the bottom.

Specific request for repetition (SRR)
Speaker:	To the house with two trees and a chimney and two windows and a door at the side.
Listener:	With what at the side?
Speaker:	The door.

Specific request for confirmation (SRC)
Speaker:	Go to the church with the point on it.
Listener:	The point?
Speaker:	Yeah. The point at the top.

Specific request for specification (SRS)
Speaker:	You go near the petrol station.
Listener:	Which one?
Speaker:	There's some swings with zig-zags on.

Potential request for elaboration (PRE)
Speaker:	Well go up and go turn and then . . .
Listener:	Go up and turn where?
Speaker:	Left and then . . .

Potential request for confirmation (PRC)
Speaker:	Go straight up and turn a bit and then to the house.
Listener:	What the one with two trees?
Speaker:	Yeah. Not the first one, the second one.

Potential request for specification (PRS)
Speaker:	Now go to the one with the line across.
Listener:	In the window or at the top?
Speaker:	The one with the line across at the top, the second one.

purpose with the addition of one category – the potential request for specification – which our data seemed to demand. The scheme, with an example of each category taken from our data, is fully set out in Table 4.2.

The results of the clarification request analysis summarized in Table 4.3 show that although the younger children are asking for more straightforward requests for repetition than the other age groups (perhaps because they do not attend as well as the other subjects), there are no significant differences in the other categories. This is surprising given the demanding nature of the potential category, and at first sight disappointing, since it casts no light on why the youngest children (57 per cent success) do so much worse at the task than the older children (86 per cent success). Two explana-- tions for the result suggest themselves. One is that younger children ask as many questions as older children but do not get the degree of cooperative response from their partners. However, data do not support this hypothesis. The other explanation is that because seven-year-olds produce more inadequate messages than older children, their partners need to do more than equal the performance of the other age groups – they need to exceed it considerably. This seems to be correct. If clarification requests are divided into just two categories, potential (being those categories where the listener actively contributes to the negotiation by introducing new information), and simple (the remaining categories), and these are set against the number of inadequate messages produced, a number of interesting findings emerges. Confining the analysis to the children, we find that the younger children produce almost twice as many inadequate messages as the older children. The younger listeners also produce about three times as many simple requests as the older listeners. A

Table 4.3. *Incidence of clarification requests given by listeners in the route-finding task (mean number per route).*

	7 years	10 years	Adults
Repetition (NRR + SRR)	1.13	0.67	0.08
Confirmation and Specification (SRC + SRS)	1.71	1.33	1.50
Potential information (PRE + PRC + PRS)	3.25	4.75	3.25

score can be computed which might be called the listener communication repair index. This is the number of inadequate messages
received, divided by the number of potential requests sent. For the
ten-year-olds this score was 1.86, and for the seven-year-olds it was
4.25, a difference that was statistically significant. Another way of
expressing this would be by means of correlation. In the case of the
ten-year-olds, the correlation between inadequate messages received
and potential requests for clarification was 0.86, but only 0.49 for the
seven-year-olds. In other words, the younger children were much
less likely than the older children to respond to an inadequate
message with a request for further information.

The Notion of a Communicative Support System

Let us return briefly to the standard referential studies reviewed
earlier. The various explanations for communication failure that have
been proposed – including not taking account of properties of the
stimulus array, not asking questions, failing to perceive the role of the
message, and having insufficient cognitive space to monitor the
activity – seem to account for many of the experimental findings.
Nevertheless, a feeling of unease persists about the face validity of
these accounts. Why is it, for instance, that young children are not
asking questions given that they have detected an ambiguity? Is it
that they lack the processing space to monitor the input effectively?
This may well be why older children do succeed at these tasks – they
have independent resources on which they can rely – but it seems
less convincing as a reason for the failure of younger children.
Anyone familiar with five- and six-year-olds would be puzzled to
learn that they do not ask questions when they do not understand
something: if five-year-olds have a failing it is that they never stop
asking questions! If this everyday observation is accurate, what is
happening in referential communication tasks?

My contention is that what is really strange is not the behaviour of
the child but that of the adult. It is reasonable to suppose that children
enter a communication task as active interactants ready to ask
questions and generally negotiate meaning because that is what they
do all the time in the world outside the laboratory. Then they
encounter an odd situation. The other 'player' in the communication
game is not observing the customary rules. The usual cues, for
instance, to indicate puzzlement or uncertainty are not being responded to; the child's feedback is not being acknowledged. In other
words, the communicative support that the child has every reason to

expect from an adult, or any competent communicator, is not forthcoming. The effect of such behaviour is, we know, very dramatic even for babies (Murray and Trevarthen, 1985). I suggest that the impact is just as forceful for older children. When the communicative support system with which they have grown up fails to function in the usual way, the effect, arguably, will be to make the children regress or behave in some other aberrant manner – for instance, to stop asking questions or to agree with whatever the adult suggests.

The argument, then, is that for the young child, the familiar adult (e.g., parent) is seen not only as a resource from which the child obtains all sorts of information, but also as an extension of the child's cognitive and communicative system – a communicative support system (CoSS). The term 'support' is used in a way analogous to the notion of 'scaffolding' in some accounts of language acquisition (Bruner, 1983). It is argued that the adult enables dialogue to take place by providing a number of important communicative functions, such as the following:

Directing   Focusing the child's attention on what is relevant rather than merely salient.

Organizing   Introducing information at the appropriate time and at a rate that can be absorbed by the child.

Simplifying   Filtering and interpreting information for the child.

Defining   Defining terms whose meaning is unknown or obscure to the child.

Storing   Holding in working memory and long-term store items beyond the child's capacity.

Reminding   Reminding the child of what is known and what needs to be known – that is, keeping the goal in sight.

Sounding out   Providing a sounding board against which the child can sound out hypotheses.

Monitoring   Alerting the child to communicative success and failure.

Prompting   Shifting the child to an alternative procedure when the present procedure is failing.

Supporting   Providing emotional support – praise for success, commiseration for failure, and encouragement to continue.

Some simple examples of the system in operation are provided in the following protocols involving an adult (myself) and various children from the research nursery of the Edinburgh Cognition Project, directed by Margaret Donaldson. The task required the child to select one of a series of plastic pieces varying in form, size and colour, and to tell the adult which one had been selected so that he could select the identical piece. Screens hid the material from the view of the other person.

6   *(A big red square had just been chosen and adequately described.)*

Child:	A little square angle.
Adult:	A little square.
Child:	Like the big one.
Adult:	Like the big one.
Child:	But not the big one. A little one.

7   *(Three shapes are left, all red.)*

Child:	A little white one.
Adult:	A little white one.
Child:	A red one! Sorry *(smiles)*.

8   Child: A wee round square one.
   Adult: Wee round – a wee round square one.
   Child: No *(smiles)*. A wee round red one.

9   Child: A white square.
   Adult: A white square.
   Child: Just a wee one.

In these examples the adult is doing some simple cognitive monitoring for the child. It is well known that when parents talk to young children they repeat a great deal of what the child says (and, of course, also expand it). This helps to pace the dialogue, model turn-taking, and give the child time to organize the next utterance. But it also gives the child feedback on his or her own utterance. Children do not listen to themselves in the way that adults (sometimes) do. The echoic response provided by parents can alert children to possible inadequacies in their messages. This seems to be what is happening in the examples above, where the adult is acting as a simple feedback loop. The significance of the support system is that these messages are not held for inspection by the children themselves; rather, it is the action of the adult doing this – by simple repetition – that brings the message into the children's awareness. Inadequacies can then be noted and remedied.

A communicative support system sounds a rather arid notion and so it is important to reiterate that it is embedded in a social relationship and only has meaning in such a flesh and blood context. My claim is that it functions regularly whenever an adult or older child is in contact with a younger child. To be sure it is not always functioning 'with all the stops out' as it might be in a problem-solving task. But, even when simply passing the time of day with a child, I would maintain that we are backing up this interaction with the support system outlined. The occasions when we fail to do this, I would further maintain, include the psychological experiment. In which case, one must ask what effect does this have on the child subject?

Evidence pertaining to this question is available from the eye movement research described briefly above. It suggests that disengaging the support system is not simply an all-or-none affair. The likelihood is not that the whole system is 'switched off', but that parts of it are turned off in a very unsystematic way. For example, in a normal conversation between a child and an adult, if the child said 'er . . . um' or looked puzzled in response to a question, the adult would attempt to resolve what appeared to be some problem of understanding by rephrasing the question or asking what the problem was. In many experimental contexts this does not happen. A demand is made, often not explicit to the child (and not always to the experimenter either), to which only a certain response is acceptable.

In the case of the eye movement study, subjects were presented with an array of four different squares, two large, two small, two with and two without a cross. The procedure followed ensured that only a certain response would disambiguate the message. In (10) the child's response in 'normal' conversation would be entirely successful in eliciting the response, 'No, the small one'.

10 *Adult:*   I'm looking at the one with no cross.
    Child: The big one.

It is impossible to be certain that the child is making explicit his indecision about which square is being targeted (though the eye movement record suggested that this was the case). What does seem to be a reasonable inference, however, is that this child would normally offer a response to an ambiguous or unclear statement on the confident expectation that his choice will be either confirmed or disconfirmed by the speaker. This is an expectation which may well have been frustrated in the experimental situation.

On other occasions in this eye movement study the adult was behaving more like an orthodox communicative support system by repeating what the child said. This sometimes led to a recognition of the problem. More often, however, it did not, probably because the adult failed to respond to other cues given by the child. It could be objected that too much onus is being placed on the contribution of the adult. It could rather be the context itself that is determining the nature of the exchanges. The context in the eye movement study was unusual in that only verbal communication was possible. But this is precisely the situation used in our telephone work, and the dialogues resulting from this are of a different nature.

The following example of a telephone dialogue comes from a study carried out by Elena Lieven and myself, in which one child (the hider) was asked to explain to a friend where she had hidden an object in a room in which the friend was sitting. All the communication was by telephone, and the finding child was instructed to look only where her partner told her to look and to make use of the telephone to discover the exact location of the object. The details of the experiment are not really relevant; the point of extract (11) is to show how eight-year-olds use one another as a resource in the exchange of information.

11	*Clare (hider):*	Hello.
	Emily:	Hello. Where's the first one?
	Clare:	Under the table.
	Emily:	Under a table (*looks round*). Which one?
	Clare:	The one with the bricks on.
	Emily:	The what one?
	Clare:	The one with the bricks . . . the little houses.
	Emily:	Right. Be back in a minute. Byee (*searches*).
	Clare:	Emily!
	Emily:	Yeah?
	Clare:	It's under the third table near the curtains.
	Emily:	Near the curtains?
	Clare:	It's under the table – right?
	Emily:	Right – be back in a minute.
	Clare:	It's not the one that you're on – not the second one but the third one.
	Emily:	There isn't a third one.
	Clare:	Yes there is . . . you know. Right. There's the one that you're sitting at – the one that we sat at with the weighing things on.
	Emily:	Yeah.
	Clare:	Then the other one – the last one.
	Emily:	Right – be back in a minute (*searches*).
	Clare:	Right. Have you, have you found it?
	Emily:	Found the elephant.

We can return now to our results in the telephone route-finding task. The difference between ten-year-olds and seven-year-olds may be that ten-year-olds are able to provide communicative support for each other in a way that is generally denied to the younger children. The support is reflected, for example, in the way the older pairs draw the attention of their partner to information that is lacking from the original description – see (2) and (3), and the way information is presented in manageable chunks in (5). The experience of the seven-year-olds outside the communicative system is still limited, and their limitations are particularly exposed when it comes to repairing inadequate instructions. Nevertheless, we should not lose sight of the fact that even such relatively immature communicators – in terms of message evaluation – as the seven-year-olds are able to progress with a substantial degree of success given the opportunity to use their negotiating powers. Their problem seems to be that very often they appear content to conclude the negotiating process before a satisfactory outcome has been achieved.

Conclusion

Our knowledge of the development of language in the primary school years has been informed by two approaches. According to the experimental tradition, communication ability is a compound of fairly independent skills: speaking and listening, skill in composing the initial message and in asking questions. In contrast, the sociolinguistic tradition has studied communicative competence in a broad sense, explaining it in terms of social and contextual variables rather than cognitive processes. Standard referential communication tasks have used a structured setting and precisely specified tasks with the emphasis on the accurate transmission of referential information. In contrast, sociolinguistic research has sampled natural settings, usually chosen and organized by the children themselves, and has stressed the maintenance of verbal exchanges and the role of social intent. It has been argued that the limited success of children in referential communication tasks is due to a large extent to the tasks being extracted from a meaningful framework. Too little attention has been given to pragmatic factors, many of which Donaldson drew to our attention with notions such as human sense as well as her analysis of the contextual factors which operate to hinder the child's grasp of intended meanings. A communicative support system has been outlined to try to amplify the sorts of competencies in which the child must become autonomous before the skills which referential communication is measuring are functioning fully.

This critique should not be understood to imply that experimental referential communication research is wasted effort. On the contrary, as Donaldson argued, perhaps the major task for the child during the school years is to learn to handle information that is decontextualized. The strength of the referential communication approach, sensitively employed, is that it can model the decontextualized world of the classroom. A teacher cannot hope to function as a normal communicative support system in most classroom interaction since it is a one-to-many rather than a one-to-one situation. Accordingly, we would predict that communication failure must take place rather frequently in the classroom. This seems to be precisely what happens (Walkerdine, 1982; Edwards and Mercer, 1986), and it is undoubtedly significant that classroom studies have exposed children's unwillingness to ask questions (Hargie, 1978).

Experiments in referential communication allow us to study, outside the classroom, ways in which children learn to recognize communication failure and discover how to overcome it. Some of the procedures of discourse analysis will make for a more profound examination of this process. There is also a need for comparison studies to see what differences there are between the experimental situation and the classroom. Research of this nature has begun, but there are many problems to be overcome before any direct extrapolation from laboratory to classroom is possible. In the meantime there is surely more scope for capitalizing on the situation which appears to work remarkably well outside the classroom, namely peer communication. If there is force in the claim that information exchange is best achieved through negotiation, then a programme in which pairs or small groups of children work together on tasks will be valuable. But much more bridging research in this field is needed so that we can get beyond pious exhortation to tested procedures that have been shown to work in the classroom as well as in the laboratory.

The map in Figure 4.1 is adapted from an original in Concept Seven-Nine, *published by E. J. Arnold for the Schools Council.*

5 Children's Reading

Jessie Reid
University of Edinburgh

In education, as in other disciplines, bodies of opinion may develop from time to time which present an unusually sharp challenge to accepted wisdom. Within recent years, one such challenging view has taken shape concerning the teaching of reading. Typical statements of this view come from Smith (1978):

> Learning to read involves no learning ability that children have not already been called upon to exercise in order to understand the language spoken at home . . .

and from Goodman (1972):

> Reading is a language process, the direct counterpart of listening . . . As long as they get some exposure to written language, most learners will acquire at least a modicum of literacy.

These two statements are striking in their optimism and confidence. If Smith and Goodman are right, becoming literate ought to be an easy achievement which normal children can readily accomplish. Why, then, has it given so much trouble to so many?

According to Smith and Goodman, the reason is that systematic attempts to teach reading have interfered with the natural processes of language learning, processes already well developed during the acquisition of speech. They consider that reading, like listening, should rely on children's ability to 'predict possible meanings' (Smith, 1978) and find their own answers to questions about written language. They hold that the adult's role should involve helping children to understand the functions of print, including those of 'public print', reading stories aloud to them, and sharing books with them, but little else. Thus supported, children will go on to extend their knowledge of written language by themselves. The process is usually known as 'learning to read by reading'.

To understand how this view developed we have to recall the effect of the insights into oral language acquisition that came from the work of Chomsky. For psychologists and educators concerned with the reading process or with the teaching of literacy, these insights marked a new beginning. They shed much fresh light on the nature and development of reading skill. They opened the way to more powerful 'theories of literacy'. Older associationist models gradually gave way to interpretations based on concepts of language learning.

For many, including myself, this meant looking at children's early attempts at reading in the context of what was known about the strength of their urge to find meaning, about their acquisition of grammar and syntax, and about their language awareness. It meant a new way of looking at reading errors, seeing them as evidence of children's use of linguistic knowledge. It had implications for the ways in which children should be introduced to written language, not just to its visual form but to its structure and purposes. It argued for finding and using linguistic and conceptual links between the oral and written modes (see, for instance, Mackay, Thompson and Schaub, 1970; Reid, 1973).

For some, however, the implications went much further: they appeared to remove altogether the need to regard reading as something new and potentially hard to master – as an activity to which children had to be introduced in carefully planned ways with thoughtfully constructed material. Seen thus, they resulted in the evolution of a language-based view of reading taken to one extreme position.

This view has been extremely influential. Understandably, it has appealed to teachers reacting against older traditional methods, particularly if these divorced learning to read from any kind of true reading experience, or if they involved the use of books containing – as many older schemes did – unnatural and stilted language which prevented children from using the linguistic knowledge they already had. But such reaction can take many forms. Where the extreme view differs from more moderate views is in playing down – or even ignoring – crucial differences between the contexts of learning that obtain for oral and for written language, and between the language modes themselves.

In the first place, the 'making sense' that is the foundation of a young child's acquisition of speech can operate because the language is met in, and relates directly to, experiences in which the child is immersed. The basis for making hypotheses about possible meanings is present. Speech is, in Margaret Donaldson's (1978) term, 'embedded' in a context of relationships and personal concerns.

By contrast, written language found in books has no such contextual support. Instead, the context has to be discovered and constructed from the text itself and from other existing knowledge the reader may have. Some help may come from illustrations, but these have a limited role. At best they are 'stills' from a sequence of actions; and they cannot portray anything that goes beyond visual observation.

Again, the interpersonal exchanges in which spoken language is first met may have strong emotional significance (Donaldson, 1984). The language young children hear comes mostly from people who are closely involved with them. It comes imbued with all the energy and variety of the living voice, the meaning pointed and enhanced by intonation, stress, volume and pace. Voices may sound loving, or angry, or anxious. On the other hand, the author of written language is absent and usually unknown. The print itself is featureless and does nothing visually to capture the attention or involve the emotions. We know that for people who can already read, the first sight of a foreign script can give the impression that all the words look alike. Words spoken in a foreign tongue, on the other hand, though they may be unintelligible, have many audible contrasts.

The interpersonal exchanges in speech have other important advantages for the learner. They limit the amount that has to be grasped in any one utterance. Moreover, they allow the adult participant to supply prompts and respond to difficulties which the child may appear to have in comprehending or replying. The author of written language, however, cannot respond in this way. It is specious to claim, as some do, that there is interaction between text and reader comparable to what takes place in a conversational exchange. The reader may question, but he must find the answer for himself (if indeed it is there). The reader may object or contradict, but the text will not change by one word. The reader may feel perplexity, but the text will not amplify what is there or rewrite itself in a simpler form.

For beginners, then, there is loss and change in the transfer to print – loss of immediacy of relevance, loss of vividness, loss of support in the search for meaning. This is true even though they bring to the search the knowledge they already possess about how spoken language works.

But the problems do not end there. As many people now recognize, learning to read entails massive amounts of new language learning. It entails the acquisition of a repertoire of words, syntactical forms and organizing principles that are seldom – and sometimes never – heard in unplanned speech (see, for instance, Perera, 1984).

As long ago as 1908, E. B. Huey pointed out the difficulties for readers caused by the style of the written English of his own day. He believed, however, that these difficulties would vanish when the 'language of books' and the 'language of men' became much more alike – a process which he thought would be hastened by the practice of dictating instead of writing (Huey, 1908).

We know today that things have not worked out as Huey hoped. It is true that much contemporary prose has a clarity and directness that was often lacking at the time when Huey wrote, while technical aids have developed beyond what he could have imagined. But the differences between our unplanned speech and the language we write are still there. We now see more clearly than Huey did that they are not differences which improved technology will remove.

The differences have many origins. Some of them result from the need for text to be explicit in ways that speech need not be. Some arise from the need to achieve coherence over extended passages of text. Many have to do with the aims and purposes of the writer, who may strive after qualities such as brevity, or elegance, or drama, or precision, or logical clarity. The resulting language varies from one author to another, but as written language it has many general features which can be described and analysed (Perera, 1984).

Learning to be reasonably at home with this formal and stylized 'language of books' – primarily as readers but also as writers – is undoubtedly one of the major learning tasks for children in the upper primary and early secondary school. It is true, as we have seen, that some attempts to teach reading have been unfortunate in having no psycholinguistic roots. But it is equally harmful to swing to the opposite extreme: to claim that the enterprise of becoming literate is hard only because teachers make it so, and that children would succeed perfectly well if they were just provided with suitable books and left to themselves. The enterprise is hard because it has to involve mastering new language in new ways.

To demonstrate something of the scope of the task which children have to undertake, this chapter examines one area of written discourse where language use deviates widely from the nearest oral counterparts, and where many variants have no oral counterpart at all. This area is the handling, in fictional or factual writing, of the speech and thoughts of people other than the author.

Written Speech and Thought

In fiction, information about what the characters say and think is woven into the texture of the narrative. In non-fiction, the other people whose words and thoughts form part of the information may be historical or contemporary figures, or they may be groups, or even humanity in general. But all instances share one characteristic: the author's words become for a time the transmitters of other voices, voices that come from inside someone else's head.

There are certain precedents for this voice switch in oral language. Children are not unfamiliar with situations in which they tell, or are told, what someone else said or thought; or in which they tell what they themselves said or thought at some point in the past or think at the time of speaking. So it is all the more striking to see what happens when those known language experiences are translated on to the page of a book.

Two dichotomies are helpful in examining this area of discourse. I shall use them first to illustrate the handling of written speech and then locate the way thoughts, beliefs, etc. are dealt with. All the examples are taken from texts written for children, most by established authors. (A list of texts appears at the end of the chapter.)

The speech of others

Firstly, the speech of others may be either quoted or reported. (The traditional grammatical terms for this distinction are 'direct' and 'indirect' speech.) In the standard form of quoted speech, the actual words spoken appear, signalled normally by punctuation ('quotation marks'). In standard reported speech, the words of the speaker typically undergo certain rule-governed transformations affecting pronouns and verb tenses. Also, they commonly appear as subordinate elements in a sentence where the main clause indicates the speaker. For instance: 'Henry said "I was there"', may become 'Henry said (that) he was there'.

The former branch of this first dichotomy takes written language at once into a mode which speakers seldom use. In conversation, direct quotation of the words of someone else is relatively rare. Its most likely function would be to enable one speaker to convey not only the matter of a remark by another speaker but also the manner in which it was made. For instance: 'I asked her where David was, and she just said "I don't know" very rudely.' It can also occur in the handling of exclamations. There is no appropriate way of turning 'She said "Good heavens"'' into reported or indirect speech. In general, however, the reported form is the normal conversational one, and is certainly the one familiar to young children in ordinary exchanges. Their best chance therefore of becoming familiar with quoted speech in their preschool years is through hearing dialogue in stories read aloud. But there they meet it enhanced by the living voice of the reader.

Even in the case of the more familiar reporting mode, however, the transition to written instances of it is by no means straightforward. As we shall see, authors vary the handling of reported speech in many ways which depart from the forms which speakers commonly use and children commonly hear.

The other main dichotomy has to do with whether the dialogue is or is not attributed – that is, whether the text is *explicit* or *implicit* about who is speaking. Here we may move, for the child, even further away from familiar ground. When a child is a listener to adult conversation (which we may call 'dialogue at first hand') the identity of the speakers is normally obvious. And if an adult, speaking to a child – or to anyone – were to introduce the quoted words of a third person ('dialogue at second hand') it would be very unusual for the source not to be identified. Instances where an adult is quoting from a source too well known to need mention (e.g., saying 'take no thought for the morrow') are liable not to register with a child as quotations at all. In written language, however, instances of quoted speech without explicit attribution are by no means unusual.

What picture emerges when the two dichotomies are combined? When considered together, they produce a two-way table (see Table 5.1) in which each cell represents one of the ways in which children may meet, in a text, voices other than that of the narrator. (Later it will become clear that this picture is somewhat over-simplified, for not all instances fall neatly into one or another of these categories. There are some 'grey areas'.)

Table 5.1. *Speech.*

Form	Source	
	Explicit	Implicit
Quoted	a	b
Reported	c	d

Let us consider examples of these different kinds of written speech.

(a)   Quoted speech, source explicit

This is traditionally a standard feature of story-telling, and may well derive from the oral tradition where the story-teller would switch from a narrative role to a dramatic one. In spite of its rarity in oral language, it is widely assumed to be easy to read, and hence is freely introduced into children's fiction and other early reading materials. Observation of children reading aloud, however, shows that they can have problems in adjusting to the change from third-person narrative (the author's voice) to quoted speech (the character's voice). This can be very noticeable if the quoted speech is a question. The question form seems to be seldom expected, and the child's eye may not catch the question mark at the end.

Some of the difficulty also depends on the position of the attributing clause (or 'source marker'). If the source marker precedes the quoted words, the reader is to some extent prepared. This form is widely – though by no means universally – adopted in writing text for young children to read. It is commonly found in texts designed for use in teaching reading, as one means of freeing the beginner from problems connected with syntax. It can also appear in more sophisticated writing, used for effect rather than for simplicity:

Nick's eyes widened. He said, 'That dark place!' (a.1)

Often, however, the source marker does not precede the quotation. It may, for instance, be interpolated between two sentences:

'I can't think where it's gone', she said. 'I can't think.' (a.2)

Immediately this happens, the reader has the problem of identifying who is speaking, and using this knowledge to make sense of what is being said. The eye has to jump ahead to the source marker, or register it peripherally, and link it correctly to the preceding text. But in the case just quoted, the last-named character happens not to be the one who speaks, so the word 'she' in the source marker becomes important.

On many occasions the interpolation splits the syntax of the spoken words in ways that require the reader not only to register the speaker but to store and carry over the syntax and sense of the quoted words:

'I am afraid,' said Grimble, 'that after Christmas will be exactly too late.' (a.3)

The latter example also shows the inversion of the subject and verb in the source marker – a form never found in conversation. Yet this device, along with the interpolation of the source marker at an early point in the quotation, may well have originated in the oral story-telling tradition. It is effective when read aloud, where the voice can be used to carry over the syntax and sense. The dilemma for the author writing for readers rather than for listeners is to avoid delaying the source marker for too long, and yet to avoid destroying the dramatic effect by placing it first. For young readers, however, the medially placed source marker is liable to increase the load on short-term memory. They must take note, in passing as it were, of who is speaking, without any loss of continuity in following the quoted words. These modes of structuring dialogue have to be learned, until they become familiar and recognizable.

The choice of speaking verb in the source marker can also be significant. For instance, in Helen Cresswell's *The Night Watchmen*, Henry is listening to Caleb's description of the mysterious train:

> 'She comes whistling out of the dark when folks is in their beds and the most they'll see of her is her green eyes and the red fires blowing up her smoke.'
>
> 'Fires!' cried Henry. 'A steam engine! . . .' (a.4)

Two messages convey Henry's delighted surprise. One is the exclamation mark, used twice. The other is the word 'cried'. To understand Henry's response, the reader must see that Henry has focused on Caleb's mention of 'fires', must see that Henry infers at once that the train is due, and must grasp the importance of the speaking verb. Notice, however, the complexity of what the child reader has to process. Caleb is – or appears to be – a night-watchman. But his sentence about the train is, to say the least, an unlikely one for any ordinary night-watchman to utter. It has a poetic quality, with images of sound and colour. And it contains a subordinate clause of time, followed by a complicated subject nominal consisting of a quantifier head plus a relative clause with deleted 'that'.

Not all dialogue is as linguistically elaborate as this example. But certain kinds of children's fiction do contain quoted speech which calls on quite advanced understanding of possibilities in expression, and an acceptance of its remoteness from the way people ordinarily talk.

(b) Quoted speech, source(s) implicit

> 'Oh, all right', I said. 'I'll ride and you can follow me.'
> 'I'll ride too.'
> 'You don't have a bike.'
> 'I have a Toddle-bike.'
> 'You can't ride a Toddle-bike to school.'
> 'Why not?'
> 'Because you can't . . .' (b.1)

Written dialogue in which, as here, source markers are suspended is at once nearer to and farther from children's experience than is the form with source markers present. In one sense it is the written version of what they constantly hear – two other people talking – perhaps, as in this case, arguing. In such a situation the flow of spoken words does not need to be interrupted by information about who is speaking. But when it is transferred to the printed page, where it is read and not heard, all the clues necessary for following the exchange have to be extracted from other sources in the text. It is up to the reader to keep track of whose turn it is to speak, and to retain the distinctiveness of the characters and their roles. For in dropping the source markers the author has, for the moment, ceased to speak with her own voice – ceased to supply the narrative thread (which is what the source markers do) – and has let the characters take over.

Written exchanges with source markers omitted are thus a good example of the way in which the disembedded nature of all texts converts what might be an easy comprehension task into a difficult one. The fact that it does may underlie a great deal of the difficulty experienced by many beginning readers. For the most extreme form of quoted speech without source markers can be found on the earliest pages of certain infant reading schemes which are based on severely restricted vocabulary and a word recognition model. Sentences like 'Run, lad, run', or 'See the boats', may often be the only text on the page. Sometimes they are supposed to be said by characters in the illustrations, but there is nothing to indicate who is speaking. Sometimes, more strangely still, they seem to be merely exhortations, addressed to no one in particular. It is not surprising that many beginners find such text bewildering.

There is one type of implicit identification in which source markers are absent, but where other devices in the narrative serve as indicators. For example:

> Dad was at the top of the cliff, looking down. He seemed a long way off.
>
> 'Chutney, keep still. You can't get down . . .' (b.2)

Here it is fairly obvious that Chutney is being addressed, and that Dad is the speaker. But this is not stated: it has to be inferred.

Here is an example where two speakers are involved:

> She stood still, heart hammering. 'Is she in there?' Albert's face was contemptuous. 'Couldn't hurt you if she was, but she isn't, she's downstairs in her coffin . . .' (b.3)

This time, the signalling device consists of prefacing the quoted speech by a brief description of what the speaker does, or feels, or how he or she looks. The effect is not unlike that of the script of a play with stage directions. Again, there is no direct attribution; the child reader has to come to know the conventions which are operating and the inferences which can be made. And if the dialogue is to be experienced with vividness and flow, these inferences about language role have to be made with accuracy and ease.

(c) Reported speech, source explicit

Here we are on ground more familiar to the pre-reading child, and there is less need to analyse straightforward examples. But some of the variants are of interest. For instance, the structure of the speech may produce, in the reported form, a word-string of considerable complexity:

> Mary Lennox had heard a great deal about Magic in her Ayah's stories, and she always said what happened almost at that moment was Magic. (c.1)

This sentence contains not simply a report of something said; but of something said on repeated occasions at times later than the 'moment' which is being described. And it does so in syntax which calls for quite a feat of structuring and interpreting.

The next example shows how the reported form may sometimes have the reporting clause embedded as a parenthesis, so that the whole sentence resembles, in word order, the structure of quoted speech, but with only commas for punctuation:

> Sometimes, Spiller explained, the grating slid easily, at other times it stuck at an angle. In which event Spiller would produce a small but heavy bolt. (c.2)

The above example also shows how reported speech may carry over into a second sentence without any reinforcing signal. The reader must decide, by attending to other clues, whether the continuation is still part of the reported speech, or whether it has reverted to the 'author's voice'. The main clues here are in the linking phrase 'in which event' and the use of 'would'.

Earlier in the same text there is yet another subtle variant. Spiller is explaining to Pod how he proposes to move the grating over a drain. The author writes:

> The twine, Pod gathered, was a fixture. (c.3)

The words 'Pod gathered' tell us that the sentence which they interrupt is a report of something said *to* Pod, namely still part of Spiller's explanation. The speaker is thus identified, but in an oblique way, which the reader can comprehend only through familiarity with the idiomatic use of 'gather' as meaning 'to deduce or conclude from something heard or read'.

(d) Reported speech, source implicit

As with quoted speech (see b.2 and b.3), it is possible to find instances of reported speech where the necessary clues to the identity of the speaker are found only in preceding text. In this extract Roddy's parents want him to take up a useful hobby:

> They tried to persuade him. It wouldn't cost much. His dad would help him. If he would pay five pounds out of his savings his dad would find another five. (d.1)

In some variants of reported speech where the speaker is only implicitly identified, the words may be not so much a straight transformation of what was said as a summary or paraphrase of it. In this next example two Polish boys are telling an English girl how they came to be in France during World War Two:

> Their names were Tadek and Stefek Pulaski. Their home was in a village far away in the High Tatra Mountains. 'They are very high,' said Stefek. 'Very high and very beautiful. There are no mountains like these anywhere else in the whole world.'
>
> Their mother had been English . . . (d.2)

It may be asked whether children need to see that the paragraphs beginning 'Their names . . .' and 'Their mother . . .' are a condensed report of what the boys told Janey, and not the 'author's voice' speaking directly to the reader. From one point of view it might not matter, for the paragraphs are in part devised to give the reader information. But if they were in the author's voice, then the interpolation of Stefek's quoted description would be glaringly inappropriate. And it is important, for an understanding of Janey's changing attitude to the boys, to know that she has been told their story. This example, then, shows the need for a sophisticated awareness of how 'background' information may and may not be conveyed.

The thoughts of others

It is interesting to discover that many of the complicated variations used in handling the speech of others also appear when thought rather than speech is dealt with (see Table 5.2). 'Think' is of course an ambiguous term. It can mean to hold an opinion or a belief, it can mean to reflect, it can mean to have an idea, and it can mean to wish. All these different kinds of thinking appear in the examples that follow.

Table 5.2. *Thought.*

Form	Source	
	Explicit	Implicit
Quoted	e	f
Reported	g	h

(e)   Quoted thought, source explicit

This is very similar to the corresponding category for speech, and the verbalized thoughts are often put in quotation marks just as if they were speech. The following example occurs in *The Night Watchmen*. Henry is trying to trace the two men with whom he has struck up an acquaintance:

'If only I were a dog!' he thought desperately. (e.1)

There is, of course, a degree of artificiality in this form. A boy in Henry's situation would be unlikely to think so explicitly in words. However, the 'If only . . .' form is almost a conventional signal for the expression of a wish in story-telling, and as such is something children have to learn.

Sometimes there is no use of quotation marks, in which case the transition from author's to character's voice has to be deduced purely from the wording. The following example occurs at the beginning of a chapter:

> I don't suppose, said Grimble to himself, that we need have a very large turkey . . . (e.2)

(f)   Quoted thought, source implicit

Since thought is solitary, there is no parallel to the dramatic inter-changes without source markers which can occur in quoted dialogue (see b.1). But the next example shows an effective alternative to the use of the explicit marker 'he thought':

> And there, as he (Tethra) lay face down in the lee of an upturned boat, . . . he let his thinking catch up with him.
>
> 'I do not belong with these people; they are not my people, and I do not belong here at all. . . .' (f.1)

The key phrase is, of course, 'he let his thinking catch up with him', with its subtle implication that Tethra has been trying to run away from the knowledge that he does not belong.

(g)   Reported thought, source explicit

Like its counterpart in the handling of speech, this is common, but it may present more in the way of reading problems. For one thing, the 'thinking verbs' can be very varied. Characters may realize, suppose, guess, expect; they may doubt, hope, wish, fear, suspect, wonder; they may conclude, decide, assume, believe; and so on. Many subtleties of meaning are carried by words in this category, and these meanings have to become attached to the written forms so that they readily convey to the reader what kind of thinking is taking place.

From the syntactical point of view, difficulty can be created when the form is the reported counterpart of (e.2), with the source marker interpolated:

> . . . the air from that point onwards, Arrietty noticed, smelled far less strongly of tea-leaves. (g.1)

Impersonal forms can cause problems too. It is not uncommon to find reporting clauses in the form 'It occurred to her . . .', 'It dawned on me . . .', and so on.

(h)   Reported thought, source implicit

Examples of this were widespread in the texts analysed. Often the attribution is implied by the preceding text, as it was for speech in (b.3):

> She (Carrie) felt mean and dirty – and scared too. Suppose, when they got back, he asked her what Miss Green was up to? Suppose he said, 'I know what's going on, did you find anything out?' (h.1)

This example contains the added complication of a piece of imagined quoted speech embedded in the reported thought, and forming part of the questions in Carrie's mind. What the child reader must be alive to is that the questions *are* in Carrie's mind. They are Carrie saying 'What if . . . ?' and not the author raising possibilities in her own voice.

The next example offers even less guidance. In *The Secret Garden* Mary has been watching a robin which has let her come quite near. The text goes on:

> Oh! to think that he should actually let her come as near to him as that! (h.2)

This ecstatic thought is not the author's: it is Mary's. But nothing in the text says so. There is only the fact that a modern author would not write 'Oh! to think . . .' in his or her own voice.

A switch of a very subtle kind appears in another passage from *The Night Watchmen*. Henry is out in the countryside at a favourite spot:

> Giant trunks of trees reared on either side, their roots exposed because of the steepness of the slope. Beautiful roots they were, grey and sculpted and somehow *bony*, clutching at the steep fall of clay. (h.3)

The paragraph begins by describing the tree roots – what Henry sees. But at some point it switches to what he thinks about them. How do we know? Because of the inversion in 'Beautiful roots they were', the printing of 'bony' in italics, and the use of 'somehow'. All three features are designed to convey that Henry is not just looking at the roots but reflecting on them and struggling to think what it is they bring to mind. From 'Beautiful roots . . .' onwards, the text is reported thought.

Sometimes an author may combine two of the (e), (f), and (g) categories in ways which blur the edges but create a particular effect. In this extract, Charlie has tripped over the dog Floss in the dark, and to his astonishment someone speaks to him:

> Charlie's first, confused thought was that Floss had spoken: the voice was familiar – but then a voice from Floss should not be familiar, it should be strangely new to him – . . . (h.4)

In this instance, the 'thought' is actually a fusion of quotation and report; the use of 'should not be' in the present tense contrasts with the third person pronoun 'him'. The confusion in Charlie's mind is well conveyed, provided that there is none in the mind of the reader.

In the next example the character's thought spans more than one sentence. It begins by being reported, then switches to quotation. Note the salience of the word 'tomorrow': it is the only clue that the 'voice' is Sue's. The author in her own voice would have had to write something like 'the next day':

> Sue sighed as she regulated the dial for the toast. The holiday began tomorrow – in fact it had as good as started already, since Bill was staying at home – and holidays always seemed to point the problem more sharply. One of these days, she thought, I really shall have to make my mind up. Which am I? Bill or Fay? (h.5)

These latest examples are from books for older children. But the next extract, from a story for quite young readers, switches 'voices' in a quite complicated way.

> Then he met a man who had a goose for sale. Goodman thought, 'I'll change this sheep. I'll change it for that goose, I will.' And he did.
>
> He and his wife would eat that goose and it would be delicious. The goose was in a bad temper. . . . (h.6)

This time, the only clue to the status of the penultimate sentence (where the 'voice' switches to being that of Goodman thinking) is the use of 'would'. The sentence is not a 'prediction in the past' by the author; it is a report of Goodman's thought 'I and my wife will eat . . .'. The last sentence, however, reverts to the author's direct narrative.

Reported thought with source implicit is also not uncommon in information text. There, it often takes the form of a question. For instance:

> In the 1960s, an astronomer named Gerald Hawkins worked on another idea. Were the other stones also set up to locate other sky times? Was Stonehenge really an 'astronomy clock'? (h.7)

In the next example the topic is the cultivation of vanilla:

> The planters were puzzled. Why wouldn't the seed pods form on their vines? (h.8)

In neither of these examples is the question from the author to the reader. Both are reports of questions in the minds of the people who figure in the passages. In this third example, however, the question has a different origin. The author has been describing how Stonehenge might have been built. He goes on:

> But how, without machinery, did they get the top stones up and across the standing ones? (h.9)

Here the author raises the question in his own 'voice', as a means of focusing on a problem.

In all three examples, clues to the type of question are contained in the preceding sentence. In examples (h.7) and (h.8) there is reference to someone working on an idea or being puzzled. In the third example, the preceding sentence is straight description, with no intention of thinking or problem-solving. Yet paradoxically, the reaction expected from a reader is in the opposite direction. It is the second type of question which is aimed at arousing speculation about possible solutions. Nothing on the surface of the text indicates which kind of question is being asked; yet it is important that young readers should be aware whether they are being directly invited to find an answer, or whether they are being led, as in (h.7) and (h.8), through the history of a discovery. It is one more thing they must learn to judge.

Discussion

The foregoing samples show that the representation of dialogue in written narrative can give rise to linguistic complexities of numerous kinds. Further, they show that many of the forms evolved to represent dialogue are also used by authors to represent thought. Text of the kind exemplified makes up a significant part of what children in primary school are expected to read.

The language in the samples contains syntactic patterns and inter-sentence relationships not found in oral language. Many of these have to do with shifts of 'voice' between author and character. Often the clues to meaning lie in subtle implication rather than in explicit statement. In order to make sense of them inferential skills may be needed, as well as an understanding of certain principles not unlike the minimal distance principle that operates for pronominal reference.

In my experience these features present problems for many young readers. Yet they must not be regarded merely as 'difficulties' in the text. They are there because to have something distinctive to say can frequently call for a distinctive way of saying it – a way that will make an author's words come fresh and vivid off the page. But the existence – and the prevalence – of this rich variety raises important questions about how children's reading competence can become a match for the challenge it presents.

It is clear from reports of children's progress that at present there is, for many, no easy progression from the simpler language and narrative line of stories written for inexperienced readers. Teachers complain of problems in 'comprehension'. Children fail to become keen independent readers. They do not learn effectively from the written word; and listening to children reading aloud will invariably uncover a whole spectrum of difficulties concerned not only with vocabulary but with the ways in which words are strung together and the ways in which, even in straightforward narrative or information text, sentences cohere and relate. Children who are struggling at this level will also have problems in grasping more complex aspects of text construction, such as the shifts of voice studied in this paper. These problems, however, may escape detection.

What kinds of help can be offered? Those who are against explicit teaching of reading (e.g., Meek *et al.*, 1984) often speak of allowing children to 'predict their way through the text' with their minds focused on meaning, rather than encouraging them to attend to features of print. In ordinary usage, and also in science, the term 'predict' is used of a conscious, deliberate attempt to make a forecast of a future event on the basis of existing knowledge and assumption. But when it is used to describe what happens during reading, or any attempt at reading, it seems to stand for something less focused and further from full awareness – something which might more appropriately be called 'anticipation' or 'expectancy'. All language-based views of reading take account of it; but the prominence given to it is the main distinguishing mark of the view of reading held by Goodman and Smith with which this paper began.

Goodman sees reading as 'tentative information processing' (Goodman and Gollasch, 1980). Efficient readers 'sample' the text, make predictions about meaning, and confirm or correct these by the use of further cues. The process is seen as cyclical, but dominated by the construction of meaning. Close attention to the words on the paper is not of the essence, and is regarded as potentially counter-productive. Smith would go further and say it results in 'tunnel vision' and a loss of grasp on sense. Both Smith and Goodman believe that skilled adult reading is far from error-free, and that errors can be a positive sign that the sense of the text has been grasped.

Models of this kind, where the construction of meaning dominates – and influences – the perception of the marks on the page, are often called 'top-down' models. The reader is said to be 'concept-driven'. The derivation of these models from theories of early speech development is clear.

The reading process can however be conceptualized in other ways without necessarily abandoning a language-based position. There are many contributors to this debate who see both short-range 'prediction' (e.g., of the next word) and higher-level construction of meaning as integral to efficient reading. However, they believe that the whole process depends on the words on the page – and proceeds in phase with them – in ways that the 'top-down' theorists would not allow (see, for instance, Laberge and Samuels, 1974). These latter theories are often called 'bottom-up', and efficient readers described as being 'text-driven'.

It is not hard to see how the two positions may be invoked in support of very different views on how children should learn to read. The differences become more apparent once the earliest stages have been left behind. There are probably few people who would now dispute that beginners' use of their existing knowledge of language is important and should be encouraged. The studies of Clay (1969), Weber (1970), and Biemiller (1970) remain key sources of understanding on this topic.

Let us look now at what can happen when the 'top-down' view – that children should learn to 'predict their way through a text' – is put into action with children whose reading has fallen behind even average expectation. *Achieving Literacy* (Meek *et al.*, 1984) describes how a group of teachers of English, critical of orthodox remedial teaching, set about applying the principle of 'learning to read by reading' to some retarded readers aged around twelve years. At one point, one of the pupils renders '. . . who lived in a pretty house with a large garden' as '. . . who lived in a palace house with a little grandfather'. This reader is using prediction. The sentence begins 'Paul was a little boy . . .'; and boys in stories do, after all, quite often live in palaces. The reader then attaches 'with' syntactically to 'lived' rather than to 'house', and using few graphic cues arrives at a person with whom Paul might reasonably live. The result is not only misleading in itself: it is an inauspicious basis for predicting what may follow. Another child renders '. . . hidden in the ruins of a house' as 'happened in the rain, runs to a house'. The teacher working with this pupil tells how children would '. . . exchange one mistake for another and incidentally change the syntax so that an appalling mess developed' (Meek *et al.*, 1984: 189). The trouble in this example starts with the misreading of 'hidden' as 'happened'. Was this due to a failure of prediction – or to a failure to see that the word had 'dd' in the middle and therefore could not be 'happened'? The error certainly blocks any subsequent attempt to construct a meaningful sequence, especially since the child is totally defeated by 'ruins'. Having tried 'rain' (because a noun is called for) she presumably sees the terminal 's' and substitutes 'runs'; and is then forced (again by syntactical constraints) to misread 'of' as 'to'. An appalling mess indeed.

Does the way to make these children better readers lie through still more prediction, particularly of this haphazard kind? I do not think so. I think a more fruitful model is one which sees the role of expectancy as providing narrowed fields of options rather than firm hypotheses. I see a grasp of graphic features not just as the basis for confirming or disconfirming guesses, but as a direct source of meaning-in-context, to be called on when expectancy has nothing to say. This view comes close to that of Stanovich (1980), who describes his model as 'interactive–compensatory'.

Of course, not all examples of children in difficulty show confusion and collapse to the extent seen above. Goodman substantiates his view of reading as a 'psycholinguistic guessing game' (1972) with accounts of children who managed to battle their way through unfamiliar syntax and uncertain word recognition to some kind of understanding of the text. In Piagetian terms they assimilated the language to what they knew, yet managed to preserve at least part of the meaning. But even if we allow that this can be a beneficial experience, we must question the wisdom of seeing it as the only valid way in which reading can be learned. The avoidance of confusion at the time of reading is not the only reason for arguing that children should be helped to become aware of what is actually on the page. Learning takes place through successive cycles of assimilation and accommodation; and it is at the accommodative phase that this clearer vision is needed.

As we have seen, young readers meet many new words and novel variants of word sequence. They find new possibilities in meaning and expression. They must in some way make these their own – take them into their personal repertoire. They will not be helped in this task if the way they read does not allow them to perceive with clarity what they are learning to interpret. It is even plausible to suppose that having to depend excessively on prediction from prior context may take up so much of a reader's cognitive resources that more wide-ranging comprehension is blocked (Stanovich, 1980).

A further difficulty in relying entirely on a 'top-down' model arises because of the differing ways in which spoken and written language are received. In the spoken mode listeners receive whole utterances. These come at the speed of the speaker and the listeners do not need to make any physical adjustment. Ears, unlike eyes, do not have to be focused and moved. The words are not interrupted if a failure of comprehension occurs. Most importantly, the context remains.

Written language, on the other hand, is experienced at the speed of the reader, who also controls the sequence in which words are perceived. If difficulty is encountered, the normal result is that the input is disrupted in various ways. Moreover, owing to the limitations of short-term memory, the context may be lost, and with it the basis for an attempt at constructing 'possible meanings'.

Disintegration of this kind has implications that go beyond the children's grasp of the text they are actually trying to read. It has crucial importance for the accommodative phase of reading progress. For although individual words and syntactical patterns recur in written language as they do in speech, most actual sentences are unique, and thus cannot be 'recognized' as wholes. It is therefore necessary to become able to recognize and attach meaning to the words and to the patterns of which the sentences consist. And if these patterns, with their changing lexical content, are never experienced except in distorted or fragmented form, the necessary accommodation will not take place.

The problem is compounded by the fact that children in the junior school are increasingly expected to read silently, and thus without help. The nature of the change from oral reading assisted by a listening adult, to 'silent independent' reading, is a neglected area, partly because it is difficult to study (Pugh, 1978). But difficulties of transfer undoubtedly interact with those arising from the need to master the 'language of books'. The arguments for help in this learning task seem overwhelming. So what kind of help can be given that will not kill what Margaret Meek calls 'the magic' stone dead?

Earlier in this paper, in the discussion of the difficulty presented by quoted speech in stories, we saw how young children could become familiar with this narrative feature through listening to stories being read aloud. And it is well known that children who have been read to in their preschool years have a general advantage when the learning of reading begins. There is much to be said for continuing the practice of reading to children right through the later primary years, letting them hear the cadences of book language and, where possible, letting them follow the text as well. In the course of this reading there can be pauses for discussion at appropriate points, when carefully chosen questions can be introduced to explore possible failures in the children's understanding, not just of terms and ideas but of the interrelationships which the syntactic structures convey. All who view reading as a language process would probably agree.

Another helpful procedure would be to let children who are learning to read silently have some experience of reading aloud, to one another, passages of their own choosing, not 'from cold', as a test of reading skill, but after they have become familiar with a text in general terms and have perhaps had a chance to look closely at syntax or vocabulary found to be perplexing.

These practices may help in another important way. One area of controversy surrounding the nature of the change to 'silent independent' reading has to do with the role of 'inner speech' – what we may call 'the voice in the head'. Huey (1908) believed that some kind of internal auditory imagery of words was a legitimate feature of skilled silent reading, and devoted an entire chapter of his book to the functioning of inner speech. Some years ago, interest in 'speed reading' caused many people to think that all auditory imagery should be suppressed, a view which Smith (1978) also supported. But more recent studies have restored it to respectability (e.g., Hanson, 1981). There is a suggestion too that poor readers are deficient in an internal articulatory code (Briggs and Underwood, 1987), and that this is in itself a source of difficulty insofar as it deprives them of one lexical route – that is, one way of identifying what words mean.

What is certain is that for many competent readers the 'voice in the head' is there – flickering in and out of consciousness, audible when helpful, silent when not. There are times when we become particularly conscious of it – when we read poetry, or when we come to something we cannot easily follow. And it contributes greatly to the reading of all text in 'character's voice' – the kind of text exemplified in this chapter.

We need the sound of words, too, when we ourselves come to

write, for the prosody of written language is an important element in its clarity and power. So practices that might strengthen the inner ear are to be commended. I believe that continuing to hear the language of books as well as to see it gives developing readers a valuable resource in this domain.

So far, the kinds of help given have been what one can call 'incidental'. But I would argue that there is a place too for a more structured approach – for the inclusion in the language curriculum of some kind of planned study of the way written language works.

Some teachers and psychologists are against all study which makes language, in Cazden's term, 'opaque' (Cazden, 1974). Language, they claim, should never be other than a transparent medium through which the meaning can be seen. This again is in line with a prediction-based view of reading. Yet when written language is imperfectly identified and not fully understood it will tend to seem opaque in any case. The meaning will not shine clearly through. I believe that it is valuable for children to learn to use this experience, and to become able, at will, to look at language rather than through it, to think about it as well as with it. This gives an important role to word-recognition skills, but it is a role which recent studies are tending to support (see, for instance, Gough, 1984).

In the material analysed in this chapter there are occasions when interpretation calls for attention to the clues given by specific words (as in examples c.2, c.3, and h.3), to unusual syntax (as in examples c.1 and g.1), to unstated shifts that have to be inferred (as in category h), and to a variety of quite subtle clues to the sources of speech and thought. It seems reasonable to suggest that children should in fact learn to read in more than one way – to be mainly concerned with overall sense when the going is easy, but to be able to switch to a mode where they become more aware of and attentive to the actual text. It is in the development of this flexibility that structured language work has a part to play.

Language work is of course already done in many schools. However, much of this work is heavily weighted towards the study of individual words, even though it is widely recognized that most vocabulary growth comes from encountering words in the course of reading. Moreover, many activities do little else than test word knowledge rather than teach it. At the other extreme, language work may consist mostly of the provision of stimuli to 'creative writing'. The crucial middle ground – the exploration of how words can be manipulated on paper and the effects such manipulation can achieve – may be seriously neglected.

Most of the extracts studied in this paper were taken from accepted and acclaimed examples of literature for children, written with what we recognize as style. The remainder were from a reputable information book written for use in school. But they speak a language far removed from the home, the street, and the playground. If we offer this kind of text to children, and if the gulf between the two languages is to be bridged, then we must not play down the magnitude of the learning task which children face. And we must remember that bridges are built from both sides.

List of Texts

a.1   *Carrie's War* (Nina Bawden)
a.2   *In the Middle of the Night* (Philippa Pearce)
a.3   *Grimble* (Clement Freud)
a.4   *The Night Watchmen* (Helen Cresswell)

b.1   *Superfudge* (Judy Blume)
b.2   *Chutney and the Fossil* (Roderick Hunt)
b.3   *Carrie's War* (Nina Bawden)

c.1   *The Secret Garden* (E. Nesbitt)
c.2   *The Borrowers Afloat* (Mary Norton)
c.3   *The Borrowers Afloat* (Mary Norton)

d.1   *The Mersey Look* (Eric Allen)
d.2   *Journey into War* (Margaret Donaldson)

e.1   *The Night Watchmen* (Helen Cresswell)
e.2   *Grimble* (Clement Freud)

f.1   *The Changeling* (Rosemary Sutcliffe)

g.1   *The Borrowers Afloat* (Mary Norton)

h.1   *Carrie's War* (Nina Bawden)
h.2   *The Secret Garden* (E. Nesbitt)
h.3   *The Night Watchmen* (Helen Cresswell)
h.4   *In the Middle of the Night* (Philippa Pearce)
h.5   *Particle Goes Green* (Helen Cresswell)
h.6   *Money to Spend* (Mary Cockett)
h.7   *The Mystery of Stonehenge* (Donovan Doyle)
h.8   *Edmund Albius, Vanilla Detective* (Betty Boegehold)
h.9   *The Mystery of Stonehenge* (Donovan Doyle)

6 Children's Writing

Miranda Jones
University of Edinburgh

The acquisition of written language is perhaps the most exciting achievement of the school years, being the basis for all further academic progress. The effect of literacy on the intellectual functioning of both society and the individual has been discussed by many authors. Donaldson (1978), for example, points out that written language is essential for the development of logic, mathematics and science. According to Donaldson, the kind of reasoning which Western society values most is context-free, disembedded thought: reasoning of the kind which is known as 'formal' or 'abstract'. She suggests that this becomes possible when individuals can think about language rather than merely think with language; when they can understand that they are required to reason within the given confines of a problem. She shows that preschool children can reason if the problem is embedded in a suitable context; and claims that disembedded reasoning is the result of learning to read and write.

The importance which society places on literacy and logic means that children who find it difficult to learn are quickly made to feel inadequate. Early feelings of failure may turn them against education for life; and thus they may never fully develop their intellectual capabilities. Why, asks Donaldson, does something which begins so hopefully turn sour so easily?

Many authors have described the preschool child's experience of print in a literate society. Like Kipling's elephant's child, the 'insatiable curiosity' shown by human children means that they are thinking about and experimenting with writing long before they start school. The teacher's task, therefore, is to build on what the child has already discovered about reading and writing. Obviously this will be facilitated by knowing what sort of a knowledge base is already in existence. As the Russian psychologist Luria (1978) suggested, knowledge of the 'prehistory' of writing would greatly assist the teacher to teach writing.

Luria's Experiments

Luria carried out several studies designed to explore the development of writing in preschool children. In his experiments, children were asked to remember and repeat several sentences. Once they had, as expected, failed at this task, they were given pen and paper and asked to write down the sentences so that they could remember them better. Naturally, many children responded by protesting that they did not know how to write, but they were encouraged to think of some way of writing down the sentences.

In the earliest phase of development – the pre-writing or pre-instrumental phase – children of three to five years produced scribbles, lines, or, most often, zig-zags in imitation of adult writing. These scribbles were entirely undifferentiated, bearing no relation to the sentence which the child was supposed to be writing. (Indeed, typical of this phase is the child who begins to 'write' before he has been told what he is to write.) This kind of writing did not aid in the recall of sentences. In fact, it often reduced the number of sentences which could be recalled.

In a slightly more advanced stage, children began to use the writing as a cue. Although still appearing as undifferentiated zig-zags or lines, each sign indicated to the child that there was something to be remembered. Factors such as the position of the sign on the page seemed to assist the child to associate the sentence with the sign, although sometimes the sentence produced by the child bore little relation to the sentence dictated by the adult.

The next stage of development, found in children aged four to five years, was the beginnings of differentiation of the sign. For example, a short word or phrase would be represented by a short line, while a longer phrase would be given a longer line or a larger scribble. However, according to Luria, this was simply a representation of the rhythm of the utterance. A greater advance was seen when the child began to represent the content of the utterance. It was found that number or quantity (particularly contrasting amounts) was the most likely attribute to induce differentiation. For example, a sentence which mentioned a large number of objects would be represented with a longer zig-zag than would a sentence which described a small number. A second factor likely to induce differentiation was form. An object which had a striking colour, shape, or size would be represented in some meaningful way. For example, one child drew particularly thick and heavy lines to represent a sentence about black smoke coming out of a chimney.

At this stage the child has essentially invented pictographic writing. By five or six years, a child can successfully record and recall simple sentences about concrete objects. However, some things are impossible to record pictorially; or alternatively, it would take too long. Luria describes children who, asked to write down 'there are one thousand stars in the sky', had to be dissuaded from spending the next hour drawing one thousand stars. This sort of task may elicit symbolism: Luria claims that the child who draws two stars and says: 'I'll remember there are one thousand' is on the verge of symbolic writing.

Most children do not fully explore the possibilities of pictographic writing, because by this age they are beginning to learn alphabetic writing. However, as Luria points out, this does not result in the immediate adoption of culturally correct techniques of writing. Instead, he describes a transition period during which, although children can produce many or all of the letters of the alphabet, they still have no idea of how the writing system functions. They have yet to understand that writing is a phonetic representation of speech. And so their acquisition of conventional alphabetic symbols is an advance which results in their returning to the earliest stage of undifferentiated writing: they write letters which have no relation to the meaning of the sentences which they are asked to write and recall.

Recent Research

The research of Luria and his colleagues was for many years inaccessible to non-Russian speakers. In the West, the acquisition of writing received very little attention. In the 1970s and 1980s, however, writing began at last to be a focus for research. After a long period of concentration on the acquisition of reading, the interaction between writing and reading became evident to researchers. Marie Clay (1975) suggested that writing was a 'necessary complement' to reading: reading involved focusing on word recognition, sentences and meaning, while writing meant that the child had to pay attention to sounds and letters. Carol Chomsky (1971) even suggested that writing should come first, and that children would teach themselves to read by writing.

Clay described the writing abilities (and the progress throughout the year) of a group of children starting school in New Zealand aged around five years. She listed a number of principles which appear to control writing production in young children. The *recurring principle* allows a child to produce long messages by repeating the same symbol or word many times. The *flexibility principle* allows children to discover new letter forms (some allowable, some not) by experimenting with known symbols: rotating, reversing, adding, and deleting. The *generating principle* allows children to generate long statements by combining and recombining a small number of symbols. The *inventory principle* describes the way that children constantly make lists of what they know, be it letters, numbers, words or items. They may use the *contrasting principle* to list items which contrast in form, sound or meaning. As they continue to write, they will discover the *directional principle*: that in English, writing begins at the top left, moves across to the right, and then sweeps back to the left to begin a new line.

Clay suggests that for young children, age norms in writing ability are inappropriate because progress is dependent more on chance exposure to (or concentration on) aspects of writing than due to intelligence. She suggests that different children may acquire the arbitrary conventions of written language in a different order. Therefore it is not possible to specify fixed sequences of learning through which all children are expected to pass. Other researchers have described what they suggest is a developmentally ordered series of writing stages through which all children will pass *en route* to alphabetic writing. The most extensive and influential series of studies of writing development to date has been carried out by Emilia Ferreiro and her colleagues, mostly on Spanish-speaking children in Argentina and Mexico. Using a Piagetian framework, Ferreiro and Teberosky (1982) charted the development of the conceptualization of written language as they saw it during both the preschool years and the early years of formal education.

The main theme of Ferreiro's research is that children do not learn to write by passive receipt of instruction. As Piaget has claimed, true learning is an active process whereby children assimilate any input, changing it to fit their existing mental structures. At the same time, they accommodate by changing mental structures where they are revealed as being inadequate to explain events or to understand the world. On this view, children learn by discovering or inventing concepts for themselves. Before children learn to write alphabetically, they will therefore formulate several alternative (erroneous) hypotheses about the nature of the writing system. According to Ferreiro and Teberosky, these early hypotheses form a sequence of stages of writing development through which children will progress even if they are being taught alphabetic writing.

In the pre-writing stage, children do not differentiate between writing and pictures. Shown pictures with accompanying text, and asked where there was something to read, the youngest children Ferreiro studied pointed at the picture as well as the text. Asked to read it, children simply described salient aspects of the picture. But children soon begin to realize that writing is different from pictures, although, to begin with, writing is seen as being related to the object being written about. One of the earliest hypotheses Ferreiro found in the children she studied was the *name hypothesis*. When some children, slightly older than those described above, were shown the pictures with accompanying text, they suggested that the writing was the name of the object pictured.

Further evidence for the existence of the *name hypothesis* came from another study in which Ferreiro (1978) looked at children's reactions to text presented without pictures. A sentence – e.g., 'Daddy kicked the ball' – was first written and then read in front of the child. (Remember that all these experiments were actually carried out in Spanish.) During the reading, a pointing finger moved smoothly along the text. The child was then asked questions such as 'Where did I write *ball*?', or (pointing to a part of the text) 'What did I write here?' They found that while the oldest children accepted the adult view that each spoken word corresponded to a portion of the written text, younger ones were somewhat confused. Some, for example, claimed that the article was not written. Others said that 'la' (the), being composed of only two letters, was too small to be read.

The youngest children had an even more restricted notion of what could be written. In their view, only nouns were represented in the written text. In a sentence such as 'Daddy kicked the ball', 'Daddy' and 'ball' were written down, but not 'kicked' or 'the'. In their attempts to relate the written text to the spoken sentence, they often introduced new nouns (such as 'Mummy', or 'field', 'trees', or 'ground').

Some children found it quite impossible to segment the utterance. They insisted that no individual words were written, and that the sentence could only be located globally in the entire presented written text. A variant of this response was found in children who decided that the whole spoken sentence was located in one written segment. They then introduced related sentences and matched these to the remaining written segments. For example, a four-year-old girl, having claimed that the first word, 'Daddy', said 'Daddy kicked the ball', suggested three more sentences for the remaining three words:

'Daddy is sick', 'Daddy writes the date', and 'Daddy goes to sleep'.

As well as the *name hypothesis*, Ferreiro and Teberosky suggested that children at the first stage believed that *the text should reflect properties of the object*. When these children were asked to write, they would vary the number of symbols they used in order to reflect the size, number, or age of the person, animal or object whose name was being written. At this stage children also formed ideas about the characteristics of text. For example, they began to try not to repeat the same symbol too often in a text, or to repeat the same sequence of symbols in succeeding texts. Ferreiro called this the *variety hypothesis*. If their repertoire of letters was limited, then children would achieve variety by changing the order in which they were used. There was also a *minimum number hypothesis*: children tended to use a constant number of graphemes for each text (generally three or four), and believed that one or two symbols was too few to be considered as writing.

In all writing at this stage there is a global correspondence between the written text and the word, phrase, or sentence which the text represents. This was seen, for example, in the children who said that individual words of a sentence were not written – that the whole of the spoken sentence was located in the whole of the written text. But by the next stage, children had come to realize that writing is related not to objects but to speech. Their first attempts to segment speech into units related to units of text leads to the *syllabic hypothesis*: children at the second stage believe that each written symbol represents a syllable of spoken language.

When the syllabic hypothesis first appears, earlier hypotheses of minimum quantity and variety are temporarily in abeyance as the child concentrates on counting syllables. But when this procedure becomes more routine, the other hypotheses reappear and lead to conflict. For example, the writing of one- or two-syllable words would require one or two letters according to the syllabic hypothesis, but the minimum quantity hypothesis insists that a minimum of three or four letters are needed before the writing is complete. Various ingenious but on the whole unsatisfactory solutions to the conflict are found. Ferreiro (1984) describes how a child writes 'barque' (boat) using three symbols, and then decides that what has been written is really 'barquito' (little boat), so that the number of symbols and syllables will match.

At the same time as they produce a random selection of letters in response to a request for writing, children are beginning to learn stable strings of letters whose order and meaning are fixed: they learn to write their name, and possibly the names of other family members.

They begin to apply stable, conventional sound values to at least some of the letters they use. Ferreiro and Teberosky describe a transition stage between syllabic and alphabetic hypotheses. Children in this phase may spend many minutes trying to write something, torn between the demands of their different hypotheses. One child studied, for example, tried to write her name using moveable letters. She had some idea of what the finished product should look like; and some half-learned notions about the sound values of letters. She selected the letters she would use according to how she knew the name should look, and according to the sound values; but then she tried to read what she had written syllabically. She added and took away letters, and rearranged them many times, without ever feeling satisfied with the results of her labours. These conflicts may result in the child refusing even to attempt to write.

Finally, children achieve the highest level. They understand that writing is a phonetic representation of speech, and so they can write anything simply by phonemic analysis.

In a paper presented to the International Reading Association in Chicago in 1982, Ferreiro described a longitudinal study of children aged three to seven years. In particular, she followed the progress of over eight hundred children (median age 6;6 at the start of school), from deprived areas of Mexico during their first year at school. She discovered in these children four developmentally ordered systems of writing: pre-syllabic (i.e., Level 1 described earlier); syllabic; syllabic–alphabetic (i.e., the transition stage); and alphabetic writing. These children were seen four times during the school year, at two- or two-and-a-half-month intervals. Thirteen per cent did not show any significant advance during the school year, and another sixteen per cent jumped from pre-syllabic to alphabetic writing between visits. The remaining seventy-one per cent went through a stage of syllabic writing even though they were receiving instruction in alphabetic writing at the time. Ferreiro stresses that the syllabic hypothesis comes entirely from within the child, and that literacy development is a process whereby the child invents and constructs the writing system for himself. Only thus does he achieve true understanding of the nature of written language.

Ferreiro's publications have stimulated further research. De Goes and Martlew (1983) carried out a study in which children aged three to six years were asked to write, to write their name, to write to dictation, to copy printed words, and then to rewrite the same words without the original model. De Goes and Martlew described seven levels of conceptualization of written language. In general, these are similar but not identical to the progression reported by Ferreiro and

Teberosky. More advanced children refused to write (which was taken to indicate understanding of the principle that writing is a rule-governed activity, along with the realization that they do not yet know the rules), or had begun to use at least some letters with conventional sound values in an attempt at alphabetic writing.

De Goes and Martlew found that most of the younger children would make an attempt to copy a word constructed out of alphabet bricks, but only some letters would be reproduced, with no attempt to place them in a line or to work systematically in any direction. When the model was removed and the child asked to rewrite the same word, these children would not use their first copy as a model for their second. Older children copied the letters of a word in correct sequence, and then copied their copy when asked to rewrite.

A report by Tolchinsky-Landsmann and Levin (1985) describes the conceptualization of written language in forty-two Israeli preschoolers (aged 3;4 to 5;8). The children were first asked to draw, and then to write, four utterances: 'a house', 'a child playing with a ball', 'sky', and 'a red flower'. After each production was complete they were asked to explain what they had drawn or written. Finally they were asked to write their name.

As expected, with increasing age, the writing attempts showed more resemblances to conventional writing – e.g., in linearity, the presence of discrete units, small size, and the inclusion of recognizable Hebrew letters. Many children were more advanced at writing their own name than in writing other utterances. The youngest children tended to use consistently either one or many graphemes, irrespective of the utterance they were writing. Older children generally used around three graphemes on each occasion. Again, there was little attempt to relate the number of written symbols to the utterance. However, a small number of older children did vary the number of graphemes according to the length of utterance.

Tolchinsky-Landsmann and Levin describe five modes of interpretation of writing shown by their subjects. The first was to offer something entirely unrelated to the utterance (e.g., 'a whale'). These idiosyncratic interpretations were mainly found in the youngest group of children. Another mode was seen in children who changed the utterances but always preserved the nouns. For example, 'a child playing with a ball' was read back as 'a child and a ball'. This type of interpretation was shown by twelve per cent of three-year-olds, and decreased with age. A third group of children gave a verbatim repetition of the utterance. This was seen in fifty-five per cent of three-year-olds, but decreased with age. A mode of interpretation which became more common in older children was to segment the utterance and attempt to relate the segments to the written symbols. However, although some children used a phonetic segmentation to guide their writing, most segmentation was *post hoc*. This meant that the basis for segmentation was inconsistent, with phonemes, syllables, words, or even larger units, being used to make the utterance fit the text. One-third of five-year-olds attempted to segment utterances. The most common response, which increased with age and was seen in sixty-two per cent of five-year olds, was to give letter-names or descriptions, while insisting that they did not know the meaning of the writing.

Discussion

The research described here reveals how children explore the act of writing, both before and after receiving formal teaching. But it also raises further questions. Categorizing children's responses generally involves the imposition of order; and children tend not to fit neatly into categories or stages. Ferreiro's research is exhaustive and meticulous; and it is no doubt the desire to describe fully and to include all responses in a coherent framework which results in some confusion. For example, Ferreiro claims that Stage 1 children use a constant number of graphic symbols for each written message. But she also says that they vary the number of symbols to reflect physical changes in the object. The Israeli research suggests that the youngest children use either one or many graphemes, with older children using a constant (small) number for all utterances.

Ferreiro claims that children pass through a stage of syllabic segmentation before discovering alphabetic writing. De Goes and Martlew do not appear to find syllabic writing at all, nor is it mentioned by Clay. Tolchinsky-Landsmann and Levin find that segmentation is generally used not in writing production, but in reading back what is written. The attempt to match utterance and text (especially when utterances are of varying length and texts all consist of three graphemes), means that syllabic segmentation is only one of many ways of dividing up an utterance.

Ferreiro describes a developmentally ordered series of stages of writing development, in which children are assumed to pass through all stages on their route to understanding. Clay, however, suggests that understanding of an arbitrary system such as alphabetic writing can be reached *via* many different routes, depending on the individual experiences of children.

Ferreiro's research has been conducted mainly on Spanish-speaking children in South America. Tolchinsky-Landsmann and Levin worked with Hebrew-speaking children in Israel. Clay's observations were made in New Zealand. While some aspects of the acquisition of written language are no doubt universal, it seems likely that the conceptualization of written language may in some ways be affected by the language which is being written. For example, Ferreiro describes how children may convert a word into its diminutive (e.g., 'barque' into 'barquito' – boat and little boat), in order to achieve what they consider to be the right number of syllables. This would not normally be possible in English, although young children especially (or adults talking to children) do have the option of converting 'dog' into 'doggie', 'cat' into 'pussy-cat', or 'Tom' into 'Tommy'.

English and Spanish are written and read from left to right, while Hebrew directionality is from right to left. In Hebrew, vowels are not represented by graphemes, but are indicated by diacritical marks (dots and tiny lines) which are often omitted. Thus, Hebrew may be compared with the invented spelling described by Bissex (1980), Chomsky (1971a, b), Read (1971), and others, where children tend to record mainly consonants. This seems to suggest that vowels are not seen as salient by preschool spellers, and may imply that Hebrew is easier for young children to begin to write.

The acquisition of writing may also be affected by cultural differences, such as the age at which children start school. It may be that delaying school entry until six years, or even later, allows children who have reached advanced levels of mental competence and meta-linguistic ability to experiment with writing, and produce hypotheses about written language, which young children at school bypass.

British children start school at around five years of age, but even before school, almost all children are regular viewers of television. Although much children's television may be purely entertainment, there has for many years been a number of excellent programmes, aimed at the preschool child, which teach what might be described as 'advanced reading readiness': numbers, letter names and sounds, and even simple words. I do not know if such programmes are available in Spanish. However, it seems likely that many of the poorer children studied by Ferreiro would not have been regular television viewers. Certainly, British children may be assumed to have regular and early access to such information about reading and writing. It seems likely that this might influence their thinking about written language.

A Longitudinal Study

The rest of this chapter describes part of a longitudinal study of children attending preschool, and then moving into primary school, which I carried out in Edinburgh. The main aim of this study was to see if the development of writing in Scottish children was similar to that described by other authors. In particular, I hoped to investigate areas of discrepancy between authors: Ferreiro's *syllabic hypothesis*, for example. The claim that all children follow the same path, and that children receiving instruction at school in alphabetic writing will pass through a syllabic stage, would have particularly important educational implications, if substantiated.

Initially, there were forty preschool children in the study, though one child refused to participate. Another child moved out of the area quite early on, and a replacement was recruited. A further child who later moved out of Edinburgh was not replaced, but those who moved within Edinburgh were visited at their new school or at home. There were therefore thirty-nine children altogether, twenty-two boys and seventeen girls. They were visited at approximately six-weekly intervals (a maximum of thirteen visits), and seen individually for around twenty minutes on each occasion. Ages ranged from 3;1 to 4;9 at the start of the study, to 4;5 to 6;2 by the end.

On each visit the children were given pictures of animals, objects or activities; and asked to write the name of the animal or object, or a specific word, phrase, or sentence about the picture – e.g., 'Hanging out the washing', 'The farmer drives the tractor', or 'skipping'. Pictures of animals and objects were generally paired, with either size, length of name, or number being varied. For example, on one sheet of paper the child might be asked to write 'elephant' and 'ladybird'; or 'bear' and 'rhinoceros'; or 'snails' and 'frogs' (on a picture of two snails and three frogs). We also played games which involved the child doing some writing – e.g., producing a shopping list for a teddy who had been knocked down by a car and who was feeling too poorly to write it himself. One December they all wrote a letter to Santa. We played a version of the 'Tins game', first devised by Hughes (1986): a guessing game where toy animals were hidden in tins and the children wrote labels for the tins to improve their guesses. They wrote labels for animals in a toy farm; they showed Teddy (now recovered from his head injury) how to write his name; and on each visit they wrote their own name, and any other names they knew. The children were also given a number of tasks designed to explore their understanding of the nature of written language. For example, they were given a number of cards showing various examples of writing, letter arrangements and pictures, and asked to differentiate between those which had writing on them and those which did not.

The writing attempts produced by the children were classified into five levels of understanding. The classification was made on the basis of the style of the 'writing', and also the child's intentions if any were expressed or inferred.

Children at the first level showed no awareness of writing. When asked to label a picture they would perhaps scribble over it, or try to colour it in. Some tried to copy the picture, or made appropriate additions (e.g., buttons on a coat, or grass, or sky). Some drew a large circle around the picture, or on a blank page drew a large circle, cross, or straight line. These children seemed not to understand the difference between drawing and writing; and they did not claim to have written anything.

The productions of children at the second level – scribbles, circles, crosses, and lines – were sometimes not visibly different from those at Level One. However, these children were beginning to understand the concept of writing, in that they claimed with some confidence that they had written something. For example, Steven (4;2) scribbled over a picture of an elephant.

> *Adult:*   Tell me what you've written there.
> *Child:*   Elephant.

Later, shown a picture of ducks and swans,

> *Adult:*   Can you write their names?
> *Child:*   Yes (*and he scribbles over each one*).

Level Three children are clearly differentiating writing from drawing or scribbling. Some produce zig-zags or wavy lines in imitation of handwriting, while others produce discrete squiggles or symbols that begin to look like real letters (see Fig. 6.1). Small circles, crosses, lines and dots are included here.

By Level Four, the child's efforts approximate visually to real writing. Recognizable letters and numbers appear. Some children use them in combination with idiosyncratic signs, while others confine themselves entirely to conventional symbols. But at this level, the children generally believe that their 'writing' says what they want it

(a)

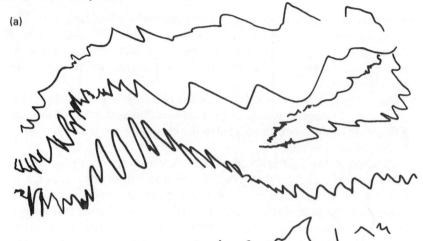

(b)

(c)

Figure 6.1 Stage 3 writing. (a) Gail (3;5) letter to Santa; (b) Steven (4;7); (c) Jamie (3;6); shopping list.

(a)

(b)

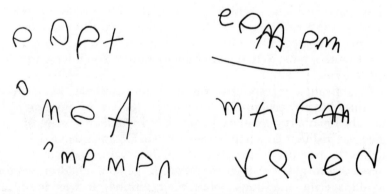

Figure 6.2 Stage 4 writing. (a) Gemma (4;3) 'Dear fish we are going to the deep pond and I'm going to swim.'; (b) Karen (4;3) 'Dear Santa alphabet tree dolly tee (?) drawing pen Karen'.

to say. They are likely to produce highly imaginative accounts of what they have written – see Fig. 6.2 – although a few children seem certain of the meaning of their written message.

At Level Five, children have achieved understanding of the phonetic principle of writing. Letters are no longer written at random, but are chosen according to the sounds of the word they are trying to write. However, children may grasp the phonetic principle before they have fully learned the letter–sound correspondences. Or, indeed, these may not have been learned at all, although the child may think she knows them. Thus Susan, at 3;9 (see Fig. 6.3a) might appear to be writing at Level Three, except that as she writes each graphic sign she mutters to herself: 'buh, eh, ih, ruh; huh, ih, puh, oh, tuh, uh, sss'. (She has named the rhinoceros a hippopotamus.) Similarly, Jennifer (3;8), given a picture of a crocodile and a dog, writes two inverted-U symbols, saying firmly 'cuh for crocodile, duh for dog'.

Some children at Level Five are happy merely to write the first sound of a word. Others, like Barbra (Fig. 6.3b), attempt the whole word. They may ask for assistance – e.g., 'How do you do a huh again?'; or 'Is it a kicking kuh or a curly cuh?' Some children would write the phonetically correct initial letter of a word and then add more letters seemingly chosen at random to complete their message. It seemed that in some children at least the phonetic principle could co-exist with a Level Four belief that any letters could be used.

Some responses did not fit into the above categories. Some pre-phonetic children, particularly when it was important to convey information, would produce a pictorial representation. Other children gave responses which indicated that they had realized that writing was a rule-bound activity, and that they also knew that they did not know the rules. Either they firmly refused to do anything ('I can't write'), or they demanded instructions ('You'll have to tell me the letters').

Classification of responses was often quite difficult. Some children produced easily recognizable letters, but others were more problematic. The child's commentary might reveal whether a series of squiggles was just that, or whether they were in fact intended to be specific letters or numbers. However, if children remained silent, it was necessary to guess at their intention. In general, children were not asked specific questions about their writing. It was found that questioning was as likely to suggest answers to an eager-to-please child, or to convince an unconfident child that his efforts were inadequate, as to elicit a reasoned reply.

At the first visit, the most common type of writing was Level Three. Fourteen children (average age 3;10) were producing zig-zags or

(a)

(b)

Figure 6.3   Stage 5 writing. (a) Susan (3;9); (b) Barbra (4;7).

squiggles that looked like writing. Another eleven children (average age 3;11) were producing Level Four writing. Three children (mean age 4;7) were writing phonetically; two wrote at Level Two, and two of the youngest were at Level One. One girl, aged 4;5, demanded that I write everything for her to copy; two children produced pictorial messages; and two refused to attempt to write.

By the end of the first year of the study, five children (average age 4;11) were at Level Five. Twelve (average age 4;7) were at Level Four, and seventeen (mean age 4;3) were writing at Level Three. One boy aged 3;10 was at Level Two, and two refused to write. After two years, eleven of the fifteen children still at preschool (mean age 4;10) were producing Level Four writing; and three (average age 5;1) were writing phonetically. One child was still at Level Three.

According to Ferreiro and Teberosky, children who had not realized that writing was a phonetic representation of speech formed several hypotheses about the nature of written language. In younger children she found the *name hypothesis*, and also the idea that characteristics of an object could be represented by the physical features of its name. Older children used the *minimum quantity hypothesis*, the hypothesis of *variety*, and finally the *syllabic hypothesis*. The writing responses given by children in this study were carefully examined for evidence that Scottish children followed the same path in learning to write.

Name hypothesis

When Ferreiro (1978) showed young children a written sentence, read it to them, and then asked where each part of the spoken sentence was written, she found a fascinating progression of responses. In particular, the youngest children believed that only nouns – names – could be written.

This experiment was tried with some of the children in my study. It was carried out in the second year, using those children (around four years old) who were still at preschool. They were shown written sentences: 'Daddy kicked the ball'; 'The boy ate a cake'; 'The baby is asleep'; 'My dog chased a cat'; and 'The baby cried', and questioned in the same way that Ferreiro questioned her children. However, this task was not a success. It was disliked intensely by the children, apparently because they were being asked questions which were meaningless. Some children refused to answer, and demanded to go back to the playroom. Others gave replies similar to those described by Ferreiro. David (4:1) claimed that each word in a sentence said that sentence. Peter (4:3) introduced new ideas so that each word said a different sentence. However, he got fixated on 'Daddy kicking the ball', so that later sentences still said things like 'Daddy kicked the ball up in the air', and 'Daddy kicked the ball into the teddy'. Older children matched the written and spoken texts word for word. But no child claimed that verbs could not be written, although Andrew (4;3) said that 'boy' and 'a' were not written; and Douglas (4;4) said that 'boy' was not written (in the sentence 'The boy ate a cake'). All in all, the results from this task were unsatisfactory and confusing, and it was decided to approach the topic differently.

At the next session, a large matchbox containing lower-case letter-tiles taken from a Junior Scrabble game was emptied on to the table in front of the child. We played with the tiles, arranging them in rows or piles, and selecting letters which the child recognized. Then I formed a word using the letters, saying to the child: 'Look, I've made a word here. It might say "kick" or it might say "kite". Which one do you think it says?' Each time, the child was offered a choice between a noun (the name of an object, substance, or creature) and a word which was either a verb or a noun describing an activity: *kick/kite*, *climb/clay*, *hurry/honey*, and *swim/swan*. Each time, the word constructed was the verb/action word of the pair (but the order of presentation of choices was varied). The children's choices are shown in Table 6.1

When making their choices, children spontaneously gave reasons such as: 'We had clay in the nursery', or 'I went swimming yesterday', or 'I had honey on my toast'. They also appeared to see the action words as verbs: one boy mimed each action as it was mentioned, and those who used the words used them as verbs. This study did not give any support to the idea that young children fail to believe that verbs can be written.

Tolchinsky-Landsmann and Levin reported a stage in the interpretation of texts where the utterance was changed but the nouns preserved. They found this type of response in twelve per cent of three-year-olds and seven per cent of four-year-olds, and suggested that these children saw writing as representing objects rather than words. However, if it is recalled that in this study there were only

Table 6.1. *Children's selections.*

kite	23	kick	11
clay	13	climb	22
swan	11	swim	20
honey	18	hurry	12
Total nouns	65	Total verbs	65

fourteen children in each age group, it is clear that this type of response was not particularly common. If a child, asked to write: 'a child playing with a ball', is then asked to read back what he has written, his response – 'a child and a ball' – may indicate a poor memory for what he was told to write, rather than a disinclination to write verbs. Certainly none of the Edinburgh children objected to writing 'skipping', or phrases such as 'skeletons swinging' or 'skeletons sleeping'.

Written text reflects object properties

In each session of the present study, children were asked to write the names of pairs of animals or objects. Sometimes the pairs differed in size (e.g., *fish/whale, elephant/ladybird*) and sometimes in number (e.g., *one swan/eight ducks, three snails/two frogs*). There was very little evidence of children varying the number of graphemes to reflect the characteristics of the object. Most children tended to use around the same number of symbols for each response. When there were different numbers of objects, it was common for the child to write a name beside each object. For example, given the *snails/frogs* picture, and asked to write 'snails' and 'frogs', the child would rather write 'snail' three times and 'frog' twice.

However, a small number of children did seem to believe on some occasions that the physical characteristics of the text could reflect those of the object. Neil (5;0) announced that because an elephant was so big, its name would have to be written in large letters. But when he had finished, there was in fact no noticeable difference in the size of the letters used for 'elephant' and for 'ladybird'. Martin (5;5), writing six letters for *whale* and three for *fish*, explained that this was because the whale was bigger. At the same session he had written fruit names, and he was asked why he had given 'strawberry' more letters than the others. He thought a while before replying, 'because it's red'. Perhaps we can believe Neil and Martin, when they proffered their statements unasked. Less credible is Lisa (5;3), who was asked why she had written 'sheep' with more letters than 'cow'. 'Because sheep is bigger than cow', she replied, inaccurately.

Questioning children about why they used the particular letters they did, or the numbers of letters they did, was more likely to produce a *post hoc* justification than evidence of prior planning. Nor can one reliably make inferences about intentions from the writing samples produced by the child.

For example, Stuart (Fig. 6.4) wrote seven letters for crocodile, and

Figure 6.4 Stuart (3;10).

only three for dog. Is this because he meant to? Or because he reached the edge of the page after three letters and was obliged to stop? Some children quite obviously get carried away when writing, and continue making letters until they reach the edge of the page. Others, perhaps having difficulty in forming the letters they want, clearly get fed up and stop prematurely. One cannot even be sure that children have written what they were instructed to write. Some children, shown a picture of a bear and a rhinoceros (selected as examples of large animals) named the bear a 'teddy-bear' (i.e., a small and friendly animal). Even though I explained that it was not a teddy but a large and fierce bear, and then asked them to write 'bear', some children persisted in their miscalling. Later asked to read what they had written, it would be: 'teddy-bear'.

Minimum quantity hypothesis

Many children in the present study used a single grapheme to represent every word or phrase they intended to write. No children objected to one- or two-letter words when shown written sentences such as 'My dog chased a cat'. When shown a number of cards which might or might not have had writing on them, around seventy to eighty per cent of children of all ages said that a single large capital letter was an example of writing, though some older children explained that it was not writing, 'just a letter'.

Variety hypothesis

If they could, children tended to vary the letters they used. Jamie (4;7), for example, knew only the letters of his name and used them in different combinations for different texts (see Fig. 6.5). But this was not invariable: his first two texts are the same. Jenny (4;3) used a row of inverted-U symbols to say everything in her shopping list, while on another page she wrote 'all her names' using quite a varied selection. Douglas had a large number of letters and symbols at his disposal, yet at 4;8 he used 'EiAO' to write 'koala bear', 'penguin', and 'cat' (on the same page). Some older (phonetic) children, asked to distinguish writing from non-writing in the task mentioned above, said the 'eeeeeeee' was not writing, because all the letters were the same. However, all eighteen four-year-olds said that it was writing.

Syllabic hypothesis

Quite often, either while children wrote or when they were asked to read back what they had written, they would attempt to break up words into smaller units, and to relate those units in some way to the written symbols. However, it is not clear whether they were trying to make the symbols fit the word, or the word fit the symbols. Short words might be expanded to match a large number of symbols – e.g., '*swoh – oh- oh- oh- on*' [swan]; or just as common, '*swoh -oh- oh – oh – swan*'. Long words would be contracted to match a small number of symbols, as in '*cat – erpillar*'. The pointing finger tended to move smoothly along the line of writing, and often the number of sounds vocalized would not match the number of graphemes. The important thing seemed to be to make the last spoken sound coincide with pointing to the last written letter. (This of course is the type of behaviour commonly observed in young children counting.) Some children achieved this by pronouncing the whole word for each written symbol, with an extra-triumphant emphasis for the last symbol. Kamler and Kilaur (1983) report similar behaviour in Coline (aged 4;6), who 'wrote' sentences and then tried to achieve a match between voice and print. She wrote groups of symbols (one group per line) and had to 'read' her sentence several times, adding either more symbols or more spoken words, changing the way in which written text and spoken words were related, until eventually she managed to be speaking the final word while pointing to the final group of symbols.

In a specific attempt to find evidence of Ferreiro's syllabic hypothesis, children were asked on two occasions to write several names of

Figure 6.5   Jamie (4;7).

varying length on the same page. The first page showed pictures of different kinds of fruit: apple, banana, plum, strawberry, orange, and pear. Five months later, they were asked to write (beside illustrations) 'umbrella', 'boat', 'house', 'television', and 'car'. The number of symbols used by those children who wrote discrete symbols was counted (excluding children whose writing was already phonetic). The average number of symbols used for each word is shown in Table 6.2.

It seems clear that the number of syllables in a word does not affect the number of graphemes used by these pre-phonetic children to write the word. Would it in fact be reasonable to expect these children to use syllables as a guide to the length of a word? In an American study, Liberman *et al.* (1974) asked children to tap out the number of syllables in a selection of words. They found that just under half of four- and five-year-olds could do this correctly; it was not until First Grade (six years of age) that ninety per cent success was achieved. In another study, Rozin *et al.* (1974) showed children two words on a card: one short word and one long, such as 'mow' and 'motorcycle'. One of the words was spoken aloud, and children were asked which of the written words corresponded to the spoken word. They found that inner-city five-year-olds did not perform well: only eleven per cent understood that the length of a spoken word would be reflected in its length when written. Suburban, middle-class five-year-olds were forty-three per cent successful.

It therefore seems very likely that three- and four-year-olds are not able to detect syllables with any accuracy. By five years of age, perhaps half the children would be capable of constructing a syllabic hypothesis, but by five years of age many of these children have begun to understand that writing involves phonemic, not syllabic analysis. It is true that phonemic analysis is an even more advanced skill than syllabic analysis; but these young children do not in general attempt to identify all the sounds in a word. Many are content to record just the first sound, while others pick out a few salient sounds – mostly consonants.

Table 6.2. *Average numbers of symbols.*

plum	3.0	boat	4.5
pear	2.9	house	3.5
apple	3.1	car	3.7
orange	2.8	umbrella	3.5
banana	2.9	television	4.1
strawberry	2.9		

Ferreiro claims that seventy per cent of the children she studied developed a syllabic hypothesis, even though they were at school receiving instruction in the alphabet and alphabetic writing. This was not found in the present study. Most children very quickly began to write phonetically once they reached primary school. Those who did not remained at Level Four, using conventional letters and numbers in an unconventional way. The syllabic segmentation which was found was similar to that reported by Tolchinsky-Landsmann and Levin: generally *post hoc*, and merely one of many alternative forms of segmentation used by the children. It is therefore possible that Ferreiro's results are due to the fact that her deprived subjects were older than those in other studies. However, in a later report (1984) of a longitudinal study of thirty-three younger children, she also reports a syllabic stage.

Name writing

On my first visit to the preschool, eleven out of thirty-six children made a recognizable attempt to write their name. These were generally the oldest children, with an average age of 4;4. Another six refused the task, saying that they could not write their name. Looking at each child in his last month (June) at preschool before starting primary school the following August, twenty-three out of thirty-seven could make an at least recognizable attempt to write their own name. Another five children could get the first one or two letters of their name correct.

Ferreiro suggests that being taught to write their own name gives children much information about the writing system: information which frequently conflicts with the hypotheses they have formed, and which may hasten progress towards a phonetic theory. For example, she described Santiago, who worried because his name had eight letters but only four syllables. It may well be true that learning how to write their name causes children to reflect on writing in general, and that they apply information about the writing system contained in their name to their attempts to write other things. Certainly children are almost always more advanced in writing their own name than at writing other texts. However, many children learn to write their name quite early on, without generalizing to other writing. For example, Lisa at 4;6, could write her own name (*Lisa* and *surname*), as well as the names of her two brothers, *Andrew* and *Christopher*. But for the whole of her last year at preschool she continued to write at Level Four, selecting letters at random to write whatever was suggested. She did not appear to reflect on the fact that her name-writing was rule-governed, while writing other texts was not. This type of behaviour is also reported by Tolchinsky-Landsmann and Levin, who note that learning how to write one's own name does not immediately raise the level of conceptualization of written language in general.

Many children in the present study seemed quite capable of holding contradictory theories about written language, believing them all at once – or at least switching quickly from one to another. A quite common phenomenon on the way to full phonetic writing was to write the first sound of a word correctly, and then to add more letters which appeared to bear no relation to the sounds of the word being written. For example, Lisa at 5;6, after a month at school, wrote 'miij' for 'mouse' and 'Cil8' for 'caterpillar'. A similar kind of dissociation was seen in Thomas, also 5;6, after seven months at school. He had already written 'worm' and 'snake' using seemingly random letters. When shown a picture of a koala bear, a penguin, and a cat, and asked 'Can you write their names?', he replied 'I know how to write a cat's name'. The tone of his voice implied that he had not known how to write 'worm' or 'snake', and that he did not know how to write 'koala bear' or 'penguin'. He wrote 'c', and then asked 'What's next after the cuh?' After I told him, ('a'), he then supplied the 't' himself. He then wrote 'penguin' ('ssil') and 'koala bear' ('ook-lom'). When he had finished I asked him to read to me what he had written. He 'read' – 'cat ... penguin ... koala bear', making no distinction between the one he could write and the ones he could not.

It is obvious that learning to write his name gives a child ideas about writing in general. For one thing, it gives him a repertoire of letters which he can then use for other tasks. But the extent to which it makes him question his beliefs about written language is dubious. Some children clearly do not worry that different kinds of writing appear to follow different rules. It may be that this is related to the way in which they are taught to write their name. Perhaps some teachers (i.e., parents, grandparents, siblings, and others) write the name out in full, and leave the child to copy and memorize it as a whole. Others teach it letter by letter – e.g., '*sss ooh sss ah nnn, Susan*'. As yet, we have no systematic information on this point.

As Donaldson (1984) points out, it has become fashionable to stress the capabilities of children: to describe them in terms of what they can do, rather than by what they cannot do. It has also been common to explain their errors in terms of their accomplishments: e.g., that they fail the traditional conservation tasks not because they do not conserve, but because they are so skilled at the rules of conversation and discourse. In this tradition, Ferreiro believes that the writing attempts of pre-phonetic children are directed by a series of complex hypotheses about the nature of written language. However, the results obtained in my Edinburgh study appear to give either only partial, or no support, to Ferreiro's ideas. This may imply that the children she studied, in a different culture, took a different route towards written language. The children in her short longitudinal study were not directly comparable to the Edinburgh children, in that they were from a particularly deprived area, and were much older, starting school at around 6;6.

The Edinburgh children divided into three main groups. Nine children (twenty-four per cent) learned to write phonetically while still attending preschool. Eleven children remained at Level Four while at preschool, but made rapid progress in phonetic writing in their first few months at primary school. Six school entrants were very slow to learn, but they showed no signs of using a syllabic hypothesis. Instead, they continued to write at Level Four. Another twelve children were still at preschool and still pre-phonetic by the end of the study. During the next year, these children would divide into those who would learn easily, and those few who would have difficulty at school.

The most striking result of this study was the absence of steady progress in writing shown by preschool children. Most learned a style of writing very early on, and continued at that level for the rest of the study – unless they were given specific teaching in writing at primary school, where most showed themselves wholly receptive to instruction in phonetic writing.

Conclusions

Writing for many young children may be seen more as a motor skill than as a meaningful method of communication. They may initially learn to form letters in imitation of parents and older siblings, without bothering too much about which letters to use when. The achievement of filling page after page with letters and squiggles, as my daughter used to do, may be enough for them. Young children who 'read' their 'writing' by pointing with a finger and breaking words up into fragments may be doing so because this is the way they see their older siblings dealing with first readers brought home from school. Evidence from my Edinburgh study did not suggest that writing production in pre-phonetic children was reliably controlled by any of the hypotheses suggested by Ferreiro. Nor have these hypotheses been described by other researchers.

It seems, then, that young children are being both over-estimated and under-estimated in regard to their ability to learn to write. Although they do form some ideas about the nature of written language, these ideas tend to be vague and unclear, and do not generally control writing production. However, this very vagueness means that many children are able to benefit from instruction in writing at an early age. Some demand – and receive – such instruction from family members, and learn to write phonetically before they reach school. Others could be able to take advantage of such information if it was presented at preschool.

Given the receptivity of young minds, and the importance of literacy to intellectual development, it would seem that preschools have been missing a great opportunity to help children towards the moment of insight described by Donaldson (1984) – the realization that marks on paper can stand for spoken language.

7 Children's Computation

Martin Hughes
University of Exeter

The Shaping of Minds to Come

In the final chapter of *Children's Minds* (1978), called 'The Shape of Minds to Come', Margaret Donaldson summarizes the main arguments of her book. She reminds us that much of the research she has reviewed earlier shows that, by the time they come to school, most young children are surprisingly competent as thinkers and language-users. Their abilities, however, manifest themselves only in meaningful real-life situations involving human intentions: '... these human intentions are the matrix in which the child's thinking is embedded'. Donaldson goes on to contrast these 'embedded' skills with the 'disembedded' thinking skills which are required of the child by the educational system – the child needs to be able 'to call the powers of his mind into service *at will* and use them to tackle problems which do not arise out of the old familiar matrix...'. Donaldson makes clear that the acquisition of disembedded thinking skills is of crucial importance both for the individual and for society: 'whether we like it or not, we need these skills – and, collectively, we know it'. She recognizes, however, that the educational system as it is currently constituted is failing to instil these valued intellectual skills in a large number of pupils, with the result that 'schooling at present turns into a wretched experience for many children, however happily it may begin, and that something most urgently needs to be done to change this'.

In the decade or so which has passed since Donaldson wrote these words, it is clear that little has been done to change the educational experience of most pupils in schools. Indeed, the recent onset of a National Curriculum and the standardized assessment of all children appear to signal, in Britain at least, a return to a more limited view of

education. There has, however, been one major educational development in the 1980s which has been greeted by many with a great deal
of enthusiasm – namely, the arrival of powerful micro-computers in
the everyday lives of children, a development which would have
been hard to predict at the time that *Children's Minds* was written. Yet
despite the recent rapid spread of micro-computer technology, and
the optimism that has surrounded it, there is still a fundamental
question to be answered. Is it possible that computers and other
forms of new technology will succeed where other educational
techniques have failed, and produce the kind of disembedded thinking skills which, according to Donaldson, society so desperately
needs? The main aim of this chapter is to look at the progress made to
date in answering this question.

The chapter has a further aim. In 'The Shape of Minds to Come',
Donaldson voices a deeply felt concern about these intellectual skills
being made available to all members of society. The second aim of the
chapter will therefore be to look at whether any benefits which might
result from using computers will be equally shared amongst all
children. In particular, we will look at the frequently voiced fear that
girls will be seriously hindered from obtaining the same benefits as
boys.

The Process of Disembedding

Computers can be used in many different ways to enhance children's
thinking. Each of these different approaches rests on a particular view
of how children can be helped to learn. If we are to see most clearly
how computers can be used to help children acquire disembedded
thinking, we need first to appreciate how Donaldson herself views
the process of disembedding. This requires a consideration of some
critical passages in *Children's Minds*.

Donaldson first introduces the term 'disembedded' by contrasting
it with thinking which is 'embedded' in the context of familiar goals
and intentions:

> So long as our thinking is sustained by this kind of human sense, and
> so long as the conclusion to which the reasoning leads is not in conflict
> with something which we know or believe or want to believe, we tend
> to have no difficulty . . . However, when we move beyond the bounds
> of human sense there is a dramatic difference. Thinking which does
> move beyond these bounds, so that it no longer operates within the
> supportive context of meaningful events, is often called 'formal' or

'abstract' ... I shall speak rather of 'disembedded' thinking, hoping
that the name will convey the notion that this is thought that has been
prised out of the old primitive matrix within which originally all our
thinking is contained. (p. 76)

Having established that disembedded thinking is difficult, Donaldson goes on to consider whether it should therefore remain the
province of a privileged minority. She is clear that it should not be so,
arguing that intelligence is not a fixed commodity but something
which can be fostered by appropriate means, including the use of
technology. The technology with which she is particularly concerned
in *Children's Minds* is that by which speech is made visible and
permanent, namely writing. Nevertheless, it is clear that the argument also applies to other forms of technology, such as the micro-
computer.

How exactly does Donaldson propose that disembedded thinking
should be made more generally available? She puts considerable
emphasis on the process of reflection, arguing that if children are to
be successful in our educational system, they will have to learn to
'turn language and thought in upon themselves'. This notion of
reflective self-awareness is, for Donaldson, very close to the notions
of consciousness and control. She quotes approvingly Vygotsky's
statement that 'control of a function is the counterpart of one's
consciousness of it', and adds that if children are going to control and
direct their own thinking, in the way she believes is desirable, then
they must also become conscious of it. She admits there is still much
we need to learn about how self-awareness grows, but she nevertheless points out that:

... awareness typically develops when something gives us pause and
when consequently, instead of just acting, we stop to consider the
possibilities of acting which are before us. The claim is that we heighten
our awareness of what is actual by considering what is possible. We are
conscious of what we do to the extent that we are conscious also of
what we do *not* do – of what we might have done. The notion of *choice* is
thus central. (p. 94)

Other notions are central too. In her subsequent discussion of
reading, Donaldson stresses the importance of the child having time
to reflect. Haste and reflective thought, she argues, do not go
together. But time alone is not enough: structure is important too.
The thoughtful consideration of possibilities, she argues, can take
place 'only when there is a situation with enough structure in it to

reduce the possibilities to some manageable set . . . No one, child or adult, can weigh up possibilities in a situation where they are infinite – or even very numerous.'

Donaldson also emphasizes the role of error in learning. She is clearly not one of those psychologists who believes in reducing children's mistakes to the absolute minimum:

> . . . it is also quite clear that error can play a highly constructive role in the development of thinking . . . [but] being wrong without knowing it is clearly not of much value! So if we are going to try to put the occurrence of error to good use in education, we must ask how we can make children aware of their errors – how we can help to bring them to the critical realization 'I am wrong!' (pp. 107–8)

Finally, Donaldson stresses the importance of the child feeling in control. In her chapter on the role of motivation in learning, she asks why extrinsic motivation, where the rewards are provided by some-one or something outside the activity, appears to be much less likely to lead to effective learning than intrinsic motivation, where the rewards come from the activity itself: 'The explanation which fits the known facts most nearly would seem to be that we enjoy best and engage most readily in activities which we *experience as freely chosen*. We do not like being controlled, we like controlling ourselves.'

We can now see more clearly some of the basic principles of Donaldson's position. She believes that we can help many more children achieve disembedded thinking by the appropriate use of educational techniques and technologies. She argues that an impor-tant part of this process is that children must become aware of and reflect on their own thought processes, and that this is an essential part of gaining control over them. In order to achieve these ends, a number of elements are important: time, structure, allowing children to make errors, intrinsic motivation, and a feeling of being in control. We can now look at how the computer might be used to help in this process.

The Use of Computers to Promote Thinking

The idea that computers can help children acquire thinking skills does not have a lengthy history: indeed, it is little more than twenty years since the first experimental projects were set up. Nevertheless, even in this brief period, the potential of computers has been advocated with a good deal of enthusiasm from a number of very different perspectives. Here we will briefly review some of the main approaches – more detailed overviews can be found elsewhere (e.g., O'Shea and Self, 1983; Solomon, 1986; Straker, 1989).

One major approach consists of using the *computer as a tutor* – that is, to deliver predetermined problems or tasks to a child at an appropriate level of difficulty. This approach is for the most part based on the traditional behaviourist theory that pupils learn best through repeatedly carrying out tasks tailored to their particular level of expertise. It is no surprise that programs embodying this principle are frequently known as 'drill-and-practice'.

One of the earliest examples of this approach comes from the work carried out by Pat Suppes at Stanford University in the 1960s (e.g., Suppes and Morningstar, 1969). In Suppes' projects the child would typically work alone at a computer terminal, carrying out arithmetic problems presented by computer. The level of difficulty of each problem was determined by the child's previous performance. Suppes reported that the children taking part in his research made significant gains on arithmetic tests, and the software on which the work is based is still selling widely in the USA today.

A more recent example of the computer as tutor comes from a series of experiments carried out by Richard Riding and Stuart Powell at the University of Birmingham (Riding and Powell, 1985, 1986, 1987). In this work children aged four and five years were individually presented with a series of computer-based activities designed to encourage 'critical thinking skills'. Typical activities involved the classification and discrimination of shapes, the use of auditory and visual memory, and perceptual matching. Riding and Powell report that children undertaking these activities made significantly greater gains on a test of non-verbal intelligence (Raven's Matrices) than did a control group of children who received no such activities. They also report that in one study (Riding and Powell, 1987) the benefits transferred to a test of reading performance, but only for the low-attaining children. There was no corresponding transfer to a test of mathematical performance.

Current developments in this area focus on the attempt to produce 'intelligent tutoring systems' (e.g., Wenger, 1987; Self, 1988) which incorporate more complex models of both the learner and the learning process. At present, however, the availability of such systems outside the laboratory is severely limited. Instead, classroom teachers are much more likely to encounter such drill-and-practice programs as 'Teacher in the Custard', in which young children are presented with a series of simple arithmetic problems on the screen. If they get these correct, they are 'rewarded' with a graphics display in which a cartoon teacher is unceremoniously dumped into a large bowl of custard. Needless to say, this is an extremely attractive piece of software for many young children.

Despite the positive findings reported by researchers such as Suppes, Riding and Powell, it is not immediately clear that the computer as tutor will have a significant part to play in helping with the disembedding of children's thinking. True, this use of the computer can certainly meet some of Donaldson's criteria: it provides structure, allows children to carry out tasks at their own pace, and gives feedback on errors. It can also be highly motivating, in the sense that children will 'freely choose' such computer-presented tasks – although the motivation appears to come more from the medium than from the tasks themselves (see Lepper, 1985, for further discussion of this issue). What the computer as tutor cannot do, at present, is to provide children with the opportunity to reflect on their own thinking. It may be useful as an aid in teaching specific, definable skills, but it is unlikely to play a major role in the process of disembedding.

A second major approach is to use the *computer as a simulator*. Here, the processing power of the computer, and typically its graphics capability as well, is used to create a simulated environment in which the pupil can have learning experiences as if in a real environment, but without the attendant disadvantages. For example, computer-controlled flight simulators are widely used for teaching trainee pilots how to fly an aeroplane – there are clear disadvantages in allowing a novice pilot to learn at the controls of a real aeroplane, and so the simulator provides the learning experiences of 'real' flying, but in a more secure manner.

Some of the most popular examples of current classroom software use the computer essentially as a simulator. In British primary schools there has recently been a great deal of enthusiasm for adventure games in which the computer presents children with simulated environments (often magical or mystical) in which tasks have to be undertaken and problems have to be solved. The most popular of these is 'Granny's Garden', in which children are invited to help a King and Queen find their six children who have been taken away by a Wicked Witch: to accomplish their task, the children have to solve a wide variety of logical and perceptual problems. A more recent example is 'Shopping on Mars' (O'Shea, 1988), in which children have to carry out shopping tasks on the alien world of Mars, where things are not necessarily what one might expect them to be.

As with the computer as tutor, the computer as simulator undoubtedly has a place in educational practice. However, it is not immediately clear how this approach can help in the process of disembedding. Rather, it seems that simulations provide environments which engage and stimulate children's *embedded* thinking and reasoning skills. This in itself may be unusual in the normal classroom, but it may not help greatly with the process of disembedding. In particular, the appeal that such games have, and the excitement they often generate at the keyboard, may act to prevent rather than encourage quiet reflection. As Lawless and Simms (1986) point out in a report on children using 'Granny's Garden', the children were so keen to play the game that they rushed through the program at a great pace. 'The children were capable of "what if" -ing, but as soon as I stopped probing for their reasons, they rapidly galloped on through the program without pause for reflection or discussion'. Of course, this may be merely the effect of novelty, but it nevertheless reminds us that there may be a considerable conflict between children 'being motivated' and 'pausing for reflection'.

A third main approach is to use the *computer as a tool*. That is, instead of presenting predetermined tasks or activities, the computer is used as an open-ended content-free device which can help learners achieve their own educational objectives. The main examples within this category are spreadsheets, telecommunication, databases, word-processing and programming. We will consider only the last two here.

At present, word-processing is probably the most common application of computers throughout the world. It is also slowly being introduced to children in school (e.g., Daiute, 1985; Pearson and Wilkinson, 1986). Word-processing clearly has many attractions: for young children it may be easier to press a key than to form a letter, and for all children the opportunity to edit and manipulate text, while retaining a professional-looking product at the end of the writing and rewriting process, is very appealing. There are, however, some problems – the QWERTY keyboard is cumbersome and outdated, and children lack the keyboard skills required for the rapid entry of text.

The use of word-processors in education accords well with Donaldson's views on the importance of reading and writing as a major form of disembedding. However, it has yet to receive systematic study from that point of view. Indeed, there have been very few systematic studies to date of children using word-processors. One exception is a comparison by Peter Hunter (1989) of children's use of word-processors and traditional handwriting. The study was carried out with a small group of ten-year-olds, and their task was to produce a class newspaper. Half the children produced the newspaper first on a word-processor, followed by handwriting, while the other half worked in the reverse order. Hunter reports that the children produced about twice as much text when using the word-processor, but that the actual quality of text was similar in both conditions. In other words, the word-processor was motivating the children to write more, but it was not influencing the way that they wrote. In addition, Hunter reports that while the children used the word-processor extensively to delete small errors as they wrote, they did not engage in the major manipulations that word-processors allow, such as changing the position of large pieces of text.

The other main use of computers as tools is for *programming*, in which children themselves write the instructions which the computer will then carry out. Programming has been much more widely researched than word-processing, and will be considered at greater length.

The Development of Thinking Skills through Programming

The idea that thinking skills can be developed through computer programming has been put forward many times over the last twenty years. The most well-known and enthusiastic advocate of this approach is undoubtedly Seymour Papert, and his book *Mindstorms* (1980) is regarded by many as the bible of educational computing. We will look at Papert's views in some detail, as there are clear parallels with those of Donaldson.

Papert is particularly associated with the programming language Logo, which he helped design in the 1960s. Logo is a full programming language with many powerful features, of which the most well-known is Turtle graphics. The Turtle is a small wheeled robot which can be made to move around on the floor or on a table, and it comes equipped with a pen which can be lowered on to a sheet of paper. In Turtle graphics, a subset of Logo, the child writes programs to control the movements of the Turtle, and thus produces patterns and pictures on the paper. The Turtle can also be simulated on a computer screen, and the Turtle's movements appear as patterns on the screen.

In *Mindstorms* Papert puts forward many claims concerning the benefits to children of using Logo. There are three main arguments which are particularly pervasive.

First, Papert argues that Turtle graphics is an especially attractive method for learning about mathematics. In order to produce a desired effect the child has to communicate a mathematical message to the Turtle – how far it must travel forward, how far it must turn and in what direction, how many times the elements of a pattern must be repeated, and so on. The metaphor Papert uses for this kind of communication is 'Mathland', i.e., 'a context which is to learning mathematics what living in France is to learning French'. Thus the Turtle makes the learning of abstract, formal mathematics more relevant to the child, and linked more to the child's own personal knowledge, compared with more traditional methods of learning mathematics.

Second, Papert is not talking just about mathematics: rather, he appears to believe that programming in Logo can produce more general cognitive gains. He argues, for example, that 'learning to communicate with a computer may change the way other learning takes place'. In particular, Papert argues that learning to program in Logo can facilitate the development of general problem-solving skills, such as breaking down a problem into smaller and more manageable parts. These skills, he argues, can then be used in situations which do not at first sight resemble the programming of computers, such as learning to juggle or learning to walk on stilts (pp. 104–5).

The third important claim which Papert makes is that Logo enables children to think about their own thinking. Programming in Logo, he claims, requires children to express their plans and ideas in a specific concrete form – as programs. Their thinking thus becomes visible, and open to inspection by themselves and others.

> Even the simplest Turtle work can open new opportunities for sharpening one's thinking about thinking. Programming the Turtle starts by making one reflect on how one does oneself what one would like the Turtle to do. Thus teaching the Turtle to act or to 'think' can lead one to reflect on one's own actions and thinking. And as children move on, they program the computer to make more complex decisions and find themselves engaged in reflecting on more complex aspects of their thinking. (p. 28)

There are clear parallels here between the processes which Donaldson believes are important for disembedding, and the claims made by Papert for programming in Logo. But there are further parallels which can be drawn between these two theorists. For example, Papert, like Donaldson, places great emphasis on the child being 'in control'. This emerges most strongly when he contrasts the way in which computers are most likely to be used in American schools (as tutors) with the approach he is advocating (as a tool):

In many schools today, the phrase 'computer-aided instruction' means making the computer teach the child. One might say the *computer is being used to program* the child. In my vision, *the child programs the computer* and, in doing so, both acquires a sense of mastery over a piece of the most modern and powerful technology and establishes an intimate contact with some of the deepest ideas from science, from mathematics, and from the art of intellectual model building. (p. 5, emphases in original)

Papert also places considerable value on children learning from their mistakes. Indeed, he argues that one of the fundamental advantages of working in a Logo environment is that it encourages a positive attitude towards error:

Many children are held back in their learning because they have a model of learning in which you have either 'got it' or 'got it wrong'. But when you learn to program a computer you almost never get it right the first time. Learning to be a master programmer is learning to become highly skilled at isolating and correcting 'bugs', the parts that keep the program from working. The question to ask about the program is not whether it is right or wrong, but if it is fixable. If this way of looking at intellectual products were generalized to how the larger culture thinks about knowledge and its acquisition, we all might be less intimidated by our fears of 'being wrong'. (p. 23)

This brief examination of Papert's philosophy reveals a number of distinct similarities with the views of Donaldson. Both theorists recognize that technology has a role to play in promoting abstract thinking; both emphasize the importance of children reflecting on their own thought processes; both see the need for the child to be in control and self-motivated; and both see errors as having a positive role to play in learning. At the same time, there are important differences between them. Papert quite explicitly bases his philosophy on the theories of Piaget: he stresses that children construct their own intellectual structures and appears to believe that adults have a minimal effect – if not a negative one – on this process. Donaldson, in contrast, is quite critical of Piaget in *Children's Minds*, and instead pays greater allegiance to Vygotsky. Accordingly, she places much more emphasis than Papert does on the role which adults play in shaping children's intellectual development, and indeed on the whole social context in which learning takes place.

While Donaldson did not argue in *Children's Minds* for any explicit connection between computer programming and disembedded thinking, she was fully aware of the connection between the two. She was deeply impressed by an incident involving a robot called FREDDY, which had been built by Stephen Salter and Harry Barrow at the Department of Artificial Intelligence at Edinburgh University. The incident in question occurred when FREDDY was confronted with various objects, including a box, which had been arranged at random on a table. FREDDY was given the instruction 'TIDYWORLD', a command which called various procedures aimed at putting all the objects on the table in the box. FREDDY picked up each object in turn and placed it in the box, and it seemed that he had completed the task in question. However, he then picked up the *box*, put it down, picked it up again, put it down again, and would presumably have continued indefinitely if the program had not been interrupted. What FREDDY was doing is clear: he had interpreted his instructions quite literally – he was to put *all* objects on the table into the box, and that, for FREDDY, included the box itself!

Donaldson used this incident to illustrate the difference between embedded and disembedded modes of thinking. A human being, asked to put 'all the objects on the table in the box', would not have interpreted the instruction in the way that FREDDY did, but would have assumed, no doubt without giving it conscious thought, that the phrase 'all the objects on the table' *in this particular context* did *not* include the box. The human would have made sense of the instructions in the context of the task. But computers do not, as a rule, make sense of instructions in this way – they operate in a much more disembedded fashion, responding exactly to the instructions they are given.

This incident is a revealing illustration of the different ways in which humans and computers operate. It is not, of course, a good advertisement for the superiority of disembedded thinking – we do not want children to behave quite like FREDDY did! But it does raise the possibility that children might benefit from the opportunity to reflect on why FREDDY went wrong. If children are to become familiar with such disembedded modes of thought, then perhaps the experience of writing and running programs themselves will provide children with relevant experience. In other words, it could well be argued that learning to program is a particularly good way of helping with the process of disembedding.

Research on the Effects of Programming

What, then, is the evidence that programming computers helps children acquire thinking skills? A good deal of research has been carried out in this area, and several reviews are now available (e.g., Ross and Howe, 1981; Pea and Kurland, 1984; Simon, 1987; Govier, 1988; Johanson, 1988). Virtually none of this work – apart from our own, which will be described later – has been carried out within the framework of Donaldson's concept of disembedding. Instead, most of the work has explicitly set out to evaluate Papert's claims, and has been carried out with the programming language Logo – quite understandably given the impact which *Mindstorms* has had on the educational world. While the overall picture emerging is still not totally conclusive, three provisional conclusions can be drawn.

First, it appears that exposure to Logo does not by itself automatically lead to generalizable gains in problem-solving abilities. While some studies have shown that programming can lead to improvements on standardized problem-solving tests, most studies have found little or no generalizable effect. Not surprisingly, this had led to feelings of disappointment and frustration in the world of educational computing, and a certain backlash against Papert. He himself has little time for such research, claiming it is based on the fundamental error of thinking that something as novel and revolutionary as the Logo approach to education can be evaluated by standard pre- and post-tests, as if it were just another 'treatment' (e.g., Papert, 1987). The debate continues, but it is clear that those who believed that Logo was an educational 'cure-all' (and Papert himself has undoubtedly contributed, however unwittingly, to this belief) have discovered that it is not. This discovery is important, but it is no reason for discarding Logo altogether.

The second conclusion is more optimistic. As several reviewers have pointed out (e.g., Salomon and Perkins, 1987; Simon, 1987), cognitive gains from programming are much more likely to occur when the learning experience is carefully structured by a teacher. For example, Clements (1986) describes a study in which small groups of six- and eight-year-old children received a 22-week introduction to Logo. The children worked through a structured sequence of activities, in which they were successively introduced to more complex ideas by a teacher who was present throughout. Key concepts, such as that of procedurality, were explicitly taught, and the importance of planning, thinking through the effects of programs, and debugging were all emphasized within a standardized instructional approach. Clements reports that the Logo group made significant gains on various tests of higher-order thinking, compared with two control groups. Such findings indicate that the negative results of other studies reflect not so much on Logo *per se* but on the unstructured method of discovery learning advocated by Papert.

The third conclusion which can be drawn from the Logo research is somewhat unexpected. Most investigators set out to discover the effect which Logo has on individual *cognitive* skills, with varying degrees of success. What many have found, however, is that the effect on children's *social* behaviour is more marked (e.g., Hawkins *et al.*, 1982; Ginther and Williamson, 1985; Clements and Nastasi, 1988; see also Light and Blaye, 1989). This finding fits in well with the case-study accounts of researchers who have not attempted to identify long-term cognitive benefits but who have been more interested in describing what children actually do with Logo (e.g., Hoyles and Sutherland, 1986), and from the many anecdotal accounts which have emerged from individual teachers using Logo in their classrooms. The finding that programming has a positive effect on children's social interaction is particularly striking given the individual nature of much of the early work with computers (e.g., Suppes and Morningstar, 1969) and given frequently expressed fears about the supposedly isolating effects of working with computers (see Crook, 1987).

In summary, the research to date suggests that exposure to Logo by itself does not usually lead to cognitive gains; that such gains are more likely to be found with structured teaching; and that the Logo environment promotes social interaction amongst learners. These conclusions offer only partial support for Papert's claims about the effects of programming on thinking, and suggest that his account does not pay sufficient attention to the role of adults and peers in the learning process. Interestingly enough, as we saw earlier, it is precisely these social aspects of learning which are emphasized far more by Donaldson than by Papert.

Logo and early mathematics

The importance of social factors in the learning process is also demonstrated in our own work, in which we have used a simplified version of Logo as a means of introducing young children to a formal mathematical language. The rationale for this work is described in more detail in Hughes (1986), but essentially it is an attempt to develop Donaldson's ideas in the area of early mathematics.

There is now substantial evidence that young children start school with considerable mathematical abilities. They appear, for example, to understand the invariance of small numbers (Gelman and Gallistel, 1978), and they can carry out simple additions and subtractions in concrete situations, provided the numbers involved are small (Hughes, 1986). These initial mathematical abilities can be considered as *embedded thinking skills*. Indeed, it seems highly likely that they have evolved from the meaningful everyday situations in which children encounter numbers before they start school. In contrast, children's difficulties at school start when they are introduced to the formal language of mathematics – either in its spoken form, 'two and two makes four', or in its written form $2 + 2 = 4$. This kind of mathematical language can be considered as *disembedded* in that it allows us to think in mathematical terms free from any specific context. While young children may acquire some superficial competence with the formal language of mathematics, they appear to have considerable difficulty in translating between this disembedded language and the embedded skills which they acquire before school. One possible reason for this difficulty is that the formal language of mathematics serves no immediate purpose for young children. When it is first introduced, it does not empower them to do anything they could not already do – the gain will come much later in their mathematical careers. One possible remedy may therefore be to devise ways of introducing the formal language of mathematics to young children so that its immediate purpose is clear.

Our interest in Logo thus arose from its being a formal language which can serve an immediate purpose – that of communicating with the Turtle. Commands such as 'forward five' or 'left three' have, in the Logo context, clear meanings. In order to achieve a particular effect, children are required to translate their embedded mathematical knowledge into the formal Logo language. In addition, the operation of debugging – trying to discover why a particular command has not had the desired effect – requires them to translate back from the formal language to their embedded concepts.

The benefits of this approach were demonstrated in a study we carried out with a group of children aged six to seven years in Craigmillar, a severely deprived area of Edinburgh (for more details see Hughes, Macleod and Potts, 1985; Lawler *et al.*, 1986). In this study, nine boys and six girls were introduced to a series of Logo-based activities over a period of five months. The children used a programmable concept keyboard which allowed them to control the floor Turtle through simple commands, such as 'F 5' or 'L 3'. The children worked for the most part in groups of two or three, and an adult was present throughout. Each session started with the children agreeing with the adult what they were going to do, usually drawing a plan in the process. The children then spent the rest of the session trying to carry out their plan, obtaining help from the adult when necessary.

As indicated above, our focus was not so much on teaching

programming or general problem-solving skills, but rather on an alternative approach to introducing a mathematical language. This focus was reflected in the evaluation which we carried out. All the children were tested before and after the project on the British Ability Scales – a standardized test which allows performance to be gauged with respect to age-related norms. The children made statistically significant gains over the course of the project, but these gains were limited to those aspects of the British Ability Scales which were concerned with number and shape. Informal evaluation was also carried out by obtaining the observations of the teachers in the school. Their comments emphasized the children's high level of concentration and absorption as they worked with Logo, and their increased confidence and self-esteem outside the Logo sessions. The teachers commented particularly on the children's increased use of mathematical language while working with the Turtle, and on the collaborative problem-solving which took place around it.

One finding which emerged from the Craigmillar project was of particular relevance for our subsequent work. When the children's scores on the British Ability Scales were analysed in terms of gender, a clear effect emerged: the boys made significant gains over the course of the project, but the girls, considered as a group, did not. The numbers involved were obviously very small; in addition, the boys' initial scores were lower than the girls' and so they may have had more to gain from the experience. Nevertheless, there was a strong suggestion that the boys benefited more from Logo than the girls did.

Gender and educational computing

There is in fact growing concern among educationalists that the increasing use of computers in schools will place girls at a serious disadvantage (e.g., DES, 1989; Hoyles, 1989). If girls are less interested than boys in using computers, then there is a real danger that they will obtain fewer of the intellectual benefits which may come from their use. Indeed, evidence is already appearing of such gender differences. A survey of 1,747 teenagers carried out from the University of Surrey found that boys used computers substantially more than girls did, both at home and at school, with the difference being particularly strong for high-level activities such as programming (Fife-Schaw *et al.*, 1986). There is a similar gender bias in the number of pupils entering for public examinations in computer studies and computer science, where boys outnumber girls by more than two to one at 'O' level, and by three to one at 'A' level. Surveys have also found gender-related differences in children's attitudes towards computers. In a study of children aged seven to ten years which we carried out in Edinburgh between 1983 and 1985, girls were just as well disposed towards computers as were boys; it was widely believed, however, by both boys and girls, that boys used and liked computers more than girls did (Hughes, Brackenridge and Macleod, 1987).

One possible solution to this problem which is frequently proposed (e.g., Culley, 1988) is that girls should be introduced to computing in girls-only groups. The assumption is that girls will be less inhibited, and will therefore learn more, if they are removed from the supposedly dominating presence of boys. While this proposal has its superficial attractions, there has been little systematic research on whether girls do in fact benefit from such segregation. However, a study we have recently carried out in Exeter throws some light on this issue.

Our Exeter study looked systematically at children working in pairs of different gender composition: boy–boy (BB), boy–girl (BG), and girl–girl (GG). Specifically, we wanted to see how these pairs performed when first introduced to the Logo Turtle. Compared with the Edinburgh study, the children were studied over a relatively brief period of time, the focus being on short-term rather than long-term effects. The study involved sixty children aged six to seven years, who were divided into three matched groups with ten pairs in each group. Within each pair, the children were from the same class at school and of similar ability. Each child used the Turtle for three sessions. In the first session the children worked in their pairs; they were shown how the Turtle worked and allowed fifteen minutes of free exploration with it. In the second session the children also worked in pairs, but this time they were given a specific task to carry out – that of taking the Turtle around a specially constructed obstacle task. Each pair had fifteen minutes in which to complete the task. In the third and final session, the children attempted this obstacle course task again, but this time they worked individually and were allowed as much time as they needed to complete the task. All the sessions were video-taped, and the children's keypressing was recorded by a continuous dribble file (for details see Hughes *et al.*, 1989).

The main findings were both clear-cut and unexpected. When the children tackled the task in pairs in Session 2, there was a major difference between the performance of the BB and BG pairs on the one hand and the GG pairs on the other. All ten BB pairs completed the task, as did nine of the ten BG pairs; however, only two of the ten GG pairs did so. A similar difference was found when the children worked individually on the task in Session 3. Girls from GG pairs took nearly twice as long to complete the task as did the boys, irrespective of which group the boys had been in. The performance of the girls from the BG pairs, however, was as good as that of the boys, and significantly better than that of the girls who had been in GG pairs. In other words, the performance of the boys was unaffected by the gender of their partner, whereas the girls did much better if they had worked with a boy.

While these findings are clear-cut, the explanation for them is less obvious. We can, however, rule out some possible explanations. The effects are not simply due to previous computer experience, for there were no differences between the groups on this measure. Nor were the GG pairs less interested or involved in the task – they applied themselves readily to the problem, and maintained their involvement throughout. Not is it simply a case of the boys in the BG groups teaching their girl partners: our analyses of the video-tapes reveals little evidence of the boys either telling or showing the girls what to do.

Instead, it seems more likely that at least part of the difference is due to the way in which the different pairs react to a situation involving *failure*. Closer examination of the children's performance on the obstacle course reveals that the differences between the groups were most marked when the Turtle crashed into an obstacle. The GG pairs not only crashed the Turtle more often than the other groups, but, more strikingly, were much worse at freeing the Turtle when it had crashed. Analyses currently under way are looking at the way in which the different pairs react when a crash occurs. It appears that the GG groups tend to react in a more emotional and fearful manner to a crash, criticizing and blaming themselves and each other, rather than engaging in a reflective analysis of what went wrong. If confirmed, this would suggest that the difficulties experienced by girls in our study are due not so much to any innate or acquired cognitive deficiency, but rather lie in the particular attitudes and expectations which girls have towards using computers. Moreover, the fact that these attitudes and expectations appear to manifest themselves most clearly in a situation involving failure is particularly pertinent, given the emphasis which both Donaldson and Papert place on the need to use errors constructively in learning.

Whatever their cause, it is clear that such findings could have important implications. They cast doubt on the notion that the disadvantage of girls in this area can be overcome by single-sex grouping, for this was the least advantageous condition for the girls. Moreover, if we are hoping that the computer can provide a way of giving disembedded thinking skills to children, then it is disturbing to find that the children's performance is so strongly affected by gender. At the same time, we must be very tentative in generalizing from the findings of a single study, in which the children were studied over a relatively short period of time.

Conclusions

We started this chapter by asking how computers might be used to produce the disembedded thinking skills which Margaret Donaldson has argued that our society desperately needs. We then looked more closely at what Donaldson meant by disembedding, and how she thought such skills might be fostered. An examination of the main ways in which computers are currently used suggested that the most promising approach is that in which computers are used as a tool, and in particular those in which children program the computer themselves. The main advocate of this approach is Seymour Papert, and indeed there are clear parallels, as well as important differences, between the views of Papert and Donaldson.

Research to date on the effects of programming on thinking skills is only partially conclusive. Nevertheless, it appears that the maximum benefits will occur only with a carefully structured teaching approach, and that the social benefits are often more marked than the cognitive ones. This emphasis on the social environment in which learning takes place fits in more closely with Donaldson's views than with Papert's. It is also illustrated by our own work with a simplified version of Logo.

It is clear that we are still some way from fulfilling Donaldson's vision of promoting disembedded thinking skills in the large majority of children. Nevertheless, it is also clear that the computer could well play a major role in this process. The work reviewed in this chapter indicates three areas to which attention must be paid if this promise is to be fulfilled.

First, further work is required which clarifies and elucidates the nature of disembeddedness itself – what exactly it means in any particular area, how it can be measured, and how far we can realistically expect it to be developed at any given age. Our own work has assumed that the acquisition of a formal language, such as mathematical symbolism, is an important part of the process, but it is not clear if this is either a necessary or a sufficient condition. It does seem unlikely, however, that the focus on a single context, such as Turtle graphics, is sufficient, given that the capacity for disembedded thought involves the conscious application of this capacity in a range of familiar and unfamiliar contexts. There is still much that we need to know about both the nature of disembedding and the contexts in which it can best be acquired and applied.

Second, we need to give further attention to the social nature of the learning environment. The research reviewed here highlights both the role of an adult, in structuring the learning experience and providing guidance, and the role of other children, in enabling communication and collaborative problem-solving to take place. Nevertheless, we are still some way from understanding how these social aspects of the learning environment can best be organized to promote learning. What type of adult intervention produces what type of effect? Is the presence of other children always beneficial, or are there some conditions under which it is of no benefit, or even harmful? Further research is needed on these issues.

Third, our work has raised the issue of gender, and the danger that using computers in the way envisaged here may benefit boys more than girls. Naturally this is of considerable concern to anyone who shares Donaldson's vision that the benefits of disembedded thinking should be available to all children. At present we are still unclear as to the true nature and extent of this problem, although our work indicates that children's different attitudes towards computers, and their responses to what they perceive as failure, may be an appropriate location for further enquiry. Given the widespread association in our society between technology and masculinity, the issue is not likely to disappear as easily as one might wish.

Our final point concerns the time-scale on which progress might be made. As we have seen, there is already an impatience and disillusionment with the role that computers might play in the development of thinking. Because they have not produced instant results, there is a danger of discarding them altogether and looking for another more fashionable approach. We would instead argue for determination and patience. The technology is still young, and its power is still growing. The importance of the exercise is vast. The shaping of minds to come, in a way that benefits both the individual and society, remains a realizable goal, and one in which computers must surely have a crucial role to play.

I am extremely grateful to the Nuffield Foundation for supporting both the projects on Logo with young children described here, and to Ann Brackenridge and Pam Greenhough for their comments on an earlier draft of this chapter.

8 Children's Pictures

Roger Wales
University of Melbourne

The pictures children make are intriguing. Indeed, Sully (1895) referred to the child as 'The little artist'. How can such a little person create pictures so 'different' from those of adults? What is the basis of the child's creativity? Or, are we being seduced by the attraction of the 'little person' image into believing that there is anything very special here? Is the apparent 'creativity' of children simply the product of their limited skills, and does this underlie our sense of difference between the child's productions and ours?

Such questions, and a multitude of related ones, are raised as soon as we try to make sense of what children are about in their picture making. Some, understandably, might argue that creation, perhaps especially that of the child, is both magical and mysterious, and best left well alone. However, there are aspects which should encourage us to attempt some kind of understanding. One is that children's pictorial productions seem to change as they develop in a fairly regular, perhaps even predictable, way. Another is that at almost any given stage in their development, a child's various pictures will bear striking resemblances to each other. These aspects encourage the belief that the child's pictures are a product of, at least partially, explicable processes, the understanding of which can tell us something about the workings of children's minds.

To start with, it may be helpful to summarize some of the characteristics of children's pictures as they are said to develop and change through childhood. As we do so, we will soon see that our observations are themselves the product of our interpretations: our 'facts' accompany our theoretical conceptions.

The basic pattern of development is typically seen as progressing from scribbles, to simple forms, to more complex graphic structures which allow more natural representations of the 'real world'. Rhonda

Kellogg (1969) itemized up to twenty different basic 'scribble' patterns – lines, patches, circular blobs, spirals, and other definite shapes. She saw these as the basic building blocks of later graphic development. In trying to make sense of the sorts of factors which organize and constrain later productions, Goodnow (1977) discussed a number of strong candidates. One is the starting point on the page, since the figure will be distorted simply by how much of the page is left available for the figure. If the movement of the production is towards a corner, the figure may well become cramped for space. Goodnow also suggests that children use similar graphic strategies when producing a given figure – for example, going the same way, from the same point, in drawing a person. While this may seem to be the case in some situations, I have more frequently observed that a child, say of 5 years, will draw the sub-parts of a figure in a variety of different orders and orientations when drawing several similar figures – members of their family, for example – or when drawing the same figure on different days.

Norman Freeman (1980) has also contributed some elegant studies, which complement those of Goodnow. These suggest that a child's apparent inability to produce a 'complete' representation may be a function both of graphic constraints at a given point in development, and what the child is trying to do with the resources available to him or her at that point. Freeman suggests that some of the child's apparent 'deficiencies' in representation are better understood as the child producing something that works like caricature. The child includes only what is needed for a given graphic communication, often in apparently exaggerated form. In Freeman's view, this is in part a consequence of how the child is able to conceive of the world at a given point in time.

However, we must again be careful how we understand this sort of claim. One of Freeman's studies, for example, requires a child to draw a mug which has a picture on it opposite the side with the handle. The child is seated so that only the side with the picture can be seen – the handle cannot. It is reported that up to the age of seven or eight years, children usually draw a rather stereotyped side-on-view of the mug and handle. In trying to repeat this observation, Maggie de Vore and I have noted that younger children often start by trying to draw the picture, but are defeated by the graphic demands. In trying to keep the picture on the mug small enough to be on the drawing, they move on to the stereotypical image. This result suggests that the kinds of drawing constraints that Goodnow reports may be as important as the conceptual constraints that Freeman appeals to. Both sets of observations and approaches seem useful in helping us understand what constraints children encounter as they attempt to draw 'under instruction'. They are constrained by how they see visual/physical relations, how well they can control their physical movements, how successfully they can place the layout of the drawing on the paper, and how they understand what is being asked of them.

Focusing on one or other of these issues, many studies have tried to elucidate some aspect or other of the child's ability to depict. Perhaps the majority of studies by psychologists have concentrated on exploring the relevance of the child's sense of space, tacitly assuming Bergson's (1913) assertion that space is 'ballasted with geometry'. Some recent fine studies include Willats's observations (1983) of children's ability to take perspective into account in their drawings. Here, children were seated before a table with objects on it and asked to draw what they saw. Willats claims a developmental sequence of the following sort:

1   5- and 6-year-olds do not represent depth, but draw the table top as a rectangle with the objects above it;
2   7- and 8-year-olds draw the table top as a line with the objects resting on it;
3   at 9 years of age children first approximate recognizable attempts to represent depth, drawing the table top as a rectangle with the objects in or on it, and with the nearer objects at the bottom of the page;
4   young adolescents draw oblique lines representing edges receding in space, but not converging.

Points (5) and (6) in the sequence involve less, then subsequently more, successful attempts to represent perspective using convergence. Clearly, these developments are not a single matter either of how the child sees, nor how he or she has been taught. Rather, they involve progressively better ways of inventing solutions to the given problem.

More detailed studies of the varieties of ways in which children see and represent simple lines, angles, and forms are described in Van Sommers (1983), and Freeman and Cox (1985). An example of the sort of technique used is where a comparison is made of children's representational drawings of solid objects, and their ability to copy drawings. The point is to try to elucidate the relevance to the child of translating the three-dimensionality of the solid object to two dimensions, compared to their ability to operate with two-dimensional depictions.

So far, terms like 'pictures', 'productions', and 'drawings' have been used rather loosely and several more could have been used – notably 'painting'. Much of what has been said so far is assumed to be relatively neutral between these ways of talking about what children are doing and producing. Of course, whether they are using a paintbrush or a pencil may fundamentally affect how they use up the available space, conditioned at least by the breadth of the line (not to mention the likely, though not necessary, variety of colours). However, a standard working assumption is that what the child is trying to do will remain constant across varieties of graphic medium. Although we will later see that this assumption is questionable, for the moment it is not too bad a working assumption. At present, trying to characterize what children are doing when they produce a picture is a deep enough problem. Be it with paints or with pencil, it may be that one of the things that children do early on, and continue to do if given the opportunity, is 'express' themselves.

The educational issues raised by this aspect of children's art have been discussed by Derham (1976), who makes a strong case for not imposing on young children expectations of 'representational art'; rather, they should be encouraged to come to this of their own volition. There are of course interesting questions as to what children 'like'; and as to what scribbles, and then patterns, are found to be expressive. It is not clear whether the expression derives from the picture itself, or the processes of its creation (nor perhaps does it need to be clear – this could vary from occasion to occasion, or from person to person). For the present our attention will be concentrated on the forms which children use to 'depict'. In the sense of a 'picture', the picture stands in some symbolic relation to that which is being depicted.

Pictures as Representations

Some studies seem to suggest that we can concentrate on visual or motoric aspects of development, since if we understand these the rest will follow. Plainly, such an approach begs a major question concerned with when and how children come to treat their graphic patterns as representations. Franklin highlights the issue in summarizing a 1972 Harvard PhD study by N. R. Smith:

> Initially, Smith suggests 'the child stumbles into symbolisation with little or no intention'. He makes a pattern and sees it as a representation, apprehending some correspondence between the pattern and a known object. This is followed by a shift toward deliberate preplanned symbolisation. (Franklin, 1973: 43)

Variations on this belief are longstanding and widespread. For example, Vygotsky (1978: 107) asserts: 'In general we are inclined to view children's first drawings and scribble rather as gestures than as drawing in the true sense of the word'. Although we are here hardly likely to solve the problem of the child's symbolization, nevertheless it is in many ways the *key* issue raised by the attempt to understand how and what children draw.

In trying to tackle this issue, what is explored is a long-established notion that young children draw what they know, not what they see – or even that children may be drawing what they want others to know they (the children) know. In considering this issue, we are faced with two main developmental traditions. One is that the progress of developmental change – the structure of the form, the presence or absence of detail – is sufficiently fixed that aspects of the process can be used either to give content to a systematic developmental theory (e.g., Piaget and Inhelder, 1956, 1966), or to translate into the sort of robust data which provide norms for development, sometimes finding expression in intelligence tests (e.g., Goodenough's Draw-a-Man Test revised by Harris, 1963).

The fundamentally contrasting tradition does not dispute the overall trend in development from less to more complex cognitive structures, but sees the focus as that of interpreting what children are doing in the interactive context in which their behaviour is typically rooted. This involves trying to construe children's behaviour, not in isolation, but in terms of their ability to interpret the contexts in which the tasks occur as an integral part of their performance with these tasks. The classic formulation of this tradition was given by Vygotsky. More recently it has been applied by Donaldson (1971) to produce trenchant criticisms of intelligence tests, and by Donaldson (1978) in a critical analysis of the Piagetian tradition.

In pursuing our immediate goal of trying to make sense of children's symbolization in terms of these traditions, let us now concentrate our attention on children drawing a person.

Draw a Person

Much work has been devoted to young children's ability to draw a person. The developmental sequence of such drawings is held by many to be so regular that a test of intellectual ability has been developed on its basis (Harris, 1963). When asked to 'draw a man', children's earliest productions seem to consist of an irregular circular figure, with a couple of lines projecting from the bottom and perhaps a couple more from the side. This is known as a 'tadpole' figure. In time, this figure comes to be elaborated by the child, adding a trunk, or giving features to the face, etc. We may speculate as to whether children really see us this way. Golomb cites Ricci's humorous remark that the child draws all he needs – a head for seeing and eating, and legs for walking.

However, this process of elaboration is not simply the basis for a test. It is also discussed by Piaget as evidence in favour of the effect of the progressive restructuring of the child's cognitive structures, which is at the heart of his theory of intellectual development. Though poles apart in their concerns, both Harris/Goodenough, and Piaget, interpret the development of the child's drawing of a person as involving an acceptance that such drawings reflect the child's representations of this key symbol. For Piaget, the child draws like this due to a deficient analysis of the object, and an inability to synthesize the parts into a coherent, whole representation. Since the child could obviously see, the problem was shifted to the child's knowledge.

As already noted, both Goodnow and Freeman seriously qualify aspects of this account. They show that we must be careful to observe other aspects of the problem facing the child – for example, the place of the drawing on the page – before making hasty or overly strong claims about what the child's drawing tells us about what the child can think about what is being depicted. Winner (1982) reports observations by her colleagues that indicate that very young children – less than 2 years of age – often betray some understanding of what they are aiming to depict. When asked to show where various features were – tummy, head, legs, arms – such very young children made their marks on the page in correct relative positions.

Much of the problem here may be our inability to recognize or decode the child's representation. Golomb (1974) showed that children could often represent appropriate bodily relations if they were asked to model them in clay. An anecdote may serve to illustrate the broader issue. When one of my children was about 3 years old, he produced a very colourful picture of what appeared to me to be more or less random coloured dots running obliquely across the page. Was this a case of him 'just expressing himself'? When asked about the picture, he said it was an 'Easter fire engine'. This seemed as incoherent as the coloured dots, until I remembered that a week or two before, he had been travelling by car at night past a candlelit Easter celebration at a local Greek Orthodox church. This church was just around the corner from one of his favourite stopping places – the central fire station. It seems not unlikely that the picture had a coherence which I was at first not inclined to give it. The situation may be similar to those children who start their language production with what sounds like nonsense, but which can at times be given contextual interpretation (compare Peters, 1983). It is of course unwise to argue that whatever mess the child produces, it is as developed and coherent as a drawing by Leonardo. Nevertheless, the fact that we see it as a mess does not entitle us to make elementary errors of psychological interpretation by assuming that the eye of the beholder is unprejudiced. The adult observer's prejudice is hardly confined to his or her view of children's pictures. Any inspection of a major art gallery will note the variety of descriptions given to the pictures. 'Pastoral Scene', for example, covers a multitude of sins – especially if depicted by Rubens.

If the problem for the child is to invent structurally adequate forms which can stand for the complex object – as argued by Arnheim (1975) and Goodnow (1977) – then clearly part of our problem as adult observers is trying to recognize what a 'structurally adequate form' might be. This way of viewing the problem is fundamentally different from that which views a drawing as 'copied from reality', and which holds that conceptual development can be measured by counting the represented parts. It raises deep and different questions about the nature of symbols. Part of our difficulty may be that even in a framework such as that espoused by Arnheim, we may also be conditioned to believe that there is some general system of signs which cuts across language and non-verbal representations, within which graphic symbols may be interpreted. This pursuit of semiotic generality has been a persuasive force in conceptual studies this century.

What lies behind this pursuit is the idea that the system of symbolic representation is unitary, in that the representation of verbal, and various non-verbal domains are assumed to be indistinguishable. As Sperber and Wilson (1986) point out, this view produces more problems than it solves. The chief problem of course is that it has nothing to say, by definition, on the difference between verbal and non-verbal representations. Hence it cannot elucidate how aspects of one might influence aspects of the other. Even within a more constrained domain such as pictorial representation, the pursuit of semiotic generality tends to act against trying to determine why using a representation – e.g., of a person – in one medium, like drawing, may apparently give different results from those obtained using another medium like modelling in clay. At the very least, this semiotic pursuit may be seriously misleading. To illustrate, let us now consider some observations of drawings by children from cultures and environments which are very different from Western, industrial cultures.

Cross-cultural Variation

In looking at children's drawings in another cultural context, surely the basic elements will be the same? This must be the expected view if we follow Piaget, or the general semiotic tradition. The following statement by Kellogg and O'Dell (1967: 105) captures the received Western view:

> Cultures the world over . . . use the same forms to express what they wish to say. The forms may appear to change from one country to another but at heart they remain alike. The art of young children everywhere is identical. Not until the weight of culture lays a burden upon the child can the art of one country or century be told from that of another. The child then assumes the style of his own time and place.

That children everywhere draw, if given the material means, is if true, not uninteresting. That their production can be categorized by the use of lines and shapes *is* uninteresting – the 'similarities' are a product of the description, rather than intrinsic to the child's mode of thought. The question is begged if we assert, without independent evidence, that lines, circles, etc., symbolize the same things for young children everywhere. What is critical about the Kellogg and O'Dell claim, and others like it, is when and how 'the weight of culture lays a burden upon the child'. If the tradition of Vygotsky, Luria, and Donaldson is to be believed, it may be that the burden is laid from the outset of the child's intellectual life.

If we look at the productions of children from a very different culture to ours what do we find? Certainly the youngest will seem to produce (often colourful) scribbles. Somewhat older children may have some aspects of their drawings in common with us. This is hardly surprising given the pervasiveness of Western cultural influence. The critical question is, are there differences? And if there are, are they important?

Let us consider the productions of young Walbiri children. The Walbiri are an Aboriginal group, who have maintained their traditional language and culture, and are found in the centre of Australia in groupings of several thousand. To make sense of what their children might do pictorially in the context of their culture, some knowledge of their cultural world view is needed.

There are many different Aboriginal groups, each with its own language and cultural emphasis – Dixon (1980) indicates that there are two to three hundred different languages. Nevertheless, all groups share the view that the immediate physical environment is a product of mythical creatures enshrined in the 'dreaming' stories of their culture, with a continuity of tradition which results in their immediate ancestors being part of their actual physical environment. Though probably apocryphal, the story that some aboriginal school children drew mountains and rocks when asked to draw 'their family' illustrates the inherent importance to them of their landscape, and how their perception of it differs fundamentally from ours. Within this overall view, there are two main traditions of pictorial representation among the groups. One, typical of the far north of Australia, is characterized by so-called X-ray figures, showing the skeletal structures of the animals, etc., represented in the dreaming stories. The other, associated with central desert tribes, uses simple graphic devices like straight and wavy lines and circles to represent relations between different elements in the stories (compare Berndt and Berndt, 1982; Issacs, 1982).

This summary is ludicrously brief, since it leaves out of account the sort of variation introduced by body painting, fibre craft, rock engraving or painting, bark painting, carving and sculpture, ground painting, etc. Nevertheless, the essence of the use of symbols by central and western desert peoples has been expertly described by Munn (1973). In characterizing Walbiri iconography, Munn shows that they will use a variety of some sixteen or so signs to signify a variety of things or relations to varying contexts. So a circle may be a circling movement, an encircling object, a campfire, a tree, a hole, a waterhole, an egg, or a dog (curled up in camp); an open semicircle may be a person or a windbreak; a wavy line may be a serpent, a watercourse, or dancers, and so on. Munn points out that women use these symbols, drawing in the sand, as they tell each other dreaming stories beside the campfire, and that young children will hear and see these from their earliest years. Munn remarks that the Walbiri 'regard sand drawing as part of (their) valued mode of life, and as a characteristic aspect of their style of expression and communication. To accompany one's speech with explanatory sand markings is to "talk" in the Walbiri manner' (Munn, 1973: 58).

A young Walbiri child when asked to draw a person is as likely as not to draw a semicircle in the dust. Often a family group is depicted as a set of such signs surrounding a circle – the campfire. The picture by Judith (Fig. 8.1) illustrates this nicely, mixing such traditional symbolism with more Western conventions. In her drawing, the semicircles are people (at middle left, top left, top right of Fig. 8.1).

Figure 8.1   Drawing by Judith, a young Walbiri child.

Where a larger semicircle contains a smaller one (top left, top right), this is a mother and child. In the original, these semicircles are in blue. The oval shape is a hollowed-out wooden vessel of that shape, often used to hold food. Though not certain, it is interesting to speculate that the two figures at top centre and top right of Fig. 8.1, completed in red in the original, are representations of white people in the community. Whatever the truth of this latter speculation, it is clear that she has and uses two very different ways of representing people. The picture as a whole has a very topographical feel to it, and the traditions for graphic symbolism of the Walbiri are consistent with this.

It is surely no accident that the Walbiri children's representation of people can be so different from ours. Even when they approximate 'tadpole' figures, a more characteristic variant has a clearly defined head, with a cross below it for the arms and trunk/leg. It is when schooling has laid its cultural burden on them, that a mix of symbols will be found. A classic instance of this, observed by David Wilkins, was produced by a child aged about ten years in Alice Springs, where there is a wide cultural mix. The child drew a Toyota Landcruiser in standard Western profile, but used traditional symbols (semicircles) for the people in it.

The drawings of children from another Aboriginal group, the Pitjandjara, show less obvious cultural symbolism – as seen in Figure 8.2, a drawing by a four-year-old girl. This may be a sampling problem. Nevertheless, even here the triangulated dwellings are in fact aptly drawn – this is what 'humpies' (temporary shelters) may look like. Also, in older children there often occurs a floral pattern of a quite elaborate form – as in Figure 8.3. This seems to be derived from symbolic forms used in women's body painting. Perhaps it is to keep the symbolism secret that knowledge of its significance is widely denied, despite the fact that these distinctive floral patterns are produced as tourist souvenirs near Uluru (Ayers Rock). In fact, the ritual significance may be far removed from the 'floral' name I have given it.

It must surely be clear even from these few examples (from samples of two dozen children in each cultural group) that we need to use great care in making claims about the universality of the forms of children's art. Not unsurprisingly, the culture plays a fundamental role in orienting the development of symbolic representations. It is presumably because of this that when visiting Chimbu in Papua New

Figure 8.2   Drawing by a 4-year-old Pitjandjara girl.

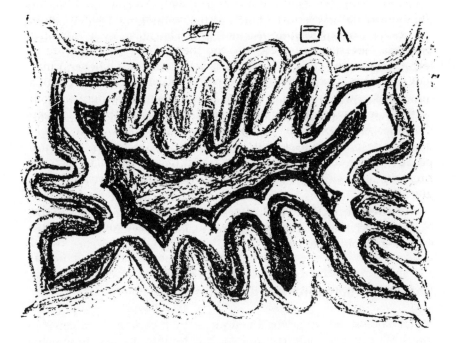

Figure 8.3 Drawing by an older Pitjandjara girl.

Guinea, Catherine Baker (1980) found teenagers – who had never had the opportunity to draw before but now given that opportunity – immediately produced pictures of great complexity, obviously anchored in local cultural symbolism. It is worth noting in passing that the anthropologist Margaret Mead was sufficiently persuaded of the reliability and cultural understanding revealed by children's drawings that she used them as a prime source of data in her studies in Papua New Guinea.

What is minimally necessary in considering these cross-cultural data is to realize their primary significance. They do not show that the children from these different cultures have different conceptions of a person (though that might be the case). What they do show is that even if the mental representation of a person is essentially the same, the way in which that representation may be pictorially realized can differ fundamentally as a function of the representation's place in the culture and its iconographic conventions. The heart of the theoretical problem here is that the term 'representation' takes several different interpretations (Goodman, 1969). We need to avoid confusing the conceptual representation of something with the conceptual means for expressing that representation as that something. Distinguishing (at least) these senses of representation will enable us to ask pertinent questions about the different aspects, and also to see how they are related. Questions having to do with what we (or children) need to know in order to express such things as forms or dimensions are presumably primarily about 'representing as'. Questions having to do with what we (or children) need to know in order to understand what is being symbolized are primarily about 'representing that'. Iconographic conventions presumably involve relating the one to the other. Since this is no simple thing, it is more understandable why we have such difficulty accounting for children's representational processes in the pictorial domain. It is also clear that when we are compelled to credit the young child with representational abilities, even of the simplest sort, we are at the same time attributing symbolic processing of considerable complexity.

Differences between Individuals and Styles

What should be apparent by now is that various parameters – physical, cognitive, and cultural – can enter into the way in which a given child constructs and interprets a drawing at a given time. We therefore have to be very careful that we do not take too literally the notion that levels of drawing reflect cognitive level – a view that we have seen advanced on theoretical grounds by Piaget, and by Goodenough and Harris in the construction of their 'Draw-a-Man' test. O'Connor and Hermelin (1987) have shown convincingly that severely retarded people can vary dramatically in their artistic ability, both in terms of their ability to draw and their ability to remember visual material. A particularly famous case is that of an autistic child, Nadia, who was studied by Selfe (1977). The Nadia data illustrate a number of problems of interpreting individual case-studies.

From an early age Nadia drew with a fluency and manner which reminded some observers of her pictures of Leonardo da Vinci's drawings. The horses were particularly noteworthy, especially since it was claimed that she had never seen horses or drawings of them – a claim that was, however, hard to check. In her early teens, her drawings became less distinctive, in parallel with the advent of her ability to use language productively. Some interpreters have drawn a causal link between these two events, suggesting that one symbolic system was displacing the other. Apart from the questionable logic of this inference, such arguments ignore the fact that the change was also consequent on the death of Nadia's mother. In fact, her later drawings betray the classic blacking out of faces consistent with expectations from the literature on the effect of trauma expressed through drawings. The advent of language could well have been occasioned by the communicative needs consequent on losing a mother to whom Nadia had been very close.

Again, we see the need to exhibit caution in interpreting a child's drawings. The case of Nadia is famous for illustrating a child's drawings at an extreme end of the distribution of individual differences. That having been conceded, we do not have to accept the simple inferences with which some have sought to account for the sources of such talent. There is often more than one option available for explaining what is going on. This does not mean we need to leave the issue in such cases in the realms of mysticism, but we do need to find ways of determining which is the better account, without too direct an appeal to our own prejudices.

Even within one culture there are of course differences in the ways in which children draw, and it is hard to see how all these differences can be accommodated simply to the variations following from age and intelligence. One way of evaluating this is to ask whether there is something both distinctive and stable about the pictures a given child produces through time. A pioneering study on this topic was conducted by Susan Somerville (1983). She obtained a sizeable number of pictures from a few children of a particular age (3 years). Then she did the same again at two later points in time. Using the first set, she trained adult observers on the different styles – simply by showing them the pictures and saying that that was a picture by child A, this one by child B, and so on. Then with the subsequent two sets, the adults had to try to say which child painted which picture. It transpired that the adults could do this very effectively. What were the stylistic variations which the adults were able to use? This promises to be a fascinating area of study. If subsequent findings are consistent with these early ones, then such findings will serve to challenge from another direction the view that the pattern of children's pictorial development is determined simply by the same mould.

On the receptive side, there are also several stylistic issues. These include whether children are aware of the expressive properties of their own pictures, and whether they are responsive to variations in the styles of other people's pictures. On the latter point, Winner *et al.* (1983) have reported that children can often respond to quite small stylistic differences – for example, changing the wavyness of the hair line in a Leonardo drawing of a head. The same authors have also reported that children aged between 5 and 10 years were able both to label and match mood type (happy, sad, excited, calm) to their pictures once they had produced them. Although much still needs to be done, it seems clear that there is already evidence that style is not something which is merely added as a later development on to a robust cognitive/perceptual base. Concomitant recognition and expression of emotion seems to be implicated from an early stage. There are all the signs that the study of children's pictures needs to take in a wide variety of cognitive, personal, and cultural factors.

Concluding Remarks

We began this chapter with a number of questions about the distinctiveness, originality and creativity which children reveal through their pictures. In distinguishing creativity from originality, Johnson-Laird (1988: 255) proposes the following three characteristic properties of creative processes:

> First, like all mental processes, it starts from some given building blocks. One cannot create out of nothing. Second, the process has no precise goal, but only some pre-existing constraints or criteria that it must meet. One creates pictures, poems . . . theories . . . and so on. One creates within genres or paradigms. Third, a creative process yields an outcome that is novel for the individual, not merely remembered or perceived, and not constructed by rote or by a simple deterministic procedure.

Although, as Johnson-Laird acknowledges, framing such definitions does not solve the psychological problems, it does serve to limit the domain of the study. Even from the little evidence that has been considered here, children's pictures meet these criteria for creativity. In asserting that, we are making a strong claim, but not an excessive one. We are not supposing that children's creations are to be placed on an aesthetic pedestal. We are, however, proposing the strong claim that their creations are as they are because children have some independent cognitive control of at least some of the decisions they take in producing. Their pictures do not vary one from another because of random variation, or merely through external determining factors. In our brief look at children's pictorial processes, we have seen how some sense can be given to the description of the building blocks they use, and the outcomes they achieve.

In order to evaluate further the interplay of the factors which affect these creative processes, we will also need to know more about how children are able to use language to talk about their graphic representations. This is especially true of their use of metaphor. On this point, it is critical that we do not get sucked into believing that there is some special 'stage' at which children are able to understand and use metaphor. When anyone is using a metaphor of the form *an A is a B*, they construct a relation (the ground) between A (the tenor) and B (the vehicle). As Wales and Coffey (1986) have shown, the key variable in the child's ability to understand metaphors is the ease with which the child can relate the meanings of the tenor and vehicle in order to construct the ground. This is very similar to some of the interactions observed in the changing symbolic skills that children evidence through their drawings. The more meaningful and accessible the meanings being represented, the greater the child's graphic fluency.

The nature and implications of this kind of task-dependent account for understanding young children's thought has been pointed out by Margaret Donaldson (1978). As she indicates, the child 'uses his skills to serve his compelling immediate purposes' (p. 121). In trying to extend this approach, it is important to recognize several things about the child's thinking. It is embedded in the construal of the context in which the actions take place and are interpreted – as Donaldson makes clear. Also, the mode of symbolic representation used to interpret and 'drive' the actions – be it language, drawing, or problem-solving – may itself impose its own task-dependent constraints. At least trying to view the child's thinking in this way leaves open to question (and hence possible answer) how these modes of cognition go together. What is already clear is that the variations of children's pictures can be a useful, if not essential window on the myriad parameters of the child's mind.

I wish to thank Edith Bavin and Penny Evans for their help in obtaining the pictures produced by the Aboriginal children referred to in the chapter, and also for their encouragement and comments. They are of course not responsible for any of the wrongs I may have done to the subject matter.

9 Children's Awareness

Robert Grieve
University of Edinburgh

While the role of awareness in children's intellectual and linguistic development has been of abiding interest (e.g., Vygotsky, 1962; Piaget, 1962a, 1976), in recent years the topic has attracted a considerable amount of renewed attention. While some attention has been given to children's metacognitive awareness – their awareness of the nature and functions of cognitive abilities such as memory (e.g., Brown and DeLoache, 1978), much more attention has been devoted to children's metalinguistic awareness – their awareness of the nature and functions of language. It is with language awareness that this chapter will mainly be concerned.

In the past ten years or so, two volumes of collected papers have appeared, plus a variety of other chapters and papers reporting analyses and the results of various studies on language awareness in children – see, for example, Sinclair, Jarvella and Levelt, 1978; Tunmer, Pratt and Herriman, 1984; Karmiloff-Smith, 1986; Bowey, 1988; and Garton and Pratt, 1989. However, despite this increase in interest in the topic of language awareness in children, there remains no clear answer to a question basic to developmental psychology – namely, when does language awareness develop in children?

In the literature, two main answers have been advanced:

1 language awareness develops relatively late, around seven years of age;
2 language awareness develops relatively early, around one to two years of age.

The first view is notably associated with the work of Margaret Donaldson at Edinburgh, the second with the work of Eve Clark at Stanford. While the two views appear incompatible, let us first outline

Donaldson's and Clark's positions, and then see what conclusions can be drawn.

Donaldson's Position

Donaldson's position is presented in her book *Children's Minds* (1978). To appreciate her views on language awareness, we first need to understand her distinction between embedded and disembedded thought. We can do this with reference to children's performance on two tasks first studied by Piaget: perspective-taking (Piaget and Inhelder, 1956), and class inclusion (Piaget and Inhelder, 1964).

In his well-known Three Mountains task, Piaget presented children with a *papier mâché* table-top model of three mountains, which were readily distinguishable from each other in terms of their colour, size, etc. Children were seated at the table to view the model. They were then presented with a set of pictures taken from several different perspectives round the table, one of which included a perspective from the position occupied by the child. Asked to select the picture which showed his or her present perspective of the model, children could do this successfully. However, asked to select the picture which showed the perspective of someone else seated at another vantage point – e.g., opposite the child – children failed to complete the task successfully until about seven or eight years of age. Piaget suggested that this illustrated young children's cognitive egocentrism – young children have difficulty in adopting a perspective other than the one they can see from their current position.

However, in more recent work on Hide-and-Seek games, Hughes (1975) has provided evidence which challenges the notion that young children are unable to adopt perspectives other than their own. In his studies, children were presented with a model consisting of a set of walls which intersected at right angles – as shown in Figure 9.1, viewed from above. The children, aged four years, were given a small doll, said to be a naughty boy being chased by a policeman. If the naughty boy wanted to hide from the policeman, where could he hide? From the child's perspective, the boy would be hidden in quadrants (a) and (b), for the child cannot see into these quadrants. However from the policeman's perspective, the boy would be hidden in quadrants (a) and (c). Hughes found that the great majority of four-year-olds responded correctly – that in the game illustrated in Figure 9.1A the successful hiding places were (a) and (c) – indicating their appreciation of a perspective other than their own. Indeed, if a

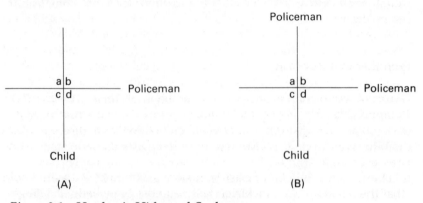

Figure 9.1   Hughes's Hide-and-Seek game.

second policeman joined the chase, as illustrated in Figure 9.1B, children indicated that the only quadrant in which the naughty boy could hide was quadrant (c), indicating their ability to appreciate and co-ordinate two perspectives other than their own.

Donaldson accounted for these discrepant results between Piaget's Three Mountains task and Hughes's Hide-and-Seek game by suggesting that the former involves *disembedded thought*, where the child has to stand back, reflect on possibilities, and work out the correct choice after considerable deliberation and cognitive processing. By contrast, the Hide-and-Seek game involves *embedded thought* – the point of the activity is immediately apparent to the child, the intentions are clear, and the game makes 'human sense' to the child. Children understand what is involved in being naughty, and in hiding from irate, pursuing adults. Donaldson suggests that young children, aged three to five years, are adept at embedded thought, but not yet adept at more abstract, disembedded thought.

As with thought, so with language. Young children of preschool age are highly adept at using language in day-to-day society and in commerce with the environment. What they are not good at is considering language in a disembedded way, where language must be considered without the everyday props of its use – for example, the clear intentions of the speaker, and non-linguistic and extra-linguistic cues as to intended meaning.

This is well illustrated in Piaget's class inclusion problem, where the child is asked to compare a class of objects with one of its constituent subclasses. For example, the child may be presented with a bouquet of flowers (class), containing seven roses (larger subclass) and three daffodils (smaller subclass). Asked if there are more flowers or more roses (comparison of class with larger subclass), most children before the age of about seven years will reply that there are more roses, for 'there are only three daffodils'. Children aged younger than seven years compare the two subclasses, not the whole class with the larger subclass as requested. Piaget accounts for this error of young children by maintaining that their thought lacks 'reversibility'. Having mentally decomposed the class into its constituent subclasses, young children cannot reverse the mental operation of decomposition to recompose the class from its constituent subclasses.

Donaldson's account of class inclusion is different. She would hold that the standard class inclusion task requires disembedded thought, where the child must stand back from the readily apparent perceptual contrast between the two subclasses, and reflect on the intended meaning of the class term – here, what does the word *flowers* refer to? The young child is not adept at doing this, and supposes that he or she is expected to compare the two subclasses which are, after all, perceptually readily distinct. The terms in the question, *roses* and *flowers*, are interpreted by the young child as referring to what he or she supposes is to be compared – the roses and daffodils. To the young child, the adult's intended meaning of the class term *flowers* to refer to the total class is not immediately apparent.

While young children may often think and use language adeptly in everyday contexts where the adult's intentions and the point of the activity are clear, they are not yet aware of language and thought: 'The child acquires linguistic skills before he becomes aware of them' (Donaldson, 1978: 87); and 'The child is more concerned to make sense of what people do when they talk and act than to decide what words mean' (p. 88).

In Donaldson's view, then, children come to school with language use and thought directed outwards towards the real, everyday world. However, to achieve success in our system of formal education, at school the child must learn 'to turn language and thought in upon themselves' (p. 89). The child must learn to consider possibilities, and to manipulate symbols. As the principal symbolic system for young children is oral language, they must first learn to become aware of language as an independent structure, freeing it from its embeddedness in everyday events. This view can be summarized by saying that *language must become independent of its use.*

How does this come about? Donaldson suggests that awareness typically develops when something gives us pause for thought, and instead of proceeding with an activity, we stop to consider possibilities. 'We heighten our awareness of what is actual by considering what is possible' (Donaldson, 1978: 94).

In this regard, the child's learning to read makes a highly significant contribution, for as a child once observed to Margaret Donaldson: 'You have to stop and think. It's difficult.' And so it is. In learning to read, children have to pause and consider possibilities, for there is no one-to-one correspondence between the marks on the page and the sounds they represent. Donaldson illustrates this by pointing out that the most common letter in written English, the letter *e*, is pronounced in a great many different ways – compare, *me*, *he*, but *hen*; *here*, but *there*; and *were*. So in learning to read, the child is constantly faced with different possibilities, and these have to be considered and choices made. Unlike the spoken word, where the non-linguistic context often determines the interpretation and excludes the need for considered choice, the printed word, being enduring, allows the child the opportunity to stop and think, giving a chance for possibilities to be considered, and awareness thereby heightened.

Clark's Position

Clark's views on language awareness appear to be quite different from those of Donaldson, for she suggests that there is evidence that children are aware of language at an early age. (Indeed, some authors posit an awareness operator functioning from the start in models of language acquisition – see Marshall and Morton, 1978.) Such evidence, summarized by Clark (1978b) under various headings, comes from a variety of observations made by a number of investigators of young children's language abilities. For example, young children can make judgements about various aspects of language. From an early age (two years), they can judge that statements like *Bring me the ball* are better formed than *Ball me the bring* (Gleitman, 1979). They can also make judgements about complexity, and have been shown at age five years to be able to assign the more complex *What can the cow say?* as more likely to have been produced by an adult, compared to the less complex *What the cow say?* which is more likely to have been produced by a child (Scholl and Ryan, 1975). At age four years, they have been found able to make various judgements about the appropriateness of statements. They know that the more indirect *I would like a sweet* is considered more appropriate and more polite than *I want a sweet* (Bates, 1976). They can also make judgements about speech registers: a four-year-old can correctly distinguish the 'voices' of father, mother, and baby in games of 'doing the voices' (Anderson, 1977). They will also use the baby-talk register used by older children and adults when talking to babies, where language is adjusted in various ways – use of higher pitch, increase in pause length, simplification of syntax, use of diminutives such as *doggie, horsie*, etc. (Shatz and Gelman, 1973).

Young children also make corrections to speech. Though they rarely seem to correct the speech of others, even if they are twins (Savić, 1980), they will correct their own speech. Language is a high-level, complex skill, and in using it mistakes often occur whether the user is adult or child. We frequently correct the mistakes we make as we speak, and these corrections are referred to as 'speech repairs'. This whole process, of making errors in speech and correcting them, is so mundane that we may often fail to notice its occurrence – it is typically 'edited out'.

Speech repairs are of two main types – prompted and spontaneous. An example of *prompted repair* in a four-year-old child is given by Marshall (Marshall and Morton, 1978):

Child:	I brang it home from school.
Father:	What?
Child:	I bringed it home.
Father:	Eh?
Child:	I brung it home.
Father:	Oy vay!
Child:	Brought!

It is interesting to note that though the adult indicates that there is something amiss (*What?*), he does not specify that the problem lies with the verb. The prompt is quite unspecific.

Another type of speech repair, of greater interest in the present context, is the *spontaneous repair*, which is spontaneously effected by the speaker. Presently, we will return to this topic in more detail. In the meantime, the phenomenon can be illustrated from these three examples from Snyder (1914):

(i) Addition of modifier: 'Dat water . . . Dat dirty water';
(ii) Correction of word: 'Might, take paddle out boat . . . Might take paddle out canoe';
(iii) Correction of word order: 'Down sand beach I been . . . I been down sand beach'.

In each case, the speech is spontaneously repaired by the child – whether for purposes of modification, selection of a more appropriate noun, or use of more congenial syntax – without any prompting by a listener.

If young children can make judgements about various aspects of language, and if they can correct errors or inelegancies in their speech either spontaneously or through prompting, this provides some evidence that they are not wholly lacking in awareness of their own language and the language used by others. Clark (1978b) advances evidence under a number of other headings, not considered here in detail, in further support of the conclusion that children are aware of aspects of language from an early age, including the ability to analyse language into linguistic units; the supplying of appropriate inter-pretations for aspects of language; and language practice and lan-guage play.

From this evidence, Clark proceeds to distinguish different *types* of language awareness, which she relates to different underlying skills such as monitoring, checking, learning, predicting and reflecting on utterances (Clark, 1978b: Table 1, p. 34). What is clear from Clark's account is her view that language awareness appears early. As she says:

> With age, children show an increasing awareness of language. From the start, they seem to be aware of both form and function. In monitoring what they say, they make spontaneous repairs and practice sounds and sentences from as early as one-and-a-half or two. They also check on whether their listeners have understood them. A little later, by three or four, they begin to adjust their speech style to their listeners, comment on their own utterances and even comment on what they can't do, ask the occasional question about linguistic forms, and begin to correct other speakers. They also practice different speech styles through role-playing, and grow progressively more sensitive to what their listeners will and won't be able to understand.

However, Clark clearly appreciates that the methodological problems involved in studying the language awareness of very young children are considerable. As she notes: 'judgements of appropriateness, complexity, and form are next to impossible to elicit from very young children and therefore tell us too little too late' (Clark, 1978b: 37). The same is true of other aspects of awareness, such as making judge-ments about linguistic rules, making interpretations, and completing analysis into structural units. Spontaneous rather than elicited phe-nomena, such as spontaneous speech repairs or spontaneous practice and play, provide valuable insights into children's early language awareness, and spontaneous repairs seem to Clark to be 'an impor-tant source of information about linguistic awareness' (1978b: 37). Let us therefore consider the phenomenon of spontaneous speech repair in more detail.

In a systematic study of spontaneous repairs made to their speech by a small sample of young children (age range 2;2–3;8), Clark (1982b) notes that for repairs to occur, we need to suppose that a mismatch occurs between what was said (incorrectly), and what should have been said. A mismatch may occur due to a simple slip – of the 'tongue', in a mispronunciation; or of the memory, in the use of an inappropriate term. However, mismatches more commonly consist of a discrepancy between the child's actual production and the child's knowledge of the appropriate form. Repairing involves knowledge of the appropriate form, against which the child *monitors* his or her speech production, *checks* to ensure that the uttered production matches that intended, and *repairs* when a mismatch is detected. The sorts of repairs that two- to three-year-old children make are illustrated by Clark (1982b):

> *Lexical repairs* (word choice)
> What – who's that?
> You have to squeak – squeak – scrape it.

> *Morphological repairs* (pronoun gender)
> It's – it's – he's too big.
> . . . but it – he climbs up – she climbs up in it.

> *Phonological repairs* (addition of final consonants)
> Where's that anima – where's that animal?
> Hair o – on your arms.

> *Syntactic repairs* (choice of subject)
> The kittycat is de – de spider's kissing the kittycat's back.
> She – he didn't give her any food.

Clark is suggesting, then, that the phenomenon of spontaneous speech repair requires the supposition of some form of language awareness in very young children. When the child speaks, the actual output is monitored and checked against knowledge of the appropriate output. If these outputs do not match in the check, then a repair occurs with production of a new, corrected, output.

Although she acknowledges that the very young child's awareness of language may be more explicit than the explicitly formulated indications of language awareness found in older children following reflection or deliberation, she nevertheless wants to argue that the evidence she advances is an indication of language awareness at some level. The point is illustrated with reference to the past-tense inflection in English (where for regular verbs *-ed* is added to the present tense form – e.g., *walk, walked*):

> One could argue that in order to apply the past tense ending, two-year-olds must be aware of it at some level to identify and select it rather than other possible verb endings to denote completed actions. But not until five or so at the earliest do children appear able to identify the *-ed* ending explicitly as the linguistic unit that adds a past tense meaning . . . (Clarke, 1978b: 36)

Comparison of Donaldson's and Clark's Positions

Donaldson's position emphasizes that children's awareness of language is a comparatively late development occurring around seven years of age. Awareness involves conscious processes of deliberation and reflection, and awareness of language comes about when the child has learned to consider language *independently of its everyday use*. This learning process is significantly enhanced by the child's acquisition of literacy, particularly learning to read, and such awareness is much involved with the type of disembedded thinking required for success in our system of formal education. Clearly, the sort of awareness that Donaldson is concerned with is *reflective awareness*, which involves processes of deliberation and reflection.

Clark's position appears quite different from that of Donaldson. For Clark, language awareness appears early, from the age of one to two years. Though it may initially be implicit, in contrast to the later, reflective awareness that Donaldson is highlighting, the young child is nevertheless aware of language at some level. Otherwise, the commonly observed phenomenon of spontaneous speech repair would not occur. In young children, awareness of language is *an integral aspect of language use*. While young children are not aware of language to the extent that they could, for example, give an articulated account of awareness that is fully conscious, they are nevertheless aware of aspects of language at some 'tacit' level.

At this point, we could presumably try to answer our question of when children become aware of language by saying that they are tacitly aware of language from the age of one to two years, and only later are they reflectively aware of language from around the age of seven years. Clark's primary concern, with an aspect acquisition, draws attention to one type of awareness – tacit. Donaldson's primary concern, with the effect of language awareness on the child's increasing control of his or her own thought processes, draws attention to another type of awareness – reflective. Though their views on when language awareness develops in children appear initially to be entirely discrepant, there is in fact no real discrepancy, for they are talking about different types of awareness that are typical of children of different ages.

While this way of resolving the matter may have some appeal, it nonetheless encounters a difficulty. Namely, on occasion, young two-, three-, and four-year-old children provide evidence that they are fully aware of aspects of language. That is, their language awareness is *not* invariably tacit, for occasionally, young children provide evidence that they have reflective awareness of aspects of language.

Reflective Awareness in Young Children

Examples of young children's 'reflective' awareness of language, scattered across the literature, have been noted by Clark (1982b). As far as I can see, they almost invariably involve children's observations on how things are said – in their own speech or in the speech of others. Sometimes, there is an indication that the child's observation arises through puzzlement; or from irritation at being teased by another child or an adult. Thus these are not instances of the everyday ebb and flow of language use. Rather, they seem to arise when the child is puzzled or intrigued by some aspect of speech, or when something or someone challenges the child's way of speaking. First let us consider a number of such examples.

Observations on own production

In examples (1) and (2), children have been mis-pronouncing words. When able to pronounce the words correctly, they announce the fact.

1   Child (aged 2½ years)

    After saying *quick* as *kip* for about a year:
    'Daddy, I can say *quick.*'
    (Smith, 1973)

2   Child (aged 4 years)

    After saying *merry-go-round* as *mekariround*:
    'Watch my mouth: *merry-go-round.*'
    (Leopold, 1949)

In example (3), a child makes an error in what she says, and then observes that she has made a mistake ('no'), and produces the word that she meant to say ('I mean'):

> 3 An adult points to the child's foot and asks: 'What's that'? The child replies: 'A footsie'. This reply, 'A footsie', is repeated when the adults points to the child's other foot. The adult then indicates both feet and asks: 'What are these'?, to which the reply is:
>
> Child (aged 2½ years)
>
> 'Two footsies . . . no, two feetsies, I mean'
> (Pratt and Grieve, 1984)

In example (4), the same child, now seven months older, observes that two things she has said rhyme.

> 4 The child, sitting at the table, asks for a bit of cheese:
>
> Child (aged 3 years)
>
> 'Can I have a bit of cheese, please? . . . *cheese please* – that's a rhyme.'
> (Pratt and Grieve, 1984)

Observations on other's production

In example (5), the child is puzzled as to why her grandfather produces an incorrect form, saying *yourn* instead of *yours*.

> 5 Child (aged 3 years)
>
> 'You know, Granpa says *yourn*. This is *yourn*. Why does he do that?'
> (Leopold, 1949)

In example (6), the child notices that an adult, Opa, pronounces the child's name differently in English and German.

> 6 Child (aged 4 years)
>
> 'Opa might call me *Hildegard*. In German, though, *Hildegart*.'
> (Leopold, 1949)

General observations on production

In example (7), the child notes what you have to say in German when there is one shoe, and what you have to say when there are two shoes:

7   Child (aged 4 years)

'If there is one, you have to say *Schuh*.
If there are two, you have to say *Schuhe*.'
(Leopold, 1949)

In example (8), the child is uncertain about how to segment words, and offers alternative ways of doing so:

8   Child (aged 4 years)

'Mummy, is it *an adult*, or *a nadult?*'
(Gleitman *et al.*, 1972)

Challenges to production

In the following examples, children's productions are challenged in some way. In example (9), a young child mis-pronounces *merry-go-round* as *mewwy-go-round*. This results in an older child teasing him, the older child using the same mis-pronunciation as the younger child. The younger child's attempt to reprove the older child reveals just what the problem is. And though he knows what the problem is, there is nothing he can do about it!

9   A young child, David, asks if he can go on the 'mewwy-go-round'.
An older child teases: 'David wants to go on the mewwy-go-round.'
David: 'No, you don't say it wight.'
(Maccoby and Bee, 1965)

Example (10) illustrates a similar phenomenon. When an adult asks the child what he wants to be when he grows up, the child replies:

10   *Child* (aged 4 years):   'A dowboy.'
     Adult: 'A dowboy, eh?'
     Child: 'No, not a *dowboy*, a DOWBOY!'
     (Campbell, 1967)

The child knows that the correct form is *cowboy*, but he cannot produce it. When the adult produces the child's incorrect form *dowboy*, this is a tease, for the child appreciates that the adult *can* produce the correct form. Also notice the child's valiant attempt to correct the adult: not a *dowboy*, but a − − and here the child wants to say 'cowboy'. But he cannot, and he is left trying to correct the adult through re-iteration of his incorrect form, albeit produced with great emphasis and frustration.

In example (11), we see a young child's appreciation of the correct form of the word *fish*. The child cannot produce it, the approximation being *fis*. But notice the distinction the child makes. The child's production of *fis* for *fish* is acceptable if unfortunate. But the adult's production of *fis* for *fish* is not acceptable:

11 *Adult:*   'This is your *fis*?'
    Child: 'No, my *fis*.'
    Adult: 'This is your *fish*?'
    Child: 'Yes, my *fis*.'
    (Berko and Brown, 1960)

In example (12), the father of a 2½-year-old child endeavours to get his son to produce the correct form *jump*. The child's approximation is *dup*. Note the child's final observation that in producing *jump*, it is the father and not the child who can succeed.

12 *Father:*   'Say *jump*.'
    Child: 'Dup.'
    Father: 'No, *jump*.'
    Child: 'Dup.'
    Father: 'No, *jummmmp*.'
    Child: 'Only Daddy can say *dup*!'
    (Smith, 1973)

In the final example here, (13), the child makes a common error, over-generalizing the final addition of *-ed* to indicate the past tense of an irregular verb. Note that the child is aware of, and quite explicit about, the fact that the incorrect production belongs to the child, not the father.

13 *Child:*   'Mummy goed to the store.'
    Adult: 'Mummy goed to the store?'
    Child: 'No, Daddy, I say it that way, not *you*!'
    (Bever, 1975)

What these examples appear to illustrate is that young children aged two to four years can be aware of how things are said, or should be said, by themselves, and by others. And on occasion, children are sufficiently explicit to reveal to us the existence of their awareness.

Conclusion

How does this affect the question of when children become aware of language? To date, the debate seems to have been somewhat confused. We can begin to try to disentangle some of the issues by referring to the different views summarized in Table 9.1.

Table 9.1. *Views on language awareness in childhood.*

View	Early childhood	Later childhood
I		Awareness
II	Tacit awareness	Reflective awareness
III	Tacit awareness	Tacit awareness Reflective awareness
IV	Tacit awareness Reflective awareness occasionally expressed	Tacit awareness Reflective awareness

In View I, awareness develops in later childhood, around 7 years of age. Early childhood, from around 1–2 years of age is marked by a lack of language awareness. In this view, young children's spontaneous speech repairs do not provide evidence of awareness, for they are held to involve 'automatic' processing which does not require conscious control. This view is described by Garton and Pratt (1989: 127):

> In order for some ability to be labelled as involving metalinguistic awareness, it is essential that it consists of reflection at a level at which the individual is explicitly focusing attention on the language. The monitoring of language which occurs automatically as part of the speech production mechanism does not require metalinguistic awareness unless it also involves conscious reflection on the language.

Related views are to be found in Tunmer and Herriman (1984), and Bialystok (1986). However, as Bowey (1988) points out, if one builds the notion of conscious control (in her terms, an 'intentionality criterion') into the definition of what is to count as language awareness, then this 'amounts to a foreclosure of all important questions regarding the emergence and function of metalinguistic performance in children' (p. 19). Those who emphasize conscious control appear to be talking about *reflective* awareness.

The distinction drawn earlier between tacit awareness and reflective awareness in comparing the positions of Clark and Donaldson would appear to be illustrated in View II in Table 9.1 – the former is characteristic of early childhood, the latter of later childhood. However, this is incorrect, for tacit awareness in early childhood does not merely translate into later reflective awareness. Tacit awareness continues, into later childhood and indeed into adulthood – for example, the phenomenon of spontaneous speech repair does not disappear during development. View III is therefore a more accurate representation of the contrast between the positions of Donaldson and Clark. Early childhood is characterized by tacit awareness which continues into later childhood and beyond; and reflective awareness is typical of later childhood and beyond.

However, this view is still incomplete, for we need to incorporate the evidence referred to earlier, which indicates that in early childhood, noticeably before the age of seven years, we can, if fortunate, observe instances of reflective awareness. This is indicated in View IV in Table 9.1, which acknowledges that the tacit awareness evident in early childhood later continues; that reflective awareness is typically observed in later childhood; but that *reflective* awareness is occasionally expressed in *early* childhood.

The phrase 'occasionally expressed' requires comment. Does the fact that young children occasionally express reflective awareness mean that they are reflectively aware only occasionally? This is one possibility. Another is that young children are reflectively aware more frequently, but give no evidence of this: either because there is no particular reason to do so; or because they are unable to do so – recall that very young children are still engaged in acquiring the means of expression. It may well be no accident that in our baker's dozen examples above, the youngest age at which children provide evidence of reflective awareness is $2\frac{1}{2}$ years, an age when some children have sufficient means of expression at their disposal to convey to us something of their knowledge and experience. Whether children below the age of $2\frac{1}{2}$ years have unexpressed reflective awareness remains unresolved.

So when do children become aware of language? In the present chapter it is suggested that they are aware of language from an early age. Initially, their awareness of language is typically tacit, though they may on occasion express the results of reflective awareness – when they have acquired sufficient means of expression from about the age of $2\frac{1}{2}$ years onwards, and when they are puzzled or challenged about the way things are said. As children grow older, tacit awareness continues, and reflective awareness becomes more frequently expressed, as problems about language and thought become increasingly apparent to the child, as opportunities for social interaction, problem-solving and reflection increase, and as the child becomes more able to articulate the results of his or her experience and knowledge.

10 Children's Perception

Lesley Hall
Deakin University

The development of humans from infancy to adulthood is marked by the increasing selectivity, specificity and discrimination of which individuals become capable in their cognitive, perceptual and physical activities. This present chapter will focus on the development of visual search strategies, viewed within the larger context of the development of mechanisms of selective attention. The chapter will also be concerned with the question of how children come to gain control over their own visual attention; as Bruner has put it – 'How does the child learn to visually orient and search in a way that reflects the needs of problem solving rather than the mere tracking of sensory change?' (1968: 6)

Attempts to answer such a question can provide information not just about the basic perceptual skills needed for efficient visual search, but can also, to the extent that search is driven by cognitive processes and knowledge, indicate developmental changes in memory capacity, logical inferential reasoning, planning capacity, and comprehension of specific concepts and linguistic structures. It is therefore of practical as well as theoretical interest to know how children of various ages organize their visual searches. The assumption that children can quickly direct their visual attention to some particular aspect of the immediate environment being talked about, and can efficiently select just the information required to answer a question or solve a problem, has implications for learning. Preschool and school-aged children are increasingly placed in situations where they are expected to explore, seek out and maintain attention on just those parts of the visual world that are relevant to the task at hand, extracting visual information in as efficient a manner as possible. If a specific kind and amount of information is required to solve a problem, then failure to search thoroughly enough may lead to the wrong decision, while looking more exhaustively than necessary may result in a cost of time and effort. A teacher may allow only a brief time for children to find some particular information, and any limitations in children's ability to find and organize that information quickly will result in a situation which is confusing, rather than adding to their knowledge.

In partial answer to Bruner's question, it seems reasonable to suggest that with age, language will begin, however inadequately at first, to serve a regulative function. This is not to suggest that language necessarily determines the perceptual experience, but rather to propose that, depending on the situation, it may influence the order and nature of the visual information which is acquired as sensory input to the perceptual systems.

The importance of language for the development of voluntary behaviour has been emphasized by Russian researchers. For example, Luria (1975) described the development of this function from the early stages in infancy, where language can serve to produce an orienting response, through to the six-year-old child who is able to inhibit certain behaviours while executing others – without the need for external speech of his own or from someone else. However Luria's studies on the effect of language on voluntary behaviour examined only the control of manual behaviour such as pressing or not pressing a hand-held rubber bulb. The effect of language on visual search, which provides the child with so much more precise and yet comprehensive information about the world, has not been studied extensively nor systematically.

Some clues about the regulative function of language for visual search can be gained by drawing on a range of studies where on-going search behaviour of various kinds is considered. In the present chapter, reference will be made to studies where children's visually guided locomotion around a natural environment constitutes the operational 'search' unit. In other studies, visual/manual search is the unit, while in yet others, eye movement and eye fixation measures are used. The studies involving visual search will be restricted to those concerned with search of pictorial rather than textual material since this will allow for more direct comparisons across the age range of interest.

In the following discussion of these various search behaviours, it will become apparent that many of the theoretical and methodological concerns, which have provided a continuing impetus for Donaldson's work, have direct relevance for any attempt to summarize what we know about visual search development. Some of the older studies to be described emphasize children's limitations when compared to adults', while more recent studies have adopted the more positive attitude noted and espoused by Donaldson (1978), whereby the focus is on the child's capacities and on the conditions under which these capacities are most likely to emerge.

Also, the distinction drawn by Donaldson (1978) between 'embedded' and 'disembedded' tasks would seem to provide an important clue as to the conditions under which children will find it most easy to exercise cognitive control over their general and visual search activities. By exploring this distinction, Donaldson reminds us that young children may have difficulty in recognizing the burden of meaning that falls on language to define strictly the nature of the tasks we present to them. In drawing conclusions about visual search development from children's performance on such tasks, we need to be conscious of how they understand the task and perform with respect to that understanding, not simply in terms of the adult-defined task.

Visual Search in Infancy

In an extensive review of developmental trends in visual scanning, Day (1975) has summarized how children and adults differ in terms of speed, efficiency, systematicity, and exhaustiveness. A most valuable aspect of the review was that it drew attention to the need to adopt a broad perspective when studying the development of visual processing, whereby the viewer's intentions, expectations, and cognitive strategies are considered in the light of task demands and stimulus materials.

This has led to modification of the view that infants and young children are generally able to carry out searches only of limited areas. Certainly studies of infants have indicated that in the first few months infants scan visual stimuli in a very restricted way, looking only at particular features when presented with two-dimensional geometric figures (Salapatek, 1968, 1975). There are also reports (Posner and Rothbart, 1981) of a phenomenon called 'obligatory attention', which refer to difficulties young infants may have in moving their fixation from one informative area to another. Instead, the infant becomes increasingly agitated during the course of a prolonged fixation with gaze finally being broken only by crying, closing the eyes or turning the head. However, by three or four months of age, infants appear able to scan more extensively and in a way that is responsive to the higher level characteristics of stimuli. For instance, Ruff (1975) found that infants of three months and over more often shifted fixations between two stimuli when they were the same than when they were different. Moreover, the extent to which restricted scanning patterns are representative of all the visual encounters of young infants is challenged by Hainline and Lemerise (1985), who have argued that a number of methodological problems may have led Salapatek to underestimate infants' ability to scan whole figures without necessarily being captured by particular stimulus features. When studying the visual scanning of one- to three-month-old alert infants held in an upright position for viewing, while they did not find age differences in extensiveness of scanning, they did find that infants were differentially responsive to certain stimulus characteristics – small (5°) shapes were more likely to be examined thoroughly than large (30°) shapes. They conclude that our knowledge about visual scanning in young infants and what such scanning signifies is less certain than has been believed.

The picture of the infant as easily 'captured' by salient perceptual features, even if accurate for very young infants, certainly does not fit the picture of the slightly older infant as revealed by studies of the development of the object concept and of object permanence. Bower (1974) reports some findings of Moore that Stage II infants (two- to four-month-olds) searched for an object in the location where it had previously been presented, even though it was placed in full view in a different location. He also reports that using opaque and transparent cups, Stage IV infants (six- to twelve-month-olds) looked to the place where they had previously found a hidden object, ignoring the location where they had just seen it hidden and where, in the case of the transparent cups, it remained visible.

Consideration must also be given to the finding of Bower *et al.* (1971) that Stage II babies continued to track along the path of a moving object after the object had stopped moving. They also looked to the place where a stationary object had been seen resting before it moved, ignoring the observed movement. This behaviour did not seem to result from an inability to arrest on-going head and eye movements. Rather, Bower interpreted the behaviour as a conceptual failure to identify a moving object with itself when stationary. It also means that the child's visual scanning is guided by conceptual considerations, whether or not they are appropriate to the context, rather than being guided by available sensory information.

The question of just how much information is available to infants and children from peripheral vision has been raised when seeking explanations of restricted scanning. For very young infants, restricted gaze patterns may indeed indicate an inability even to detect peripheral information. However, Harris and McFarlane (1974) found that by two months of age, infants could rapidly shift their gaze to targets introduced as far as 35° into the periphery when no central stimulus was available. Findlay and Irvinskia (1984) confirmed that when a stimulus was already fixated by four-month-old infants, the probability of orienting to a peripheral stimulus was decreased. However, cardiac measures of the infants indicated that on trials when the peripheral stimulus did not elicit orienting movements, the stimulus was nonetheless still being detected, even if detection of the peripheral stimulus was not sufficient to result in on-going search.

To summarize, during infancy there is a growth in the capacity of the infant actively to explore the visual world, such exploration being guided not only by perceptual factors but also by the child's way of cognitively structuring the world.

Visual Search in Early Childhood

Now we need to consider how to characterize the developmental pattern of visual scanning in the years beyond infancy. What evidence is there for a growth of the kind of sustained planning and self-regulation which allows an adult to search the same pictorial array exhaustively or selectively depending on task requirements? For reasons probably closely related to the extreme wriggliness of the young child, there are very few studies of visual scanning on children younger than four or five years. However, the last ten years have seen an upsurge of interest in the development of general logical search skills in young children. Although eye fixations and movements are not explicitly measured in these studies, their findings do provide us with a very useful base from which to proceed to discuss the performance of the older child on visual search tasks.

Sophian and Wellman (1980) provide convincing evidence that children as young as three years show a definite, if still developing, ability to utilize both their knowledge of the world, and verbal information provided by an adult, to guide their initial selection in a search task. Three- to seven-year-old children were asked to select one room of a doll's house to search for a target object. The doll's house consisted on an upstairs kitchen and bedroom, and an identically furnished pair of rooms downstairs. The target objects were recognized by the children as being ones which were typically located in a particular room (e.g., a fork in a kitchen, a pillow in a bedroom) or else as being ones which had no typical location (e.g., candle, dog). Children were shown the target object, and following its removal, they were given either complete ('it's in the upstairs bedroom'), partial ('it's downstairs'), or no information about where the target had been placed. Children were then allowed to select one room to search.

Sophian and Wellman found, not surprisingly, that children made most correct selections when a complete specification of the target was provided. When the verbal information specified a location that was incongruent with the target's typical location ('the pillow is in the downstairs kitchen') there was some reduction in the children's correct selections, but for the most part (60 per cent of trials) even the youngest child followed these instructions. When only partial instructions were provided, children combined them with their knowledge of typical location to guide their selection. In these young children, regulation of the initial aspects of search appeared to be coming under cognitive control, although it must be remembered that since only one room could be selected, we do not know how the children would have continued their search if they were initially unsuccessful. The restrictions of their search to one location may also have maximized the children's performance in accordance with Wellman's (1985: 143) belief that 'planning a course of action occurs first on tasks when planning is required in order to succeed at all, and only later on tasks where planning is needed to honour other constraints like those of efficiency'.

This point is worth bearing in mind when considering inconsistencies in the reports of young children's capacity for efficient search. Indeed the search task in the study by Wellman *et al.* (1979) generally elicited a comprehensive search of eight locations by three-, four- and five-year-olds, even though information was available to the children to enable them to restrict their search to only three locations. Why did the children not demonstrate the sort of selectivity observed by Sophian and Wellman? This question will be taken up later, but it is worth noting that in the study by Wellman *et al.* (1979) there was no forewarning that the children would be required to carry out a search; the cupboards were not particularly distinctive; the children were not limited in the number of locations they could search; and an exhaustive search was fairly readily accomplished.

Some of the conditions pertaining to the task set by Wellman *et al.* (1979) also characterized the search task used by Miller *et al.* (1986), who asked children to search arrays consisting of two rows of six doors each marked with a symbol (house or cage) to indicate whether that door covered a picture of a household object or one of an animal. Three search tasks were performed by each child, who was asked to remember the locations of all the pictures, and to decide if the two rows were the same or different. They found that eight- and ten-year-olds were better able to match their search strategy to the particular task, whereas the six-year-olds tended to carry out exhaustive searches even on trials where they needed only to open doors marked as showing one of the picture subsets. Using a similar selective recall task, Miller and Weiss (1981) reported that only 63 per cent of thirteen-year-olds consistently made selective searches of the arrays.

The contrast between these results and those to be discussed later, highlights the need to be sensitive to task variables which may promote or prevent the demonstration of appropriate search strategies by children. In the task set by Miller *et al.*, the two subsets of pictures were distributed across both rows, requiring the child to carry out an exhaustive visual search of the symbols, even when a selective manual search was required. Younger children may have been better able to search selectively if all the relevant doors had been located together spatially, so that a selective visual and manual search could be carried out.

Evidence that young children can demonstrate some capacity for selective search comes from a naturalistic study by Wellman, Somerville and Haake (1979) who asked three-, four- and five-year-old children to find an item which might have been lost at four of eight marked locations in their familiar preschool playground. The opportunity to search the locations occurred after the child had been taken round each one, had had their photo taken at the third location, and had witnessed the discovery that the item was missing at the seventh location.

In the control condition only 20 per cent of the children first searched for the lost item in locations 3, 4, 5 or 6. It was a very different story, however, when children were provided with information which allowed them to infer the critical regions where the item might logically be found. In this situation 76 per cent of the children first searched either location 3, 4, 5 or 6, and no age differences were found. Comparable results emerged from further studies which were designed to rule out the possibility that children were guided simply by associating the item with a particular location, or the possibility that children might succeed due to idiosyncrasies of particular settings like the popularity of the sandpit location.

Further studies, reviewed by Somerville and Haake (1985), set out to replicate and extend the findings of these naturalistic studies by developing hiding-and-finding tasks with four table-top locations, where the presence or absence of objects could be demonstrated to children in a controlled way. Even with children as young as two years of age, the success rates for making an initial selection of a logically correct location to search for a missing object was essentially the same as in the naturalistic task. Somerville and Haake concluded that to some extent quite young children could make inferences about the unseen displacements of an object, and use such inferences to constrain their search. They also recognized the children's perform-ance as 'better-than-chance but less-than-perfect' (p. 83). This was particularly evident on those trials where the first search location selected was logically correct but nonetheless unsuccessful. In the playground study by Wellman et al. (1979), the second locations searched by three-year-olds were less likely to be correct than those of four- and five-year-olds. Younger children were also more likely to repeat their search of a location which had already been unsuccess-fully checked. One interpretation of this result is that young children believe that their inference about an object's location will hold true for only one location and that they do not appreciate that there is a range of possible, but not necessarily correct, locations. An alternative explanation is that although children may recognize that there are several possible locations, they are easily distracted from im-plementing more than an initial part of the search.

To conclude, as do Somerville and Haake, that the young child's search efficiency is imperfect rather than totally erroneous, is both to acknowledge those search skills which young children can demon-strate, and to recognize that young children are not without intellec-tual limitations. Such a conclusion also leads to questions about the conditions under which children are most likely to recognize a need to be efficient, and how that recognition relates to their ability to plan and execute a sequence of steps in order to achieve a particular goal. Wellman (1985) reports some findings that suggest young children of 4;6 but not 3;6 can benefit from a simple reminder to 'go the quick way' when asked to visit locations A and B (equidistant from the child and eighteen feet apart), collect a baby toy at each location, and deliver both animals to a mother animal located near location A. With no instructions about being quick, children were just as likely to go to location A first as to go to location B. With instructions, the older children chose the more efficient B-first route on 73 per cent of trials. However, even the older children's efficient performance was re-duced to chance level when location B was placed at some distance from the child's starting point while location A and the endpoint were moved closer to the child. Only a group of children aged 5;6 were able to use instructions to overcome a bias to search first the location that was perceptually salient by virtue of being closer.

What picture emerges from this brief overview of the logical search capacities of young children? Certainly there is evidence that young children can be responsive to external demands for efficiency, particularly if the demands are explicitly stated or if there are clear costs attached to inefficiency. They are also able to organize at least the initial stages of a selective search according to logical constraints, particularly when the logical constraints do not conflict with perceptual saliency. Children have also shown an ability to carry out organized exhaustive searches, albeit unnecessarily, particularly when supported by an organized spatial arrangement.

However, efficient search also involves knowing when particular search strategies are appropriate, and how to co-ordinate them for different tasks. One further area of concern for the development of search, be it general or purely visual, is the process by which external demands for efficiency are internalized so that efficient search is more or less automatic even when not obligatory. In the next section we will be concerned with how these aspects of search develop.

Changes in Children's Visual Search

A consideration of studies concerned specifically with visual search measures indicates that the most significant changes with age may relate to children's abilities to select and implement the most appropriate strategy for a particular situation. For instance, when Zinchenko, Chzhi-Tsin and Tarakanov (1963) asked three- to six-year-old children to inspect an unfamiliar irregularly shaped figure in order to identify it later, they found that the younger children focused their eye fixations on a limited and irrelevant part of the figure, whereas the older children scanned more extensively, attending to the figure's contours. However, during the recognition phase of the task, the search patterns of another group of children showed the reverse, the older children restricting their search to a few relevant features while the younger children scanned the contour more thoroughly. The familiarity of the visual stimulus seemed to influence the extent and relevance of the young children's visual search.

A study by Mackworth and Bruner (1970) also found that developmental differences in visual scanning were most likely to occur in situations that reduced children's chances of recognizing relevant information. They recorded the eye movements of six-year-olds and young adults while they inspected slides which were presented in either a blurred-to-focused sequence or a focused-to-blurred sequence. When viewing an initially blurred slide the children often started by making long 'leaping' eye movements, but the areas they fixated were not ones chosen as informative by adults. When a slide was presented in focus, it was the adults who made longer eye movements, enabling them to link information from various parts of the picture, while the children tended to make fixations which were concentrated on fewer areas. However, these areas were among those selected by adults as informative. Thus it seemed that children, while able to make detailed searches on some occasions and able to scan more broadly on others, failed to co-ordinate both sorts of search in a way that optimally located informative areas.

The importance of the child's understanding of the nature of the search task has been emphasized by Vurpillot (e.g., Vurpillot and Ball, 1979), who asked children from four to nine years of age to compare pictures of two houses in order to decide if they were 'just the same or not the same'. The similarity or difference in the houses lay in the features which defined the identically located windows in each house. An analysis of the children's judgements of sameness or difference, as well as the scan paths they used to compare the windows of the houses, indicated that the younger children rarely made a systematic paired comparison of each of the window locations. Judgements of 'same' were often made on the basis of one common element between the two houses, or because scanning was not carried out exhaustively enough to detect differences. This contrasted with older children who were more likely to make sufficiently exhaustive paired comparisons to make correct decisions. Even when young children were induced to examine each window systematically before a decision was made, the same kinds of decisions occurred. This led Vurpillot to conclude that it is changes in children's criteria of identity that will lead to selection of more appropriate search strategies rather than *vice versa*.

The interrelations between understanding and visual search has also been studied by Hall (1975). In one study, three groups of viewers – four-year-olds, seven-year-olds, and adults – were asked to search arrays of six pictures in order to judge the truth or falsity of quantified descriptions such as 'All the pictures are horses', or 'None of the pictures are shoes'. The pictorial arrays consisted of six identical pictures or pictures of six different objects. As with Vurpillot's task, exhaustive and selective search patterns both constituted possible efficient search patterns, with exhaustive search being necessary on true trials, and selective search as far as the first disconfirming instance being sufficient on false trials. As Vurpillot found, there were developmental differences both in the correctness of judgements and the nature of visual searches. While 96 per cent of the four-year-old children made correct judgements about positive quantifiers like 'all', only 13 per cent made exhaustive searches on 'true' trials, and most did not search as selectively as possible on false trials. When it came to statements with negative universal quantifiers, for the most part the four-year-olds treated these as 'all' statements, and regardless of which criterion was used they rarely used appropriate search strategies.

The seven-year-olds were markedly better at judging negatively quantified statements, and their capacity to sustain exhaustive searches increased to an average of 73 per cent across all true trials. However, the seven-year-olds also made exhaustive searches of all six pictures on 73 per cent of false trials when the search could have been terminated after one picture was inspected.

Adults were wholly correct in their judgements of both positive and negative quantifiers. In addition, they demonstrated a further improvement in the ability to select a search strategy appropriate to the logical demands of the task, inasmuch as exhaustive searches were made on 87 per cent of true trials and 7 per cent of false trials. However, even adults rarely made their judgement having inspected only the minimum amount of information.

The developmental sequence found both in Hall's quantifier study and in Vurpillot's identity study showed children using partial search before exhaustive search, then finally demonstrating an ability to use either an exhaustive or a selective search as appropriate.

A further study by Hall (1975) confirmed that the way in which a linguistic description maps on to a visual array can influence the efficiency of a viewer's search, particularly that of the young viewer. Groups of four- and seven-year-old children were asked to search arrays beginning at a common central starting point so as to judge descriptions about the spatial location of a picture in the array – such as 'the picture of the dog is at the top', or '. . . the shoe is at the bottom'. Even the youngest children were able to make true and false judgements appropriately but there were considerable differences between the groups in the ability to make efficient selective searches to gain the information needed to make the judgements. These differences related both to the presence of irrelevant pictures in the array (none, one or three) and, more interestingly, to the criterion by which a false judgement could be made. To explain this latter point more fully, true judgements were required on trials when the named picture was indeed located at the specified location, but false judgements could arise either because some other picture was in the specified location (False Present trials) or because no picture at all was in the specified location (False Absent trials). In all cases, inspection of the specified location alone provided sufficient information to make a decision.

In the simplest condition, when no irrelevant pictures were present in the arrays, both groups were immediately able to look either up or down from the central starting point as appropriate, and for 95 per cent of True and False Present trials, to make a decision on the basis of their inspection of only that picture location. On False Absent trials, however, while all the children were able to use the linguistic specifications to guide them to the location which, by definition, was not defined by the presence of a perceptual stimulus, many children appeared unable to make an immediate decision based on their inspection of that location. Instead, the children scanned across the array, with the four-year-olds inspecting 4.5 locations on average and the seven-year-olds 3.1 locations before making a decision. Across both age groups only 37 per cent of searches were efficient for False Absent trials as compared to 89 per cent of True trials and 83 per cent of False Present trials.

The impact on search of the addition of one irrelevant picture to the arrays was assessed by asking three further groups of viewers – four-year-olds, eight-year-olds, and adults – to carry out the same task except that when the description specified the top there was an additional picture in the bottom picture location, and *vice versa* if the description specified the bottom location as the relevant one. In this condition the performance of even the adults was less than optimal, with the specified picture location being first inspected on 76 per cent of trials, and with a decision being made immediately after that inspection on only 50 per cent of trials. Efficient searches were rarely made on either False Present (25 per cent) or False Absent (37 per cent) trials. The search performance of the children was even more severely disrupted than that of adults, with virtually no efficient searches being made on either kind of false trial and with only 28 per cent and 44 per cent of true trials resulting in efficient searches by the four- and eight-year-olds respectively. So while some degree of cognitive control over the initial direction of search had been evident when no pictures at all were present in the visual field, perceptual salience won out in the False Absent trials in this condition, where children looked first to the irrelevant picture and not to the relevant but unoccupied specified location.

Despite the lack of search efficiency evident when one irrelevant picture is introduced, performance was found to be somewhat better when four further groups of viewers – four-year-olds, eight-year-olds, thirteen-year-olds, and adults – carried out the same task, but with three pictures present in irrelevant positions. In this condition, both the teenagers and adults were nearly always (98 per cent and 96 per cent trials) able to search the specified location first regardless of the kind of trial. Generally teenagers (71 per cent trials) and adults (87 per cent trials) were also then able to make their decision before inspecting irrelevant pictures. While less efficient than the adults and while showing the same pattern of results, the younger groups of children were also performing at a higher level than when only one distractor was present. Here four-year-olds were successful in first inspecting the specified location on 69 per cent of True and False Present trials but on only 25 per cent of False Absent trials. Some increases in efficiency occurred with age with the percentage of appropriate first searches rising from 69 per cent to nearly 100 per cent for true and false positive trials. However, on False Absent trials even the eight-year-olds continued to be attracted to a location defined by the presence of perceptual stimuli rather than one defined only linguistically. Both of the younger groups also had difficulty in restricting their search only to the relevant location, with only 8 per cent and 21 per cent of all trials being totally efficient.

The performance of the viewers of different ages on this task indicates something of the variety of factors which can influence search patterns. Full efficiency is only gradually achieved as the viewer acquires concepts (like *top* and *bottom*) and begins to use them; becomes aware of what constitutes sufficient information to make a decision (the identity/presence of a picture in a specified location); and becomes able to inhibit inspection of irrelevant parts of visual arrays. One further factor may also relate to the viewer's criterion about when it is cost-effective to be 'efficient', so that knowledge and strategies are more likely to be put into operation if search would otherwise be lengthy and difficult, but less likely to be used if there is only one additional area to be inspected.

Being able to relate linguistic and visual sources of information about the world is clearly an important part of development and, as we saw from the studies using sentence verification tasks, establishing such relationships is often carried out inefficiently by young children. However, this kind of task represents only one way of examining how visual search may be influenced by language. Another less complex way is to ask viewers to find a designated target picture in an array, and to signal its detection as quickly as possible. The viewer can be provided with general information about the location of the target such as 'The picture of the frog is at the bottom', or 'The shoe is not at the top', and the extent to which this information constrains their visual search can then be determined. Since in this 'Find' task the viewer is given every reason to believe that the information about target location is correct, this should lead the viewer to search the specified area for positive instructions, but to search all areas other than the one specified when instructions are given in a negative form.

In such a task used by Hall (1985), viewers were asked to search arrays containing six different but easily identifiable pictures – see Figure 10.1 – in order to 'find' a named target picture quickly, and to signal this by pressing a button. Viewers were asked initially to fixate the centrally located starting point, and begin to look around only when the array appeared, following the instructions.

On six trials the location of the target was indicated (top/bottom), and in six trials the location was indicated in a negative form. Practice trials were used to establish the potential locations, and that the target was always present and in the general location provided.

The performance of five groups – four-year-olds, seven-year-olds, nine-year-olds, thirteen-year-olds, and adults – supports earlier conclusions that efficient visual search strategies are only gradually acquired, and that perceptual and cognitive factors will influence when such strategies are most likely to be demonstrated.

The most consistently efficient searches across the different trials came from adults. When no instructions were given, they, like the other groups, were no better than chance in directing their gaze from the starting point to the row containing the target. However, in these

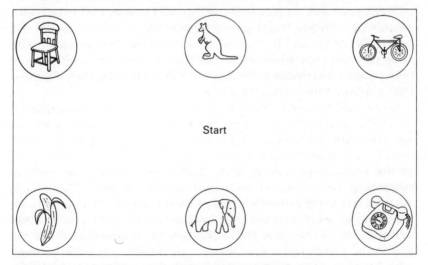

Figure 10.1   Example of pictorial array for 'Find' task.

no-instruction trials they did search systematically, either moving from one picture to an adjacent one in a cyclic manner, or adopting a left-to-right scan of first the top and then the bottom row until the target was found. When instructions were given, adults always looked immediately to the appropriate row and on 99 per cent of trials looked only within that row. The only apparent inefficiency occurred on 19 per cent of trials when search continued after the target had been fixated, but before its location had been signalled. However, there was no evidence for adults that such redundant search increased the overall search time.

The performance of the four-year-olds contrasted with that of the adults in a variety of ways. When no instructions were given, the children typically made unsystematic searches, not proceeding from one picture to the adjacent one, and often back-tracking to already inspected locations. Importantly, the provision of instructions did modify their search patterns such that first eye movements were appropriate significantly more often than the chance level which occurred under no-instruction trials. Nonetheless, on 34 per cent of instruction trials, children first searched in the wrong direction. This was most likely when instructions were in a negative form and when the target was at the bottom. Even when the initial search took account of the instructions, on 13 per cent of trials the children looked at the non-designated row before locating the target. On 50 per cent of trials the four-year-olds made redundant searches after locating the target, and unlike the adults, these redundant searches took longer than trials which were otherwise comparable but non-redundant.

Seven-year-olds showed better ability first to look to the appropriate row (82 per cent trials) and to sustain search in that row (74 per cent trials), but it was the nine-year-olds and thirteen-year-olds who came closest to the adult level of performance by being able to use both positive and negative instructions to look for targets in either the top or bottom row of pictures.

Conclusions

In the research considered here, some discrepancies have arisen concerning the ability of young children to search efficiently in various tasks, particularly when selective search is required. To resolve these discrepancies it would be valuable to compare the performance of the same children when carrying out both general and visual search tasks. This would help to answer questions as to whether efficient search strategies become implemented at much the same time across a range of task contexts, or whether the need for efficient search is more likely to become apparent when certain responses are called for, such as walking long distances, rather than other less effortful ones like moving the eyes.

Related to this question is the need to devise tasks where the child's motivation to locate visual information efficiently is maximized. Perhaps with the kind of interactive technology now available for monitoring eye movements during the reading process, it may be possible to provide children with rewarding visual events, contingent upon the performance of certain visual scanning patterns.

In addition to these questions about the efficiency of search behaviours, meta-attentional processes need to be considered. Only recently has interest in metacognitive processes focused on children's awareness of the attentional process, and of factors that might influence this process (Miller, Haynes and Weiss, 1985).

Certainly this would be a worthwhile area to examine in terms of specific visual search measures as well as the more general ones concerned with the physical location of objects. The ability of children to benefit from being asked to reflect upon what makes a given task easy or hard has important educational implications. As Donaldson (1978: 94) points out: 'If a child is going to control and direct his own thinking he must become conscious of it.' Much however remains to be done to find out what makes children think about how and where they look.

A further topic which requires consideration concerns the regulative role of speech. While evidence has been presented to indicate something of the role language may play in helping young children control the processes involved in acquiring visual information, much more needs to be done in order to map out how the control and monitoring of these processes is achieved. In Fuson's (1979) excellent review of the development of self-regulating aspects of speech, she raises a number of issues which need to be addressed if we are to increase our understanding of how language comes to be used for the spontaneous regulation of behaviour. She points out that much research has concentrated on the regulatory function of speech where the source is external to the child, or else has focused on the self-regulating speech that children produce spontaneously, but there is little information on how children learn self-regulating speech.

Another limitation of recent research relates to the fact that, for the most part, the activities which are supposed to be regulated by the child's speech or that of an adult, are not goal-directed activities selected by the child from a range of attractive alternatives, nor does the child usually have much to say about when the task is completed or whether a new one needs to be selected. As Fuson points out, these are just the aspects of situations where self-regulating speech might be most useful and most likely to occur.

Finally, Fuson suggests that while research has gone some way to examining how behaviour may be affected by speech sounds, the physical act of speaking, and the meaning of spoken words, there is almost no research concerned with the process of choosing words to speak, and how specification of an intended referent relative to a set of alternatives may have a regulating effect in itself.

Although many questions remain to be answered about the relative contributions of language, cognitive and perceptual systems to the regulation of visual search at various points during development, it is hoped that this chapter has conveyed something of the multifaceted nature of visual search and the gradual nature of its development, as well as indicating the need to find out more about how the visual system develops in efficiency and flexibility.

11 Children's Thinking

Robin Campbell and David Olson
University of Stirling
Ontario Institute for the Study of Education

The study of children's thinking has been dominated for a very long time now by a concern to explain, or to explain away, the phenomena first explored by Jean Piaget (1896–1980). These phenomena – the slow and faltering approach which children make towards a grasp of the central notions of quantification, measurement and logic – have a typical and special character. In almost every case, the endpoint of development is commitment to a proposition, or set of propositions, which is neither clearly dependent on experience (i.e., not an inductive generalization) nor attainable by deduction from other propositions which are dependent on experience. Principles such as the Piagetian conservations are *abductions*. Like the conservation principles of classical physics and chemistry, they make the best possible sense of the phenomena in their domain; they are interpretations or construals of the world. (For decisive historical analysis, see Meyerson, 1930, an undoubted source of Piaget's interest and approach.) This formal property of the phenomena studied was perhaps not Piaget's reason for studying them: his interest in the origins of scientific notions may have been the determining motive. However, it is a property that ensures that what the child is *not* doing in these tasks is detecting some manifest property of the material presented. Rather, the child's achievement is to invest the presented material with a property of his or her own devising. We shall argue that selection of tasks that can be characterized in this fashion is an essential methodological step in the study of thinking (of child or adult), if thinking is to be effectively distinguished from perception or attention.

Why has there been this long attempt to explain the phenomena studied by Piaget? What is wrong with Piaget's own explanations? To begin with, his explanations look like descriptions, albeit perspicuous ones, with only unsatisfactory gestures in the direction of a causal account. The pattern of Piagetian analysis is a fairly constant one. In any specific domain of children's thought, he sought first of all to establish a stage-like progression towards adult understanding – an essentially descriptive enterprise. Then, by way of explanation, he sought to relate the observed progression of stages to his general account of stages of cognitive development. Thirdly, to preserve this explanatory move from circularity, he would suppose that the transitions between stages were to be accounted for by domain-independent processes of functional reorganization, involving the co-ordination of established structures and somewhat mysterious regulatory processes known as *equilibration* and *reflective abstraction*.

Explanation by assimilation to stages is often thought of as unsatisfactory, for much the same reasons as explanations in terms of powers is thought unsatisfactory – e.g., the dormitive power of opium explains its sleep-inducing property. However, this objection is hardly cogent. If a general sequences of stages can be characterized in such a way that individual developmental patterns from different domains can be related to it, and therefore to one another, then such a general sequence has clear explanatory force. The ordering of stages in the different patterns has thereby been attributed to a common cause. The most successful application of this technique in Piaget's works is perhaps the sequence of sensori-motor stages, which has been applied to developmental patterns in such diverse domains as imitation, object representation, and tool use, with undeniable success, particularly in the field of comparative primate cognition (see Piaget, 1954; Chevalier-Skolnikoff, 1983). Of course, although a common cause is identified by this means, there remains obvious scope for further illumination! The situation may be compared with genetic explanation: patterns of inheritance of characters in diverse animal and plant species were seen to follow a common, Mendelian pattern long before the explanation of that pattern in terms of recombination of genes was formulated.

Equilibration, too, insofar as the process is described in a comprehensible way, has been criticized as logically unfounded (Fodor, 1976) and indistinguishable from nativism (Haroutounian, 1983).

The pattern of Piagetian explanation is thus often seen as intrinsically weak. In addition it fails to fit comfortably into the dominant modes of explanation in Anglo-American psychology. There have been two such dominant modes during Piaget's working life. Until around 1960, the infant was generally seen as a *tabula rasa* and the development was characterized as (a) the acquisition of new response functions, and (b) the gradual elimination of error. The sole mechanism of development was the learning of new stimulus and response connections by variants of the conditioning processes isolated in experimental animals. Viewed against this reductive and empiricist backcloth, Piaget was seen as a rationalist, since he attributed unwarranted mental structures to children, represented these structures as *constructions*, and represented children as *imposing* their thought on the world. He was also accounted a nativist, since the emergence of these structures was either not explained at all, or explained by means of an appeal to complicated and mysterious inherited mechanisms. Thus, Wohlwill (1962: 95) – by no means a firm adherent to the behaviourist hegemony – worried that:

> ... the non-operational, and at times frankly mentalistic, terms used by Piaget ... may seem to leave his analysis devoid of empirical, and perhaps even of theoretical, significance ... his whole conceptual apparatus of schemata, operations, centrations, and so forth appears to lack direct empirical reference.

Since 1960 the behaviourist hegemony has gradually been displaced by a nativist hegemony. The infant is seen as a *tabula omnifera*, development being characterized as the unfolding of inherited flexible structures which are fixed by the phenomena which happen to be present in the child's world. The main mechanism of development is simply endogenous growth triggered or channelled by exposure to relevant phenomena. (This is slightly exaggerated, for the process of revolution is still very much in progress. Nevertheless, though pockets of 'resistance' survive, the main academic citadels have clearly fallen.)

This spectacular intellectual convulsion will doubtless be of strong interest to future historians of science: it must have amused Piaget, if it did not drive him to despair. Branded rationalist and nativist through the 1950s and 1960s, when Anglo-American psychology first took serious note of his work, he found the same set of ideas – he was not given to hasty changes of mind – condemned as hopelessly empiricist in the late 1970s by the high priests of the new cognitive science (see Piattelli-Palmirini, 1980).

Although the two extreme positions which we have just characterized could hardly be more different, there remains a unifying thread of similarity. In both accounts the child is pictured as *passive*: the course of his development is fixed by external forces. To be sure, under the present dominant view innate structure plays a paramount role in shaping development, but such structure is inherent and its establishment calls for no effort on the child's part. In contrast, Piaget's picture of the child was as an active agent of development, fabricating mental structures from the thin yarn of experience by the slow and difficult application of the instruments of understanding. Facile 'improved' performance, uncoupled from understanding and the 'grasp of consciousness', led nowhere. In this respect, as in many others, Piaget represented the ontogenesis of thinking as a process homologous to the history of thinking (see Kuhn, 1962, for a compelling account of this homology).

Between the demise of the behaviourist picture of development and the establishment of the present innatism, the study of cognitive development in Britain and North America enjoyed a brief period of harmony with Piagetian ideas, under the respective intellectual leadership of Margaret Donaldson at Edinburgh and Jerome Bruner at Harvard. In our view, the case for such harmony remains a strong one. (See also the excellent review by Mandler, 1983.) Cognitive development is a bland label for a desperate struggle, and institutions such as schools and twenty years of parental care exist neither to install new response functions nor to provide appropriately timed triggering experiences. Rather, they assist and encourage children in that struggle. In this chapter, we put (part of) the case for restoration of that harmony.

We first discuss the nature of thinking in general and children's thinking in particular, emphasizing the rarity of the phenomenon and the variety of the forms of thought. Some problems of method and proposed solutions to them are discussed, and compared with innatist remedies. Finally, we identify some differences between our view of children's thinking and Piaget's.

What is Thinking?

In our view, thinking is an effortful activity, involving mental 'work', in which the organism forsakes its normal outward orientation on the presented world and struggles instead with a world indexed only imperfectly by a shadowy inner structure of mental symbols. While we regard this form of thinking as central, we shall refer to it as *inwardly mediated thinking* (conceding the possibility of other forms of thinking), for reasons which will become clear below.

Representations of thinking by artists reflect this view. Rodin's thinker crouches in a withdrawn foetal pose, with eyes closed and head lowered. Conan Doyle's detective Sherlock Holmes, when faced with some knotty problem, retires to consume a pound of shag tobacco, his mind sharpened by the drug and his senses dulled by the resulting fog. Rex Stout's hero Nero Wolfe leans back, closes his eyes and pushes his blubbery lips in and out in infantile fashion until his imagination delivers. For Stout's detective, as for most of us, thinking is a repugnant and – or so this cameo suggests – regressive activity, to be undertaken only as a last resort. Wolfe would rather groom his 10,000 orchids, experiment with new sauces, read, or drink beer, just as lesser mortals would rather attend some spectacle or entertainment.

Of course there are, doubtless, individuals for whom thinking is a pleasurable activity. Fortunate universities and publishers have them on their payrolls. Similarly, it may be that from time to time all of us can undertake this difficult activity with equanimity at worst, if the circumstances are sufficiently propitious. Perhaps these circumstances are most often propitious when we are young! At any rate, once the novelty of inwardly mediated thinking has worn off, it seems patent that adults will take almost any pains to avoid it.

A gripping presentation of this pessimistic view of consciousness and thinking is Eugene Marais' extraordinary essay (1969), in which the taking of such steps to avoid thinking is seen as diagnostic of consciousness in the animal world. Marais argued that inwardly mediated thinking, or rather the aversion felt for it, led to a variety of depression which he called Hesperian depression, because of its association with the setting of the sun and subsequent attenuation of the presented world. He pointed to certain universal aspects of human culture which in his view constituted avoidance of inwardly mediated thinking. There were two basic remedies for Hesperian depression: maintenance of the presented world by illumination of the dwelling or other devices (thus providing the active mind with its customary aliment), and rendering the mind inactive by the use of alcohol or narcotics.

While the first of these remedies makes thinking of this sort unnecessary, and the second remedy makes it impossible, it seems to us that many other human devices constitute a third remedy: they make thinking of this sort easier and less repugnant. What we have in mind are of course the innumerable means that we have developed to represent the presented world *externally* by means of maps, diagrams, tokens, linguistic and mathematical systems. This is the reading Vygotsky presumably favoured of Francis Bacon's aphorism, which he often quoted (cited in Wertsch, 1985):

> Neither the bare hand nor the understanding left to itself can effect much: it is by means of instruments and helps that the work is done,

which are as much needed for the understanding as for the hand. (Nec manus nuda, nec intellectus sibi permissus, multum valet; instrumentis et auxiliis res perficitur; quibus opus est, non minus ad intellectum, quam ad nanum. *Novum Organum*, Book I, para. 2)

Of course, Bacon's reading was certainly different: what he had in mind was a method of scientific discovery.

A similarly restricted view of thinking was espoused by Edouard Claparède (1919). He proposed a Law of Awareness, often cited approvingly by Piaget, which took thinking to be a standby activity, invoked only when existing habits failed to deliver an adequate response. There are certain difficulties with this notion of Claparède's. For instance, one undeniable finding of laboratory studies of human 'problem-solving' has been that problem-directed thinking is itself governed by habit, like almost every other human activity – witness the many demonstrations of the potent effects of *Einstellung* or Set on problem-solving. However, this difficulty may well have been viewed as a virtue by Piaget, whose accounts of cognitive development, even in the sensori-motor stage, stressed the importance for diagnostic purposes of genuinely novel responses; that is, of thinking not governed by habit (e.g., 1953, Conclusions, Section 3). Claparède's Law may be saved by one of two additional assumptions: either habitual forms of thinking are not guided by awareness, or habitual thinking is not really a species of thinking. We prefer the second assumption, on the grounds that the processes governing *all* highly practised and skilled activities differ radically from the consciously guided processes in which they originate (see Dreyfus and Dreyfus, 1983, for some interesting discussion in the context of the claimed educational value of early programming experience). So a problem initially solved by inwardly mediated conscious activity may be solved on future occasions by some stored heuristic, requiring little or no reflection.

If these assumptions are correct, then true thinking is an activity undertaken *rarely*. Since by hypothesis solutions achieved by true thinking are rapidly replaced by stored routines, it is then evident that we are concerned with an ephemeral and evanescent phe-nomenon, and that the researcher will be faced constantly with the difficulty of distinguishing true thinking from a routine which has replaced it ontogenetically. (Ryle, 1949, argued forcefully for the rarity of thinking, in the sense of our definition. Unfortunately, he took the view that this rarity implied epiphenomenal irrelevance. In our view, the rarity of thought merely reflects the rarity of occasions when we are confronted by a genuinely novel set of circumstances – see

Dennett, 1983, for useful discussion of these views of Ryle.)

The study of children's thinking is of particular and special interest, for there are many sorts of problem which children fail to solve. By surveying these problems, we may be able to build up a picture of the thinking powers that adults possess as the union of the various powers that children of different ages lack. This is perhaps one relatively straightforward sense in which the study of children's thinking constitutes a vital element in developing an adequate theory of epistemology, a project cherished by Piaget.

The characterization of thinking we have offered is a particularly strict and conservative one, emphasizing the central importance of inwardly mediated conscious activity proceeding without the aliment of an outwardly present world or of external representations of such a world. Probably it is unduly conservative. Certainly it is common intuition that we often think about the presented world directly, or indirectly through the medium of external representations. However, there seems little reason to doubt that there is at least a gradient of difficulty applying to these three sorts of thinking. Moreover, we agree with Gibson (e.g., 1972) that there is no good reason to regard normal perceptual processes as involving inference or any other type of thinking. We suspect that the routine extensions of the presented world (a) in space – seeing parts as signs of wholes, automatic location and tracking of hidden objects – and (b) in time – limited automatic projection of the present to the past or future – should likewise be excluded. It may be, however, that the focusing of attention on some aspect of the presented world (extended in this Gibsonian fashion) constitutes a kind of thinking, particularly when our attention is *directed* there rather than simply *attracted* as a natural consequence of the salience of the aspect in question. This kind of thinking about aspects of the presented world we shall call *immediate thinking*. So far as the case of thinking guided by external representations is concerned (henceforth *externally mediated thinking*), it is at least the case that once grasp of the relation between sign and referent has been mastered, no mental effort is required to maintain that relation. We shall later return to the question of generalizing our notion of thinking to these two less clear cases.

Forms of Thinking

Following the assumptions of the previous section, the study of children's thinking should provide us with information, of an indirect sort, about the varieties of adult thinking. Children solve different sorts of problems at different ages. These developmental separations suggest that different forms of thinking are required for the solution of these different sorts of problem. This was Piaget's fundamental assumption – that thought undergoes *qualitative* development – and if it falls then the whole structure of Piaget's theory collapses.

Piaget's own ontology of forms of thought is very theory-dependent and makes only weak connections with lay intuitions. We shall adopt instead a provisional ontology which does make such strong connections, and attempt to relate it to Piaget's findings and to some contemporary research, modifying it where necessary in the course of the chapter. Our ontology is based on the idea that inwardly mediated conscious connection with some entity is correlated with immediate conscious connection with that entity, and that the essential step in thinking is to represent external subjects of consciousness internally. Our regulating metaphor is of thought as a *grasping or holding in mind of some entity*. (We shall sometimes use the locution 'being intentionally connected to some entity' with this sense, roughly following the notion of intentionality due to Brentano, 1973, and recently much discussed – see, for example, Dennett, 1987; Searle, 1983.) These entities are arbitrarily various, but we assume tentatively that at least four different kinds of entity need to be distinguished: objects (individuals), properties (including relations), propositions, and worlds. Some objects can be actually grasped, held, viewed, etc.; some properties are immanent in such objects; some propositions are facts; and some worlds are real. The power of thought is of course that we may think about non-existent or abstract objects and properties, about propositions which are false or of unknown value, and about imaginary worlds. It follows from this truism that the devices adopted for constructing mental symbols must be combinatorially productive, since actual entities constitute only a tiny subset of those which are conceivable.

It may be objected at this point that the contemplation of an object is impossible without the simultaneous contemplation of some at least of its properties; that object and properties together determine certain facts, and that these facts specify a world or class of worlds. So what sense does it make to speak here of four kinds of thinking, since no kind may be practised in isolation from the others? But if this objection were cogent, then a child who had attained the stage of object permanence – who could therefore 'hold an object in mind' – must also be able to 'hold its location (a relation) in mind', to grasp the fact that the object is located there (a proposition), and to locate that fact with respect to other facts known about the world confronting it. We will make the assumption – consistent with developmental findings – that this aprioristic argument is unsound, and that how these four kinds of thinking are ordered and related is an empirical question. After all, there is ample evidence that we can contemplate objects attentively without grasping (in the relevant manner) innumerable 'obvious' properties. For example, it is a familiar and diminishing experience to be at a loss to specify the eye-colour of a close friend. Likewise, Gombrich (1982) points out that those who know a cow when they see one are unable to say how the horns are situated in relation to the ears.

Since it is at least possible (see previous section) that the grasping or holding in mind of some entity is sometimes carried out in the presence of that entity, or in the presence of some external representation of that entity, these two generalizations enlarge our ontology of forms of thinking to twelve basic kinds: immediate, externally mediated and internally mediated thinking about each of the four sets of entity.

Evidence of Thinking

In this section we make extensive use of the notion of representation, intending by that term the symbol, mental or external, that enables the thinker to hold some entity in mind. An arbitrary entity may be externally present, internally represented by a mental symbol, or externally represented by a picture, drawing, imitation, check mark, referring expression or other public symbol. A fundamental developmental question, then, concerns the order of mastery of these two kinds of representation. Does the capacity to represent an entity by means of an external device depend upon the capacity to represent it by means of an internal device, or is the converse proposition true? As we will show, there is a reasonable case to be made for both sides of this argument, whether we are considering ontogenesis, phylogenesis or human cultural prehistory.

To investigate this question it is necessary to have independent means of assessing each capacity. For externally mediated representation we require evidence that the symbol is used as an aid in calling to mind the absent (possibly virtual or non-existent) entity. For internally mediated representation we require exactly the same kind of evidence! On the face of it, it seems that evidence for externally mediated representation should be easier to come by, since the resemblance between symbol and entity may be so strong that the intentional connection cannot reasonably be denied. But if the entity is absent and resemblance is strong, what is the *source* of that resemblance? Surely it is likely that the production of the symbol has been guided by an internal representation of the absent entity!

In human prehistory the capacity for external representation is first clearly signalled by the carvings and paintings of the Magdalenian culture, 20,000 years ago. And since these highly naturalistic paintings were often produced to 'illuminate' the walls of the caves, they can hardly have been drawn from life. Although we cannot examine these early men directly for evidence of use of internal representations, their tool-making is a reasonably secure indirect sign, since the separation of site of tool manufacture from site of tool use is also clearly established in this culture, implying contemplation of the use in its absence. (In fact, neither of these arguments is particularly compelling, the weakness that they exhibit being the same. Cave drawings may have been drawn 'from death' if not from life, or worked up from sketches made from life – see Sandars, 1968: 56–8. Equivalently, a tool may be made at the site of use and then used remotely as a guide for the manufacture of further tools.) Moreover, the great apes show no clear or compelling sign of capacity to use external representations, but likewise tool manufacture takes place only at the site of use and neither are tools retained for future use.

These examples, and the preceding discussion, make it seem likely that the two capacities are rather closely bound up with one another. Vygotsky was probably the most forthright advocate of the priority of externally mediated representation in ontogenesis, with subsequent internalization. He argued in many places that thought was internalized social speech, for instance (1981: 162):

> It is necessary that everything internal in higher forms was external, that is, for others it was what it is now for oneself. Any higher mental function necessarily goes through an external stage in its development because it is initially a social function.

Vygotsky's presentation of this idea in the context of the origins of thinking is well known, but he applied the notion more widely. For instance, the infant's unsuccessful attempts to reach for an object are first taken by adults as a sign that he desires the object and requires help; later they become attenuated as the infant comes to recognize this function; and finally they come to be deliberately produced signs. However, even in Vygotsky's discussions, uncertainty intrudes. When discussing memory he writes (1978: 51):

> When a human being ties a knot in a handkerchief as a reminder, he is, in essence, constructing the process of memorizing by forcing an

external object to remind him of something; *he transforms remembering into an external activity.* . . . It has been remarked that the very essence of civilization consists of purposely building monuments so as not to forget. In both the knot and the monument we have manifestations of the most fundamental and characteristic feature distinguishing human from animal memory.

The phrase we have emphasized shows that not even Vygotsky could resist the obvious move of taking the capacity for external representation as a *sign* of pre-existent internal representation, rather than the cause and source of it. But there are difficulties with this move, as noted above. In some cases the problem of deciding whether an external symbol truly represents an entity may be just as hard as deciding, independently of such evidence, whether the child who produced the debatable external symbol might be capable of mentally representing such an entity. This is notoriously the case with early child speech. Whether a simple one- or two-word utterance represents (i.e., expresses) a proposition is a problem which cannot be solved by examination of the form of the utterance alone. More fundamentally, to the degree that such speech is firmly rooted in the here and now, it is unnecessary to count the elements of this speech as representations mediating an intentional connection, since symbol and entity symbolized are present simultaneously (see Campbell, 1976, for discussion).

Given these difficulties and uncertainties in using evidence of externally mediated representation as a criterion for attributing capacity for internally mediated representation, there are excellent reasons to search for independent criteria, such as remote tool-making, for use of internal representation. We may identify in Piaget's methods the use of the following criterion. Children are credited with representational capacity only if such capacity can be demonstrated, roughly, 'under difficult conditions': *that is, where the actions or judgements produced are novel and where the entity represented is absent or non-manifest in some other way.* We propose this vague criterion as definitive, providing necessary and sufficient conditions, and now proceed to sharpen it. Notice that Piaget's use of the notion of representation (like ours) is thereby tied to thinking and to intentionality, and therefore different from the more common and broader notion in which anything that can be recognized or produced is said to be represented (see Dennett, 1983, for interesting, if inconclusive, discussion). This broader notion of representation is pandemic in Fodor's philosophy of mind and psychology (e.g., Fodor, 1981), and has been endorsed by many psychologists (e.g., Karmiloff-Smith,

1986; Leslie, 1987). However, it leads inevitably to premature talk of *meta-representations*, to the lethal confusion of thought and perception abhorred by Gibson, and to needless disagreements (e.g., Piatelli-Palmirini, 1980). According to our usage (and, we argue, according to Piaget's too), crediting a child with the capacity to represent some entity of given type is equivalent to crediting him or her with the capacity for (inwardly mediated) *thought* about that type of entity, and conversely.

Thinking about Objects

Although the criterion we have identified is logically impeccable, its application is hardly straightforward. While it seems plain enough what is meant by the question – Can a child represent an *object* when it is absent? – and while familiar tests of object permanence provide a diagnostic method, it is less clear what must be done to establish corresponding diagnoses for mental symbols for properties, propositions and worlds, the other elements in our provisional ontology of mentally represented entities. However, a little reflection makes it evident that even for the case of objects, and assuming a simplified perceptual definition of object based on, say, spatio-temporal contiguity, what counts as being *present* or *absent* is open to argument. As noted above, there are grounds for regarding the immediately presented world as going somewhat beyond those entities indexed directly through the senses. Surely the footbrake of a car is present (in all relevant senses) even if we cannot see it (we are looking at the road, of course), nor feel it with our foot. Certainly no mental effort is required to call it to mind: if such effort *were* required, then cars would be designed with the footbrake prominently displayed! Piaget's own method for assessing Stage 6 of object permanence (1937/1954, Chapter 1, Section 5) requires the child to make a systematic search of the possible locations of the hidden object, rather than simply to keep track of an invisibly displaced object. So perhaps the notion implied by Piaget's choice of diagnostic is that, lacking representational capacity, intentional connection with an object can be maintained by the Stage 5 child only so long as he or she *knows where it is located* in the presented world (appropriately extended). It is an interesting question, not much investigated (Huttenlocher, 1974; Acredolo, 1979) whether the Stage 5 child maintains such connections with objects in permanent locations in familiar worlds other than the presented world, for instance in other rooms of the house, etc.

Allowing for some developmental separation here, we can distinguish the following hierarchy of notions of 'presence' for objects:

1 indexed in the sensory array
2 in the 'field of immediate action' (compare the footbrake)
3 in a known location in the presented (extended) world
4 in a known location in a familiar world
5 real, but of unknown or unspecified location.

Each of these notions of presence specifies a different corresponding sense of absence. For Piaget, the objects which are present to the mind of the child who lacks representational capacity are at best those objects which are present in the sense of level (3). Once this new capacity is attained, at around 18–24 months, objects at level (5) may be present to the mind, even if not physically present in any conventional sense. The ability to *find* such objects by means of an efficient search undergoes further development throughout the preschool period (Babska, 1965; Sophian, 1986). Of course, thinking about non-existent, abstract or otherwise unreal objects may depend on later evolutions of representational capacity.

Turning now to externally mediated representation, at around the same period of development children begin to use one object as a substitute or surrogate for another in the context of pretend play (Piaget, 1945/1962a; Nicolich, 1977). However, it is by no means clear that in such play episodes the child takes the play object as representing some definitely absent other (level (5)). Rather, it may be that the play object is assimilated to the schemes associated with the represented *kind*. (For discussion, see Piaget, 1945/1962a; Huttenlocher and Higgins, 1978; for the distinction drawn, see Goodman, 1969.) Whether a two-year-old's words constitute cases of externally mediated representation is similarly unclear: the problem here is to be sure that reference is being made to (level (5)) absent others. Recently, DeLoache (1987) has reported remarkable discoveries in this field: namely, that two-year-olds can use a photograph and 2½-year-olds a scale model as a 'map' of a room in which objects are hidden and retrieved. Since DeLoache's successful subjects take the 'real thing' as representing the model, just as readily as they take the model to represent the real thing, it may be that the capacity shown here is the same capacity needed to follow the famous story of the three bears with understanding: namely, the construction of parallel analogies – since this is the biggest bed, it must belong to the biggest bear, etc. It may be, then, that the emergence of externally mediated representation lags a little behind internally mediated representation.

Thinking about Properties

We have argued that holding x in mind under difficult circumstances – where this is a novel task – provides a necessary and sufficient (albeit vague) condition for ascribing the general capacity to form mental representations of x. In addition, we have presented this condition as central to Piaget's notion of mental representation. In the preceding section we applied the condition to object representation. Of course, it is hardly surprising that it fits well here, since Piaget's discovery and analysis of object permanence strongly influenced the development of his theoretical views. What is perhaps slightly surprising is that in this hackneyed field of research so little attention has been paid to gradations of presence/absence or to familiarity and salience, factors which immediately spring to mind as soon as one thinks about what constitute 'difficult circumstances' in this context. (However, see DeLoache and Brown (1983) and other work reviewed there. This work – a development of techniques first explored by Babska (1965) – is couched in terms of 'memory', 'search', and 'delayed response'. Although it somewhat studiously ignores its connections and debt to Piaget's investigations, it may be assimilated without undue difficulty to the scheme proposed here.) In this section we shall see that applying our condition to mental representation of properties is much harder work. This may be because of some difficulty in construing the idea of an 'absent property': however, we suspect it is because past developmental research has not pursued the natural construals of this notion.

So what might make it difficult to hold a property in mind? We may begin by noting that if the property in question is *manifested by some present object* and *salient*, then there should be no difficulty and therefore no call for mental representation. Neither of these notions is easy to apply, however. The famous Paradox of the Ravens (Hempel, 1965) provides clear illustration of the difficulties involved. Seeking evidence for the proposition P that all ravens are black, we stumble on a red wheelbarrow. Since this object is not black, we make a further inspection and discover that it is not a raven either. Our confidence in P should then be boosted by an amount equivalent to the boost provided by spotting a black raven, since 'all non-black objects are non-ravens' is an equivalent proposition, logically speaking. So much the worse for logic! Yes, but the psychological lesson here is that it is almost inconceivable that we should *notice* that the wheelbarrow was not black and not a raven under these circumstances – such evidential propositions would hardly spring to mind! So deciding what properties are salient will in general depend on assumptions about the interests or expectations of the perceiver. Nor can this difficulty be resolved by accounting all negative properties non-salient (they are certainly non-manifest). So-called 'inalienably possessed' attributes provide a critical antidote to this view. Surely anyone would notice the leglessness of a legless woman; but except under very special circumstances no one would remark the possession of legs in a legged woman. Usage reflects this powerful constraint: hairless men are merely bald, but a hairy man is over-endowed; likewise to identify a woman as 'the one with the legs' draws attention not to the legs but to some higher-order property. Indeed, many such adjectives are unipolar – *headless, legless*, etc., the other pole occurring only in combinations – *two-headed, long-legged* etc. -- or in discussions like this one.

This line of reasoning suggests that consideration of a perceiver's interests and expectations may permit a decision about whether a property is salient or not, if manifested by some present object. Roughly, it will be salient if an interest resonates to it or if it violates an expectation. Notice that both object and property have to be considered: whereas an orange banana constitutes a salient presentation of the property *orange*, an orange orange may not. Likewise, the leglessness of a legless book may pass unnoticed.

This still leaves us with the problem of deciding whether a given property is manifested by a present object. An obvious necessary condition is that the corresponding proposition should be true. However, truth is not sufficient, as the previous examples show. It seems plain that what is needed is that the property should be available to direct perception, other things being equal, in objects that possess it. Notice that this criterion will exclude negative properties like leglessness and disjunctive properties.

This has been a long preamble, and the excuse for it is poor. However, similar preambles might have been constructed for each of our four categories of objects of thought. We have included it in order to make the general point that *a priori* decisions about what will constitute difficult circumstances will always be awkward and will necessarily involve the researcher in metaphysical speculation, and debate. We also hope that we have made the specific point that in this context 'manifestness' of a property is independent of its salience and is determined by quite different conditions. Returning to the general point, it is clear that any methodological decision about what constitutes 'difficult circumstances' here will have to be guided as much by the products of research as by aprioristic analysis, so we now turn to discuss these briefly.

It is evident from the most cursory reading of Piaget that he considered certain properties – e.g., the logico-mathematical properties of quantity and measurement – to be non-manifest in the sense we have described, to be *constructed* properties imposed on reality by the intelligence of the child. Moreover, he provided ample evidence that to hold such properties in mind constitutes a major difficulty for young children, a difficulty not surmounted until around 5–6 years of age. However, the conservations of quantity are by no means the most important or most obvious method adopted for investigating ability to think about properties. Researchers from Piaget and Vygotsky onwards have instead often favoured sorting tasks for that purpose. And these tasks typically involve straightforwardly manifest properties. Moreover, the saliences of object properties – while undoubtedly variable – surely lie in moderate ranges. The tasks do present difficulties, however, and these difficulties can be readily identified with features of the task. Roughly, in a conventional free-sorting task the difficulty consists in holding fast to a particular property while other properties change. We tentatively offer the suggestion that this difficulty can be characterized as a difficulty of 'holding x in mind, when x is *relatively* low in salience with respect to other manifest properties', since the variation in other properties will in general ensure that the salience of the target property is occasionally less than that of other properties. The products of research in this field have burgeoned recently: Sugarman's investigations (1983) show that the rough age-level derivable from Inhelder and Piaget's studies (1964) is strongly dependent on techniques and materials used (i.e., on manifest properties). It seems now that children will meet this criterion at different ages for different properties and materials. If 'sortal' properties are manifest (e.g., 'being a doll') and such properties are not comprehensively 'multiplied' with salient intrinsic properties (e.g., colour properties), then 2-year-olds can hold them in mind. It seems plain that 'thinking about a property' as measured by this admittedly weak criterion is an achievement heavily dependent on circumstances, with the age of achievement ranging from 2 to 6 years, depending on the target property.

This conclusion fits reasonably well with what can be gleaned from the study of language development about the external representation of properties. The acquisition of command of expressions denoting different sorts of property seems to follow a similarly staggered course, with sortal properties, locations, and temporary, undesirable states (high salience) being represented very early (compare Nelson, 1976), and intrinsic manifest 'qualities' of shape, colour, etc., appearing somewhat later (compare Rice, 1979). Rice's work and other indications also present a considerable puzzle: while external means of representing colours are established later than external means of representing shapes, internal means appear to develop in the opposite order (Bornstein, 1985). Other precise work (e.g., Levine and Carey, 1982; Halpern *et al.*, 1983) suggests fairly substantial *décalage* between the development of internal and external means.

Thinking about Propositions

This is an enormous topic. As we review developmental evidence from a theoretical standpoint similar to that adopted in this paper in Olson and Campbell (to appear) – see also Olson and Astington (1987) – we will not attempt to review it here. Our notion is that the investigations of Heinz Wimmer and Josef Perner (e.g., Wimmer and Perner, 1983) form the most direct test of the relevant ability. In these studies children are presented with circumstances in which an adult would ascribe belief in a certain proposition to another, while counting that proposition false. Children younger than 4 years will not do this. Instead, they ascribe a true belief to the other, even when that other has no grounds for such a belief. Similar findings arise from studies of lying (Wimmer *et al.*, 1984). Lying involves presenting a proposition as true, while believing it to be false, and so involves a similar disclocation between a proposition and relevant factual knowledge. So the analogue of absence for the case of a proposition will be falsity. Notice that this leads us – where Wimmer and Perner may not wish to follow – to the conclusion that children cannot hold a proposition in mind until around 4 years. Their conclusion is a milder one, that their findings show development in the young child's 'theory of mind', rather than a fundamental change of mental function. (For discussion of this subtle difference in interpretation, in a different context, see the discussion of Jaynes, 1973, in Witelson and Kristofferson, 1986.)

Thinking about Worlds

Again, we can offer here only the briefest of comments on this ability. It seems to us that deductive reasoning depends on this ability. A conclusion follows necessarily from certain facts or premises only if there is no world consistent with the premises in which the conclusion is false. The regulation of deduction therefore depends on consideration of worlds different from the presented world: this is the case whether or not the inference proceeds from facts or from suppositions or assumptions. While the investigation of deductive reasoning in children has hardly begun, there is every reason to suspect (as Piaget did) that it is a late achievement. Accordingly, it makes good sense to adopt as a provisional criterion 'holding a world in mind, when the world is inconsistent with the presented world'. There is of course a difficulty in distinguishing this criterion from that adopted in the previous section, but we assume that this can be met by an appropriate definition for 'world'.

Interrelationships

The developmental 'stagger' suggested above for mental representation of properties of different types implies corresponding staggers for mental representation of propositions and worlds. It is noteworthy, for instance, that the propositions figuring in Wimmer and Perner's studies invariably involve locations – a property (relation) represented early – as predicates. Likewise, clear cases of early deductive inference such as Donaldson's (1978: 53) case seem to involve logically simple properties (*dead/alive* in this case). If this view is correct, then we should not expect to find any simple stage-like progression, although the dependence of worlds on propositions and propositions on objects and properties will determine such progressions for fixed combinations of types.

The Innatist Alternative

Our proposals amount to a strong claim that cognitive development comprises, amongst other things, a sequence of added representational powers: children can think about increasingly complex kinds of thing as development proceeds. As we have acknowledged, this is by no means a popular opinion. A more common view admits the factual basis for such a claim, but chooses to regard the cognitive limitations of young children as merely apparent. Younger children, so the argument runs, have these representational powers, but initially can exercise them only in certain limited contexts, or with adult help and prompting. This is a perfectly natural and appealing move: presumably many learned skills begin life in this context-dependent way. Frequent application of the skill in varied contexts then leads to some release from such dependence. In fact, a similar claim was made long ago by Vygotsky, who argued (Vygotsky, 1978: 84) that children of apparently similar ability might differ in their 'zones of proximal development', meaning by that phrase that within such zones, precocious powers could be exercised given careful choice of materials and adult or peer support. Much the same point is made in an exemplary passage from Babska (1965: 118):

> In Stage I performances giving evidence of the existence of the relevant ability did not occur. There are, relatively speaking, no circumstances or conditions to evoke the ability. Nothing can help the child. What we observe here may be termed *lack of ability*. In Stage III there are no conditions, relatively speaking, which can prevent the child from giving a correct performance. There are no circumstances that would prevent the child from solving the given problem. What we observe is *presence of ability*. Stage II is the middle one in which one may observe close relations between performance and conditions. In some conditions a high level of performance can be achieved, while in others the opposite is observed. An examination of the relations mentioned above can give us criteria for diagnosing the level that the child has achieved so far in developing the given ability.

In Donaldson (1978) a test of 'disembedded thinking' – i.e., what we regard as real thinking – is often represented as an 'unfair' test of children's abilities, systematically under-representing their real competence. In recent developmental debate, however, in Britain and in North America, this sort of formulation has been extended and generalized towards an innatist position in which formal operational reasoning (or so it would seem to our jaundiced observation) lies within the 'zone of proximal development' of the neonate. A representative view is DeLoache and Brown's (1983: 888):

> ... two tasks that are structurally similar may give very different estimates depending on a variety of superficial features. Stripping away non-essential features of a task, situating the task in a familiar setting, and making the task content familiar and meaningful are some of the steps that can transform a difficult task in which young children fail into an opportunity for them to display their fledgling competence. The objective of such careful task engineering is not simply to demonstrate that some ability is present earlier than has previously been shown, but to examine the precursors and rudimentary forms of the ability and the conditions of its emergence.

Now Vygotsky's point in arguing for the existence of such a zone was not to legitimize extreme innateness claims, but to suggest improvements in the *pedagogical* assessment of children and in methods of pedagogy. He certainly did not see the performance of the child in an assisted context as providing a truer measure of cognitive powers but rather as refining that measure for pedagogical purposes. Our assessment of Donaldson's position is similar. There is no hint in her writings that she sees each episode in cognitive development as the spontaneous appearance of an ability present from early infancy. She argues merely that examining 'disembedded thinking' underestimates children's cognitive resources and that appropriate pedagogical techniques exist or can be created to promote the development of these powers in children who often fail to show command of them. We have no weighty objection to this view. However, we would insist that most of the published 'demonstrations' of precocious representational powers 'succeed' either by removing the elements of 'adverse or difficult circumstances' or novelty of task, which we have taken as crucial to diagnosis; or, alas more commonly, by straightforwardly tendentious interpretation of weak and equivocal data. Classic cases of the latter sort are 'demonstrations' (a) of number conservation in three-year-olds, refuted in Donaldson (1971), and (b) of neonatal imitation (see for example, Abravanel and Sigafoos, 1984; Hayes and Watson, 1981; Jacobson, 1979; and Vinter, 1986, for corrective experiment and comment). Numerous cases of the former sort are reviewed (and dismissed) by Gold (1987). Our discussion of this issue should make it clear that those findings, or those that survive critical examination, do not in any way constitute a refutation of the methodology endorsed here. They may provide opportunities for a more effective pedagogy, as Vygotsky suggested, but will not capture thinking, as we have defined it. Naturally, it is always possible that a particular tradition of diagnosis may change in the direction suggested by Donaldson. The criterion we have adopted for diagnosis is certainly vague enough to allow such movements to correct true underestimates.

Conclusion

We have offered a framework for a theory of children's thinking and its development. This framework is based firmly on a Piagetian notion of mental representation of x in which that notion is linked to conscious, intentional connection with x. Moreover, our framework – again, like Piaget's – represents cognitive development as the accretion and expansion of representational powers. However, we depart from Piaget in our assumption that development is configured by differences in the substantive 'contents' of thought, rather than by formal differences between distinct kinds of mental operation.

This chapter was prepared while the senior author was a Visiting Professor in the Departments of Linguistics and Psychology at the University of Toronto for the session 1986–87.

A Bibliography of Margaret Donaldson's Published Work

Books and Articles

1959   'Positive and negative information in matching problems', *British Journal of Psychology*, 50, 235–62.
Reprinted in P. Wason and P. N. Johnson-Laird (eds), *Thinking and Reasoning*, Harmondsworth: Penguin, 1968.
'The work of Jean Piaget', *Scottish Educational Journal*, 45, 780–1, and 816–17.

1963   *A Study of Children's Thinking*, London: Tavistock.

1966   'Behaviour development'. In R. W. B. Ellis (ed.), *Child Health and Development*, London: Churchill (with T. T. S. Ingram).

1968   'Less is more: a study of language comprehension in young children', *British Journal of Psychology*, 59, 461–71 (with G. Balfour).

1969   'Primary effect in short-term memory in young children', *Psychonomic Science*, 16, 59–60 (with H. Strang).

1970   'On the acquisition of some relational terms'. In J. R. Hayes (ed.), *Cognition and the Development of Language*, New York: Wiley (with R. J. Wales).
Reprinted in P. Adams (ed.), *Language in Thinking*, Harmondsworth: Penguin, 1972.
'Developmental aspects of performance with negatives'. In G. B. Flores D'Arcais and W. J. M. Levelt (eds), *Advances in Psycholinguistics*, Amsterdam: North Holland.

1971   'Preconditions of inference'. In J. K. Cole (ed.), *Nebraska Symposium on Motivation*, Lincoln, Nebraska: Nebraska University Press.

1974   'Sentences and situations: children's judgements of match and mismatch'. In F. Bresson (ed.), *Problèmes Actuels en Psycholinguistique*, Paris: Centre National de la Recherche Scientifique (with P. Lloyd).
'Some clues to the nature of semantic development', *Journal of Child Language*, 1, 185–94 (with J. McGarrigle).

'Conservation accidents', *Cognition*, 3, 341–50 (with J. McGarrigle).

1976 'On a method of eliciting true/false judgements from young children', *Journal of Child Language*, 3, 411–16 (with P. Lloyd).
'Constraints on classificatory skills in young children', *British Journal of Psychology*, 67, 89–100 (with R. Campbell and B. Young).
'The development of conceptualization'. In V. Hamilton and M. D. Vernon (eds), *The Development of Cognitive Processes*, London: Academic Press.

1977 'L'erreur et la prise de conscience de l'erreur', *Bulletin de Psychologie*, 30, 181–6.

1978 *Children's Minds*, London: Fontana and Croom Helm.
American edition published 1979, New York: Norton.
Translations: Danish, Dutch, Finnish, German, Hebrew, Italian, Japanese, Norwegian, Polish, Russian, Serbo-Croat, Spanish, Swedish.

1979 'The mismatch between school and children's minds', *Human Nature*, March, 61–7.
Reprinted in N. Entwistle (ed.), *New Directions in Educational Psychology, Vol. 1: Learning and Teaching*, Lewes: Falmer Press, 1985.
'Making sense of the written word', *Child Education*, July.
'The use of hiding games for studying the coordination of viewpoints', *Educational Review*, 31, 133–40 (with M. Hughes).

1981 'Changing attitudes in a changing world'. In *All the Time in the World*, London: HMSO.

1982 'Conservation: what is the question?', *British Journal of Psychology*, 73, 199–207.
'Children's language and literature', Open University Press.
'Piaget on language'. In S. Modgil and C. Modgil (eds), *Jean Piaget: Consensus and Controversy*, London: Holt, Rinehart and Winston (with A. Elliot).
'Language skills and reading: a developmental perspective'. In A. Hendry (ed.), *Teaching Reading: The Key Issues*, London: Heinemann (with J. Reid).
Reprinted in M. M. Clark (ed.), *New Directions in the Study of Reading*, Lewes: Falmer Press, 1985.

1983 'Justifying conservation: comment on Neilson *et al.*', *Cognition*, 15, 293–5.
Early Childhood Development and Education. M. Donaldson, R. Grieve and C. Pratt (eds), Oxford: Blackwell.

1984 'Speech and writing and modes of learning'. In H. Goelman, A. Oberg and F. Smith (eds), *Awakening to Literacy*, London: Heinemann.

1987 'Growth of the knowledge of word meanings'. In R. L. Gregory (ed.), *Oxford Companion to the Mind*, Oxford: Oxford University Press.

'The development of deductive reasoning'. In R. L. Gregory (ed.), *Oxford Companion to the Mind*, Oxford: Oxford University Press.

'The origins of inference'. In J. Bruner and H. Haste (eds), *Making Sense: The Child's Construction of the World*, London: Methuen.

1989   *Sense and Sensibility: Some Thoughts on the Teaching of Literacy*. Reading, Berks: Reading and Language Information Centre, University of Reading.

1990   Margaret Donaldson is currently writing a book in which she proposes a new analysis of different kinds of development and modes of mental functioning (in preparation).

Writing for Children

Curriculum development

1976   *Orbit* A series of fiction and information books for children aged 7–9, Edinburgh: Holmes McDougall.

1979   *Letter-Links* A new approach to decoding skills in reading, Edinburgh: Holmes McDougall (with J. Reid).

1980–84   *Link-Up* A reading programme for children aged 5–7, Edinburgh: Holmes McDougall (with J. Reid and J. Low).

1982–83   *Storyclub* Stories for shared reading, Edinburgh: Holmes McDougall (with J. Reid).

1984–87   R & D A reading and language programme for children aged 7–11, London: Macmillan Education (with J. Reid).

Novels

1979   *Journey into War*. London: André Deutsch.
American edition, New York: E. P. Dutton.
Paperback edition, London and New York: Scholastic.
Translation: Norwegian.
Mindar, London: Methuen.

1980   *The Moon's on Fire*, London: André Deutsch.
American edition, New York: E. P. Dutton.
Paperback edition, London and New York: Scholastic.

References

Abbeduto, L. and Rosenberg, S. (1985) 'Children's knowledge of the presuppositions of *know* and other cognitive verbs', *Journal of Child Language, 12*, 621–41.

Abravanel, E. and Sigafoos, A. D. (1984) 'Exploring the presence of imitation during early infancy', *Child Development, 55*, 381–92.

Ackerman, B. P. (1983) *Comprehension Failure in Children*, Delaware University: Unpublished.

Acredolo, L. P. (1979) 'Laboratory versus home: the effect of environment on the 9-month-old infant's choice of spatial reference system', *Developmental Psychology, 15*, 666–7.

Anderson, E. S. (1977) 'Learning to speak with style: a study of the socio-linguistic skills of children', Stanford University: Unpublished doctoral dissertation.

Arnheim, R. (1975) *Art and Visual Perception*, Berkeley: University of California Press (second edition).

Aronoff, M. (1976) *Word Formation in Generative Grammar. (Linguistic Inquiry Monograph 1)*, Cambridge, Mass.: MIT Press.

Astington, J. W. (1986) 'Children's comprehension of expressions of intention', *British Journal of Developmental Psychology, 4*, 43–9.

Babska, Z. (1965) 'The formation of the conception of identity of visual characteristics of objects seen successively'. In P. H. Mussen (ed.), *European Research in Cognitive Development*, SRCD Monograph No. 100, Vol. 30.

Baker, C. (1980) *The Innocent Artists: Student Art from Papua New Guinea*, Poole: Blandford Press.

Barnes, D. (1969) 'Language in the secondary classroom'. In D. Barnes *et al.* (eds), *Language, the Learner and the School*, Harmondsworth: Penguin.

Barrett, M. D. (1978) 'Lexical development and overextension in child language', *Journal of Child Language, 5*, 205–19.

Bartlett, E. J. (1978) 'The acquisition of the meaning of colour terms: a study of lexical development'. In R. N. Campbell and P. T. Smith (eds), *Recent Advances in the Psychology of Language. Vol. 1: Language Development and Mother–Child Interaction*, London: Plenum Press.

Bates, E. (1976) *Language and Context: The Acquisition of Pragmatics*, New York: Academic Press.

Bearison, D. J. (1985) 'Transactional cognition', Paper presented at the Biennial Conference of the International Society for the Study of Behavioural Development, Tours, France.

Bebout, L. J., Segalowitz, S. J. and White, G. J. (1980) 'Children's comprehension of causal constructions with *because* and *so*', *Child Development*, 51, 565–8.

Bergson, H. (1913) *Time and Free Will*, London: Allen and Unwin.

Berko, J. (1958) 'The child's learning of English morphology', *Word*, 14, 150–77.

Berko, J. and Brown, R. (1960) 'Psycholinguistic research methods'. In P. H. Mussen (ed.), *Handbook of Research Methods in Child Development*, New York: Wiley.

Berndt, R. M. and Berndt, C. H. (1982) *Aboriginal Australian Art: A Visual Perspective*, Sydney: Methuen.

Berzonsky, M. D. (1971) 'The role of familiarity in children's explanations of physical causality', *Child Development*, 42, 705–15.

Bever, T. (1975) 'Psychologically real grammar emerges because of its role in language acquisition'. In D. P. Dato (ed.), *Georgetown University Monograph Series on Languages and Linguistics*, Washington D.C.: Georgetown University Press.

Bialystok, E. (1986) 'Factors in the growth of metalinguistic awareness', *Child Development*, 57, 498–510.

Biemiller, A. (1970) 'The development of the use of graphic and contextual information as children learn to read', *Reading Research Quarterly*, VI, 76–96.

Bindra, D., Clarke, K. A. and Shultz, T. R. (1980) 'Understanding predictive relations of necessity and sufficiency in formally equivalent "causal" and "logical" problems', *Journal of Experimental Psychology: General*, 109, 422–43.

Bissex, G. L. (1980) *GNYS AT WRK*, Cambridge, Mass.: Harvard University Press.

Bloom, L. (1974) 'Talking, understanding and thinking'. In R. L. Schiefelbusch and L. L. Lloyd (eds), *Language Perspectives – Acquisition, Retardation and Intervention*, London: Macmillan.

Bornstein, M. H. (1985) 'On the development of color naming in young children', *Brain and Language*, 26, 72–93.

Bower, T. G. R. (1974) *Development in Infancy*, San Francisco: Freeman.

Bower, T. G. R., Broughton, J. M. and Moore, M. K. (1971) 'The development of the object concept as manifested in the tracking behaviour of infants between 7 and 20 weeks of age', *Journal of Experimental Child Psychology*, 11, 182–92.

Bowey, J. A. (1988) *Metalinguistic Functioning in Children*, Geelong: Deakin University Press.

Brentano, F. (1973) *Psychology from an Empirical Standpoint*, Routledge & Kegan Paul (German edition, 1874).

Briggs, P. and Underwood, G. (1987) 'The nature of reader ability differences in lexical access', *Journal of Research in Reading*, 10, 57–64.

Brown, A. L. and DeLoache, J. S. (1978) 'Skills, plans and self-regulation'. In R. S. Siegler (ed.), *Children's Thinking: What Develops?*, Hillsdale, N.J.: Erlbaum.

Brown, G. and Atkins, M. (1986) 'Explaining in professional contexts', *Research Papers in Education*, 1, 60–86.

Brown, G. and Yule, G. (1983) *Discourse Analysis*, Cambridge: Cambridge University Press.

Bruner, J. S. (1968) *Processes in Cognitive Growth: Infancy*, Worcester, Mass.: Clark University Press.

Bruner, J. S. (1983) *Child's Talk: Learning to Use Language*, Oxford: Oxford University Press.

Bullock, M. and Gelman, R. (1979) 'Preschool children's assumptions about cause and effect: temporal ordering', *Child Development*, 50, 89–96.

Bullock, M., Gelman, R. and Baillargeon, R. (1982), 'The development of causal reasoning'. In W. Friedman (ed.), *The Developmental Psychology of Time*, New York: Academic Press.

Bybee, J. L. and Slobin, D. I. (1982) 'Rules and schemas in the development and use of the English past tense', *Language*, 58, 265–89.

Campbell, R. N. (1967) Personal communication.

Campbell, R. N. (1976) 'Propositions and early utterances'. In G. Drachman (ed.), *Akten des 1. Salzburger Kolloquiums über Kindersprache*, Tübingen: Gunter Narr.

Carey, S. (1978) 'Less never means more'. In R. N. Campbell and P. T. Smith (eds), *Recent Advances in the Psychology of Language. Vol. 1: Language Development and Mother–Child Interaction*, London: Plenum Press.

Carey, S. and Bartlett, E. J. (1978) 'Acquiring a single new word', *Papers and Reports on Child Language Development*, 15, 17–29 (Stanford University).

Cazden, C. B. (1968) 'The acquisition of noun and verb inflections', *Child Development*, 39, 433–48.

Cazden, C. B. (1974) 'Play with language and metalinguistic awareness: one dimension of language awareness', *The Urban Review*, 7, 1249–61.

Chapman, R. S. and Miller, J. F. (1975) 'Word order in early 2 and 3 word utterances: does production precede comprehension?', *Journal of Speech and Hearing Research*, 18, 355–71.

Chevalier-Skolnikoff, S. (1983) 'Sensori-motor development in orang-utans and other primates', *Journal of Human Evolution*, 12, 545–6.

Chomsky, C. (1971a) 'Write first, read later', *Childhood Education*, 47, 296–9.

Chomsky, C. (1971b) 'Invented spelling in the open classroom', *Word*, 27, 1–3.

Claparède, E. (1919) 'La conscience de la ressemblance et de la différence chez l'enfant', *Archives de Psychologie*, XVII, 67–80.

Clark, E. V. (1972) 'On the child's acquisition of antonyms in two semantic fields', *Journal of Verbal Learning and Verbal Behaviour*, 11, 750–8.

Clark, E. V. (1973a) 'What's in a word: on the child's acquisition of semantics in his first language'. In T. E. Moore (ed.), *Cognitive Development and the Acquisition of Language*, New York: Academic Press.

Clark, E. V. (1973b) 'Non-linguistic strategies and the acquisition of word meanings', *Cognition*, 2, 161–82.

Clark, E. V. (1974) 'Some aspects of the conceptual basis for first language acquisition'. In R. L. Schiefelbusch and L. L. Lloyd (eds), *Language Perspectives: Acquisition, Retardation, and Intervention*, Baltimore: University Park Press.

Clark, E. V. (1978a) 'Discovering what words can do'. In D. Farkas, W. M. Jacobsen, and K. W. Todrys (eds), *Papers from the Parasession on the Lexicon*, Chicago: Chicago Linguistic Society.

Clark, E. V. (1978b) 'Awareness of language: Some evidence from what children say and do'. In A. Sinclair, R. J. Jarvella and W. J. M. Levelt (eds), *The Child's Conception of Language*, Berlin: Springer.

Clark, E. V. (1979) *The Ontogenesis of Meaning*, Wiesbaden: Athenaion.

Clark, E. V. (1980) 'Where's the top? On the acquisition of orientational terms', *Child Development*, 51, 329–38.

Clark, E. V. (1982a) 'The young word-maker: a case study of innovation in the child's lexicon'. In E. Wanner and L. R. Gleitman (eds), *Language Acquisition: The State of the Art*, Cambridge: Cambridge University Press.

Clark, E. V. (1982b) 'Language change during language acquisition'. In M. E. Lamb and A. L. Brown (eds), *Advances in Developmental Psychology*, Vol. 2, Hillsdale, New Jersey: Erlbaum.

Clark, E. V. (1983a) 'Convention and contrast in acquiring the lexicon'. In T. B. Seiler and W. Wannemacher (eds), *Cognitive Development and the Development of Word Meaning*, Berlin: Springer.

Clark, E. V. (1983b) 'Meanings and concepts'. In J. H. Flavell and E. M. Markman (eds), *Handbook of Child Psychology Volume 3: Cognitive Development*, New York: Wiley.

Clark, E. V. (1987) 'On the principle of contrast: a constraint on lexical acquisition'. In B. MacWhinney (ed.), *Mechanisms of Acquisition: The Twentieth Annual Carnegie Symposium on Cognition*, Hillsdale, N.J.: Erlbaum.

Clark, E. V. (1988) 'On the logic of *Contrast*', *Journal of Child Language*, 16, 317–35.

Clark, E. V. (1990a) 'Contrast is pragmatic', *Journal of Child Language*, 17, 417–31.

Clark, E. V. (1990b) 'Acquisitional principles in lexical development'. In S. A. Gelman and J. P. Byrnes (eds), *Perspectives on Thought and Language: Interrelations in Development*, Cambridge: Cambridge University Press.

Clark, E. V. (in preparation) *'Words and Children: Lexical Development and Word Formation in Acquisition'*.

Clark, E. V. and Berman, R. A. (1984) 'Structure and use in the acquisition of word formation', *Language*, 60, 542–90.

Clark, E. V. and Clark, H. H. (1979) 'When nouns surface as verbs', *Language*, 55, 547–90.

Clark, E. V., Gelman, S. A. and Lance N. M. (1985) 'Noun compounds and category structure in young children', *Child Development*, 56, 84–94.

Clark, E. V. and Hecht, B. F. (1982) 'Learning to coin agent and instrument nouns', *Cognition*, 12, 1–24.

Clark, E. V., Hecht, B. F. and Mulford, R. C. (1986) 'Coining complex compounds in English: affixes and word order in acquisition', *Linguistics*, 24, 7–29.

Clark, E. V. and Sengul, C. J. (1978) 'Strategies in the acquisition of deixis', *Journal of Child Language*, 5, 457–75.

Clark, H. H. (1970) 'The primitive nature of children's relational concepts'. In

J. R. Hayes (ed.), *Cognition and the Development of Language*, New York: Wiley.

Clay, M. M. (1969) 'Reading errors and self-correction behaviour', *British Journal of Educational Psychology, 39,* 47–56.

Clay, M. (1975) *What Did I Write?*, London: Heinemann.

Clements, D. H. (1986) 'Effects of Logo and CAI environments on cognition and creativity', *Journal of Educational Psychology, 78,* 309–18.

Clements, D. H. and Nastasi, B. K. (1988) 'Social and cognitive interactions in educational computer environments', *American Educational Research Journal, 25,* 87–106.

Corrigan, R. (1975) 'A scalogram analysis of the development of the use and comprehension of *because* in children', *Child Development, 47,* 195–201.

Cromer, R. (1978) 'The strengths of the weak form of the cognition hypothesis for language acquisition'. In V. Lee (ed.), *Language Development*, London: Croom Helm.

Crook, C. (1987) 'Computers in the classroom: defining a social context'. In J. C. Rutkowska and C. Crook (eds), *Computers, Cognition and Development*, London: Wiley.

Culley, L. (1988) 'Girls, boys and computers', *Educational Studies, 14,* 3–8.

Daiute, C. (1985) *Writing and Computers*, Reading, Mass: Addison-Wesley.

Day, M. L. (1975) 'Developmental trends in visual scanning'. In H. W. Reese (ed.), *Advances in Child Development and Behaviour*, Vol. 10, New York: Academic Press.

De Goes, C. and Martlew, M. (1983) 'Young children's approach to literacy'. In M. Martlew (ed.), *The Psychology of Written Language*, New York: Wiley.

DeLoache, J. (1987) 'Rapid change in the symbolic functioning of very young children', *Science, 238,* 1556–7.

DeLoache, J. and Brown, A. L. (1983) 'Very young children's memory for the location of objects in a large-scale environment', *Child Development, 54,* 888–97.

Dennett, D. C. (1983) 'Styles of mental representation', *Proceedings of the Aristotelian Society, LXXXIII,* 213–25.

Dennett, D. C. (1987) *The Intentional Stance*, Cambridge, Mass.: MIT Press.

Derham, F. (1976) *Art for the Child Under Seven*, Canberra: Australian Pre-school Association.

DES (1989) 'Information technology from 5 to 16', London: HMSO.

Deutsch, W. and Budwig, N. (1983) 'Form and function in the development of possessives', *Papers and Reports on Child Language Development, 22,* 36–42 (Stanford University).

Dixon, R. M. W. (1980) *The Languages of Australia*, Cambridge: Cambridge University Press.

Dockrell, J. E. (1981) 'The child's acquisition of unfamiliar words: an experimental study', Stirling University: Unpublished doctoral dissertation.

Doise, W. and Mugney, G. (1984) *The Social Development of the Intellect*, Oxford: Pergamon Press.

Donaldson, M. (1963) *A Study of Children's Thinking*, London: Tavistock.

Donaldson, M. (1970) 'Developmental aspects of performance with negatives'. In G. B. Flores D'Arcais and W. J. M. Levelt (eds), *Advances in*

Psycholinguistics, Amsterdam: North Holland.

Donaldson, M. (1971) 'Preconditions of inference'. In J. K. Cole (ed.), *Nebraska Symposium on Motivation*, 81–106, Nebraska University Press.

Donaldson, M. (1976) 'The development of conceptualization', In V. Hamilton and M. D. Vernon (eds), *The Development of Cognitive Processes*, London: Academic Press.

Donaldson, M. (1978) *Children's Minds*, Glasgow: Collins/Fontana.

Donaldson, M. (1984) 'Speech and writing and modes of learning'. In H. Goelman, A. Oberg and F. Smith (eds), *Awakening to Literacy*, London: Heinemann.

Donaldson, M. (1989) *Sense and Sensibility: Some Thoughts on the Teaching of Literacy*, Reading and Language Information Centre, University of Reading.

Donaldson, M. and Balfour, G. (1968) 'Less is more: a study of language comprehension in children', *British Journal of Psychology, 59*, 461–71.

Donaldson, M. and Hughes, M. (1979) 'The use of hiding games for studying the coordination of viewpoints', *Educational Review, 31*, 133–40.

Donaldson, M. and Lloyd, P. (1974) 'Sentences and situations: children's judgements of match and mismatch'. In F. Bresson (ed.), *Problèmes Actuels en Psycholinguistique*, Paris: CNRS.

Donaldson, M. and McGarrigle, J. (1974) 'Some clues to the nature of semantic development', *Journal of Child Language, 1*, 185–94.

Donaldson, M. and Wales, R. J. (1970) 'On the acquisition of some relational terms'. In J. R. Hayes (ed.), *Cognition and the Development of Language*, New York: Wiley.

Donaldson, M. L. (1980) 'The case of the disappearing train: Is it coming or going? A study of children's and adults' use of some deictic verbs', Edinburgh University: Unpublished master's dissertation.

Donaldson, M. L. (1986) *Children's Explanations: a Psycholinguistic Study*, Cambridge: Cambridge University Press.

Dreyfus, H. L. and Dreyfus, S. E. (1983) 'Putting computers in their proper place', *Teachers' College Record*, Summer, 578–601.

Edwards, A. D. (1980) 'Perspectives on classroom language', *Educational Analysis, 2*, 31–46.

Edwards, D. and Mercer, N. (1986) 'Context and continuity: classroom discourse and the development of shared knowledge'. In K. Durkin (ed.), *Language Development in the School Years*, London: Croom Helm.

Eilers, R., Oller, D. and Ellington, J. (1974) 'The acquisition of word meanings for dimensional adjectives: the long and short of it', *Journal of Child Language, 1*, 196–204.

Emerson, H. F. (1979) 'Children's comprehension of *because* in reversible and non-reversible sentences', *Journal of Child Language, 6*, 279–300.

Emerson, H. F. and Gekoski, W. L. (1980) 'Development of comprehension of sentences with *because* or *if*', *Journal of Experimental Child Psychology, 29*, 202–24.

Epstein, H. L. (1972) 'The child's understanding of causal connectives', Wisconsin University: Unpublished doctoral dissertation.

Evans, M. and Rubin, K. (1979) 'Hand gestures as a communicative mode in school-aged children', *Journal of Genetic Psychology*, 135, 189–96.

Ferreiro, E. (1978) 'What is written in a written sentence? A developmental answer', *Journal of Education*, 160, 25–39.

Ferreiro, E. (1984) 'The underlying logic of literacy development'. In H. Goelman, A. Oberg and F. Smith (eds), *Awakening to Literacy*, London: Heinemann.

Ferreiro, E. and Teberosky, A. (1982) *Literacy Before Schooling*, London: Heinemann.

Fife-Schaw, C., Breakwell, G. M., Lee, T. and Spencer, J. (1986) 'Patterns of teenage computer usage', *Journal of Computer Assisted Learning*, 2, 152–61.

Findlay, D. and Irvinskia, A. (1984) 'Cardiac and visual responses to moving stimuli presented either successively or simultaneously to the central and peripheral visual fields in 4-month-old infants', *Developmental Psychology*, 20, 29–36.

Flanders, N. (1970) *Analyzing Teaching Behaviour*, New York: Addison-Wesley.

Flavell, J., Speer, J., Green, F. and August, D. (1981) 'The development of comprehension monitoring and knowledge about communication', *Monographs of the Society for Research in Child Development*, Serial No. 192.

Fodor, J. A. (1976) *The Language of Thought*, Brighton: Harvester Press.

Fodor, J. A. (1981) *Representations*, Brighton: Harvester Press.

François, D. (1977) 'Du pré-signe au signer'. In F. François, D. François, E. Sabeau-Jouannet, and M. Sourdot (eds), *La syntaxe de l'enfant avant cinq ans*, Paris: Larousse.

Franklin, M. B. (1973) 'Nonverbal representation in young children: a cognitive perspective', *Young Children*, 11, 33–53.

Frederickson, F. (1981) 'Timing and context in everyday discourse: implications for the study of referential and social meaning'. In W. P. Dickson (ed.), *Children's Oral Communication Skills*, New York: Academic Press.

Freeman, N. (1980) *Strategies of Representation in Young Children*, London: Academic Press.

Freeman, N. and Cox, M. (1985) (eds) *Visual Order: The Nature and Development of Pictorial Representation*, Cambridge: Cambridge University Press.

Freeman, N. and Janikoun, R. (1972) 'Intellectual realism in children's drawings of a familiar object with distinctive features', *Child Development*, 23, 1116–21.

French, L. A. and Nelson, K. (1985) *Young Children's Knowledge of Relational Terms*, New York: Springer.

Fuson, K. C. (1979) 'The development of self-regulating aspects of speech: a review'. In G. Zivin (ed.), *The Development of Self-Regulation Through Private Speech*, New York: Wiley.

Gardner, H. (1980) *Artful Scribbles: The Significance of Children's Drawings*, London: Jill Norman.

Garton, A. and Pratt, C. (1989) *Learning to be Literate*, Oxford: Blackwell.

Garvey, C. (1979) 'Contingent queries and their relations in discourse'. In E. Ochs and B. Schieffelin (eds), *Developmental Pragmatics*, New York: Academic Press.

Garvey, C. (1984) *Children's Talk*, Glasgow: Collins/Fontana.

Gelman, R. and Gallistel, C. R. (1978) *The Child's Understanding of Number*, Cambridge, Mass.: Harvard University Press.

Gibson, J. J. (1982) 'A theory of direct visual perception'. In J. R. Royce and W. W. Rozeboom (eds), *The Psychology of Knowing*, New York: Gordon and Breach.

Ginther, D. W. and Williamson, J. D. (1985) 'Learning Logo: what is really learned?', *Computers in the Schools*, 2, 73–7.

Gleitman, L. (1979) 'Metalinguistics is not kid-stuff', Paper presented at the International Reading Research Seminar on Linguistic Awareness and Learning to Read, Victoria, Canada.

Gleitman, L. R., Gleitman, H. and Shipley, E. F. (1972) 'The emergence of the child as a grammarian', *Cognition*, 1, 137–64.

Gold, R. (1987) *The Description of Cognitive Development*, Oxford: Clarendon Press.

Golnikoff, R. M., Hirsh-Pasek, K., Lavallee, A. and Badirini, C. (1985) 'What's in a word? The young child's predisposition to use lexical contrast', Paper presented at Conference on Child Language, Boston University.

Golomb, C. (1974) *Young Children's Sculpture and Drawing: A Study in Representational Development*, Cambridge, Mass.: Harvard University Press.

Gombrich, E. H. (1982) *The Image and the Eye*, Oxford: Phaidon Press.

Good, T. L. and Grouws, D. A. (1977) 'Teaching effects: a process-product study in fourth grade mathematics classrooms', *Journal of Teacher Education*, 28, 49–54.

Goodman, K. S. (1972) 'The key is in children's language', *The Reading Teacher*, March, 505–8.

Goodman, K. S. and Gollasch, F. V. (1980) 'Word-ommissions: deliberate and non-deliberate', *Reading Research Quarterly*, XVI, 6–31.

Goodman, N. (1969) *Languages of Art*, Oxford: Oxford University Press.

Goodnow, J. (1977) *Children's Drawing*, London: Collins/Fontana.

Gough, P. B. (1984) 'Word recognition'. In P. D. Pearson (ed.), *Handbook of Reading Research*, New York: Longman.

Govier, H. (1988) 'Microcomputers in primary education – a survey of recent research', ESRC Information Technology in Education Programme, Occasional Paper ITE/28a/88.

Grice, H. P. (1975) 'Logic and conversation'. In P. Cole and J. L. Morgan (eds), *Syntax and Semantics: Volume 3: Speech Acts*, New York: Academic Press.

Grieve, R. and Stanley, S. (1984) 'Less obscure? Pragmatics and 3–4 year-old children's semantics', *British Journal of Developmental Psychology*, 2, 95–103.

Griffiths, J. A., Shantz, C. A., and Sigel, I. E. (1967) 'A methodological problem in conservation studies: the use of relational terms', *Child Development*, 38, 841–8.

Hainline, L. and Lemerise, E. (1985) 'Corneal reflection eye-movement recording as a measure of infant pattern perception: what do we really know?', *British Journal of Developmental Psychology*, 3, 229–42.

Hall, L. C. (1975) 'Linguistic and perceptual constraints on scanning strategies: some developmental studies', University of Edinburgh: Unpublished doctoral dissertation.

Hall, L. C. (1985) 'Searching high and low: the development of visual search in hearing, deaf and learning disabled children'. In R. Groner, G. McCombie, and C. Menz (eds), *Eye Movements and Visual Information Processing*, New York: Elsevier.

Halpern, E., Corrigan, R. and Aviezer, O. (1983) 'In, on and under: examining the relationship between cognitive and language skills', *International Journal of Behavioural Development*, 6, 153–68.

Hanson, V. L. (1981) 'Processing of written and spoken words: evidence for common coding', *Memory and Cognition*, 9, 92–100.

Hargie, O. D. W. (1978) 'The importance of teacher questions in the classroom', *Educational Research*, 20, 99–102.

Haroutounian, S. (1983) *Equilibrium in the Balance*, New York: Springer.

Harris, D. B. (1963) *Children's Drawing as a Measure of Intellectual Maturity*, New York: Harcourt Brace.

Harris, P. L. (1982) 'Cognitive prerequisites to language', *British Journal of Psychology*, 73, 187–95.

Harris, P. and MacFarlane, A. (1974) 'The growth of the effective visual field from birth to seven weeks', *Journal of Experimental Child Psychology*, 18, 340–8.

Hawkins, J., Sheingold, K., Gearhart, M. and Berger, C. (1982) 'Microcomputers in schools: impact on the social life of elementary classrooms', *Journal of Applied Developmental Psychology*, 3, 361–73.

Hayes, L. A. and Watson, J. S. (1981) 'Neonatal imitation; fact or artifact?', *Developmental Psychology*, 17, 655–60.

Heibeck, T. H. and Markman, E. M. (1987) 'Word learning in children: an examination of fast mapping', *Child Development*, 58, 1021–34.

Hempel, C. G. (1965) *Aspects of Scientific Explanation and Other Essays in the Philosophy of Science*, New York: Collier-Macmillan.

Hoenigmann-Stovall, N. M. (1982) 'Extralinguistic control of language comprehension and production in the nonfluent child', *Journal of Psycholinguistic Research*, 11, 1–17.

Hofmann, T. R. (1982) 'Lexical blocking', *Journal of the Faculty of Humanities*, 5, 239–50 (Japan: Toyama University).

Hood, L. (1977) 'A longitudinal study of the development of the expression of causal relations in complex sentences', Columbia University: Unpublished doctoral dissertation.

Hoyles, C. (ed.) (1989) 'Girls and computers', University of London Institute of Education, Bedford Way Paper 34.

Hoyles, C. and Sutherland, R. (1986) 'Using Logo in the mathematics classroom', *Computers in Education*, 10, 61–72.

Huang, I. (1943) 'Children's conception of physical causality: a critical summary', *Journal of Genetic Psychology*, 63, 71–121.

Huey, E. B. (1908) *The Psychology and Pedagogy of Reading*, New York: Macmillan (Reprinted 1969, Harvard University Press).

Hughes, M. (1975) 'Egocentrism in pre-school children', Edinburgh University: Unpublished doctoral dissertation.

Hughes, M. (1986) *Children and Number*, Oxford: Blackwell.

Hughes, M., Brackenridge, A., Bibby, A. and Greenhough, P. (1989) 'Girls, boys and Turtles'. In Hoyles, C. (ed.), *Girls and Computers*, University of London Institute of Education, Bedford Way Paper 34.

Hughes, M., Brackenridge, A. and Macleod, H. (1987) 'Children's ideas about computers'. In J. C. Rutkowska and C. Crook (eds), *Computers, Cognition and Development*, London: Wiley.

Hughes, M., Macleod, H. and Potts, C. (1985) 'Using Logo with infant school children', *Educational Psychology*, 5, 287–301.

Hunter, P. (1989) 'Children using wordprocessors' (in preparation).

Huttenlocher, J. (1974) 'The origins of language comprehension'. In R. L. Solso (ed.), *Theories in Cognitive Psychology: The Loyola Symposium*, Hillsdale, N.J.: Erlbaum.

Huttenlocher, J. and Higgins, E. T. (1978) 'Issues in the study of symbolic development'. In W. A. Collins (ed.), *Minnesota Symposium on Child Development*, Vol. 12, Hillsdale, N.J.: Erlbaum.

Inhelder, B. and Piaget, J. (1964) *The Early Growth of Logic*, London: Routledge and Kegan Paul.

Isaacs, J. (1982) *Arts of the Dreaming: Australia's Living Heritage*, Sydney: Landsowne.

Jacobson, S. (1979) 'Matching behaviour in the young infant', *Child Development*, 50, 425–30.

Jaynes, J. (1979) *The Origin of Consciousness in the Breakdown of the Bicameral Mind*, London: Allen Lane.

Johanson, R. P. (1988) 'Computers, cognition and curriculum: retrospect and prospect', *Journal of Educational Computing Research*, 4, 1–30.

Johnson-Laird, P. (1988) *The Computer and the Mind*, London: Collins/Fontana.

Kamler, B. and Kilarr, G. (1983) 'Looking at what children can do'. In B. M. Kroll and G. Wells (eds), *Explorations in the Development of Writing*, London: Wiley.

Karmiloff-Smith, A. (1986) 'From meta-processes to conscious access: Evidence from children's metalinguistic and repair data', *Congition*, 23, 95–147.

Kavanaugh, R. D. (1976) 'On the synonymity of *more* and *less*: comments on a methodology', *Child Development*, 47, 885–7.

Kellog, R. (1969) *Analysing Children's Art*, Palo Alto, California: National Press.

Kellog, R. and O'Dell, S. (1967) *The Psychology of Children's Art*, San Francisco: CRM.

Kiparsky, P. (1983) 'Word-formation and the lexicon'. In F. Ingemann (ed.), *Proceedings of the Mid-America Linguistics Conference*, Lawrence, Kansas: University of Kansas.

Klatsky, R. L., Clark, E. C. and Macken, M. (1973) 'Asymmetries in the acquisition of polar adjectives: linguistic or conceptual?', *Journal of Experimental Child Psychology*, 16, 32–46.

Kuczaj, S. A. and Maratsos, M. P. (1975) 'On the acquisition of *front, back*, and *side*', *Child Development*, 46, 202–10.

Kuhn, D. and Phelps, H. (1976) 'The development of children's comprehension of causal direction', *Child Development*, 47, 248–51.

Kuhn, T. S. (1962) *The Structure of Scientific Revolutions*, Chicago: University of Chicago Press.

Laberge, D. and Samuels, S. J. (1974) 'Toward a theory of automatic information processing in reading', *Cognitive Psychology*, 6, 293–323.

Laboratory of Comparative Human Cognition (1983) 'Culture and cognitive development'. In W. Kessen (ed.), *Handbook of Child Psychology*, Volume 1, New York: Wiley.

Lawler, R. W., du Boulay, B., Hughes, M. and Macleod, H. (1986) *Cognition and Computers*, Chichester: Ellis Horwood.

Lawless, S. and Simms, A. (1986) 'What goes on in Granny's Garden?', *Education 3–13*, 14, 38–41.

Leopold, W. F. (1949) *Speech Development of a Bilingual Child* (4 vols), Evanston, Illinois: Northwestern University Press.

Lepper, M. R. (1985) 'Micro-computers in education: motivational and social issues', *American Psychologist*, 40, 1–18.

Leslie, A. M. (1987) 'Pretense and representation: the origins of *Theory of Mind*', *Psychological Review*, 94, 412–26.

Levine, S. C. and Carey, S. (1982) 'Up front: the acquisition of a concept and a word', *Journal of Child Language*, 9, 645–57.

Liberman, I. Y., Shankweiler, D., Fischer, F. W. and Carter, B. (1974) 'Explicit syllable and phoneme segmentation in the young child', *Journal of Experimental Child Psychology*, 18, 201–12.

Light, P. H. and Blaye, A. (1989) 'Computer-based learning: the social dimensions'. In H. Foot, M. Morgan and R. Shute (eds), *Children Helping Children*, Chichester: Wiley.

Lloyd, P. (1983) 'Children's detection of ambiguity in verbal messages: insights from an eye movement study'. Paper presented at the Biennial Conference of the International Society for the Study of Behavioural Development, Munich, West Germany.

Lloyd, P., Baker, E. and Dunn, J. (1984) 'Children's awareness of communication'. In L. Feagans, R. Golinkoff and C. Garvey (eds), *The Origins and Growth of Communication*, Norwood, N.J.: Ablex.

Lloyd, P. and Beveridge, M. (1981) *Information and Meaning in Child Communication*, London: Academic Press.

Lloyd, P. and Donaldson, M. (1976) 'On a method of eliciting true/false judgements from young children', *Journal of Child Language*, 3, 411–16.

Luria, A. R. (1975) 'The role of language in formation of temporary connections'. In B. Simon (ed.), *Psychology in the Soviet Union*, London: Routledge and Kegan Paul.

Luria, A. R. (1978) 'The development of writing in the child'. In M. Cole (ed.), *The Selected Writings of A. R. Luria*, New York: Sharpe.

Maccoby, E. E. and Bee, H. L. (1965) 'Some speculations concerning the lag between perceiving and performing', *Child Development*, 36, 367–77.

Mackay, D., Thompson, B. and Schaub, P. (1970) *Breakthrough to Literacy: Teacher's Manual*, London: Longman.

Mackworth, N. H. and Bruner, J. S. (1970) 'How adults and children search and recognize pictures', *Human Development*, 13, 149–77.

Macnamara, J. (1982) *Names for Things: A Study of Human Learning*, Cambridge, Mass.: MIT Press.

Mandler, J. M. (1983) 'Representation'. In J. Flavell and E. Markman (eds), *Handbook of Child Psychology*, III, 420–94.

Marais, E. (1969) *The Soul of the Ape*, London: Blond.

Maratsos, M. P. (1983) 'Some current issues in the acquisition of grammar'. In J. H. Flavell and E. M. Markman (eds), *Handbook of Child Psychology, Volume 3: Cognitive Development*, New York: Wiley.

Markman, E. (1981) 'Comprehension monitoring'. In W. P. Dickson (ed.), *Children's Oral Communication Skills*, New York: Academic Press.

Markman, E. M. (1984) 'The acquisition and hierarchical organization of categories by children'. In C. Sophian (ed.), *Origins of Skills: The Eighteenth Annual Carnegie Symposium on Cognition*, Hillsdale, N.J.: Erlbaum.

Marshall, J. L. and Morton, J. (1978) 'On the mechanics of EMMA'. In A. Sinclair, R. J. Jarvella and W. J. M. Levelt (eds), *The Child's Conception of Language*, Berlin: Springer.

McCabe, A. and Peterson, C. (1985) 'A naturalistic study of the production of causal connectives by children', *Journal of Child Psychology*, 12, 145–59.

McGarrigle, J. and Donaldson, M. (1974) 'Conservation accidents', *Cognition*, 3, 341–50.

McGarrigle, J., Grieve, R. and Hughes, M. (1978) 'Interpreting inclusion: a contribution to the study of the child's cognitive and linguistic development', *Journal of Experimental Child Psychology*, 26, 528–50.

McTear, M. (1985) *Children's Conversation*, Oxford: Blackwell.

Meek, M. with Armstrong, S., Austerfield, V., Graham, J. and Plackett, E. (1984) *Achieving Literacy*, London: Routledge and Kegan Paul.

Menig-Peterson, C. L. (1975) 'The modification of communicative behaviour in preschool-aged children as a function of the listener's perspective', *Child Development*, 46, 1015–18.

Meyerson, E. (1930) *Identity and Reality*, London: Unwin.

Miller, P. H., Haynes, V. F., Demarie-Dreblow, D. and Woody-Ramsay, J. (1986) 'Children's strategies for gathering information in three tasks', *Child Development*, 57, 1429–39.

Miller, P. H., Haynes, V. F. and Weiss, M. G. (1985) 'Metacognitive components of visual search in children', *Journal of Genetic Psychology*, 146, 249–59.

Miller, P. H. and Weiss, G. (1981) 'Children's attention allocation, understanding of attention, and performance on the incidental learning task', *Child Development*, 52, 1183–90.

Mulford, R. C. (1983) 'On the acquisition of derivational morphology in Icelandic: Learning about -ari', *Islenskt Mal*, 5, 105–25.

Munn, N. (1973) *Walbiri Iconography: Graphic Representation and Cultural Symbolism in a Central Australian Society*, New York: Cornell University Press.

Murray, L. and Trevarthen, C. (1985) 'Emotional regulation of interchange between two-month-olds and their mothers'. In T. M. Field and N. A. Fox (eds), *Social Perception in Infancy*, Norwood, N.J.: Ablex.

Nelson, K. (1976) 'Some attributes of adjectives used by young children', *Cognition*, 4, 13–30.

Nicolich, L. M. (1977) 'Beyond sensori-motor intelligence: assessment of symbolic maturity by analysis of pretend play', *Merrill-Palmer Quarterly, 23,* 88–99.

O'Connor, N. and Hermelin, B. (1987) 'Visual memory and motor programmes: their use by idiot-savant artists and controls', *British Journal of Psychology, 78,* 307–23.

Olson, D. R. And Astington, J. (1987) 'Seeing and knowing: on the ascription of mental states to young children', *Canadian Journal of Psychology, 41,* 399–411.

Olson, D. R. and Campbell, R. N. (to appear) 'Constructing representations'. In C. Pratt and A. Garton (eds), *The Development and Use of Representations in Children,* London: Wiley.

Olson, D. and Torrance, N. (1983) 'Literacy and cognitive development: a conceptual transformation in the early school years'. In S. Meadows (ed.), *Developing Thinking,* London: Methuen.

O'Shea, T. (1988) 'Magnets, Martians and mathematical microworlds', Paper presented to the British Association for the Advancement of Science, Oxford.

O'Shea, T. and Self, J. (1983) *Learning and Teaching with Computers,* Brighton: Harvester.

Palermo, D. S. (1973) 'More about *less*: a study in language comprehension', *Journal of Verbal Learning and Verbal Behavior, 12,* 211–21.

Palermo, D. S. (1974) 'Still more about the comprehension of *less*', *Developmental Psychology, 10,* 827–9.

Papert, S. (1980) *Mindstorms,* Brighton: Harvester.

Papert, S. (1987) 'Computer criticism vs. technocentric thinking', *Educational Researcher, 16,* 22–30.

Patterson, C. and Kister, M. (1981) 'The development of listening skills for referential communication'. In W. P. Dickson (ed.), *Children's Oral Communication Skills,* New York: Academic Press.

Pavlovitch, M. (1920) *Le Langage Enfantin: Acquisition du Serbe et du Français par un Enfant Serbe,* Paris: Champion.

Pea, R. D. and Kurland, D. M. (1984) 'On the cognitive effects of learning computer programming', *New Ideas in Psychology, 2,* 137–68.

Pearson, H. and Wilkinson, A. (1986) 'The use of the word processor in assisting children's writing development', *Educational Review, 38,* 169–87.

Perera, K. (1984) *Children's Writing and Reading,* Oxford: Blackwell.

Perner, J. and Leekam, S. R. (1986) 'Belief and quantity: three-year-old's adaptation to listener's knowledge', *Journal of Child Language, 13,* 305–15.

Perret-Clermont, A. N. (1980) *Social Interaction and Cognitive Development in Children,* New York: Academic Press.

Peters, A. (1983) *The Units of Language Acquisition,* Cambridge: Cambridge University Press.

Piaget, J. (1926) *The Language and Thought of the Child,* London: Routledge and Kegan Paul.

Piaget, J. (1928) *Judgement and Reasoning in the Child,* London: Routledge and Kegan Paul.

Piaget, J. (1929) *The Child's Conception of the World,* London: Routledge and Kegan Paul.

Piaget, J. (1930) *The Child's Conception of Physical Causality*, London: Routledge and Kegan Paul.

Piaget, J. (1953) *The Origin of Intelligence in the Child*, London: Routledge and Kegan Paul (French edition, 1936).

Piaget, J. (1954) *The Construction of Reality by the Child*, New York: Basic Books (French edition, 1937).

Piaget, J. (1959) *The Language and Thought of the Child* (3rd edition), London: Routledge and Kegan Paul.

Piaget, J. (1962a) *Play, Dreams and Imitation*, London: Routledge and Kegan Paul (French edition, 1945).

Piaget, J. (1962b) 'Comment on Vygotsky's critical remarks concerning the language and thought of the child'. In L. S. Vygotsky *Thought and Language*, Cambridge, Mass.: MIT Press.

Piaget, J. (1976) *The Grasp of Consciousness*, London: Routledge and Kegan Paul.

Piaget, J. and Inhelder, B. (1956) *The Child's Conception of Space*, London: Routledge and Kegan Paul.

Piaget, J. and Inhelder, B. (1964) *The Early Growth of Logic in the Child*, London: Routledge and Kegan Paul.

Piaget, J. and Inhelder, B. (1966) *The Psychology of the Child*, London: Routledge and Kegan Paul.

Piatelli-Palmirini, M. (1980) *Language and Learning: The Debate Between Jean Piaget and Noam Chomsky*, Cambridge, Mass.: Harvard University Press.

Posner, M. I. and Rothbart, M. K. (1981) 'The development of attentional mechanisms'. In J. H. Flowers (ed.), *Nebraska Symposium on Motivation*, Vol. 28, Nebraska: University of Nebraska Press.

Pratt, C. and Grieve, R. (1984) 'Metalinguistic awareness and cognitive development'. In W. Tunmer, C. Pratt, and M. Herriman (eds), *Metalinguistic Awareness in Children*, Springer: Berlin.

Pugh, A. K. (1978) *Silent Reading: an Introduction to its Study and Teaching*, London: Heinemann.

Read, C. (1971) 'Preschool children's knowledge of English phonology', *Harvard Educational Review*, 41, 1–34.

Reid, J. F. (1973) 'Towards a theory of literacy', In M. M. Clark and A. Milne (eds), *Reading and Related Skills: Proceedings of the Ninth Annual Conference of the United Kingdom Reading Association*, London: Ward Lock Educational.

Reid, J. F. (1983) 'Into print: reading and language growth'. In M. Donaldson, R. Grieve and C. Pratt (eds), *Early Childhood Development and Education*, Oxford: Blackwell.

Reid, J. F. and Donaldson, M. (eds). (1984) *R & D: A Reading and Language Programme*, London: Macmillan.

Rice, M. (1979) *Cognition and Language*, Austin, Texas: Pro Ed.

Riding, R. J. and Powell, S. D. (1985) 'The facilitation of thinking skills in pre-school children using computer-presented activities', *Educational Psychology*, 5, 171–8.

Riding, R. J. and Powell, S. D. (1986) 'The improvement of thinking skills in young children using computer activities: a replication and extension', *Educational Psychology*, 6, 179–83.

Riding, R. J. and Powell, S. D. (1987) 'The effect on reasoning, reading and number performance of computer-presented critical thinking activities in five-year-old children', *Educational Psychology, 7*, 55–65.

Robinson, E. J. and Robinson, W. P. (1983) 'Children's uncertainty about the interpretation of ambiguous messages', *Journal of Experimental Child Psychology, 36*, 305–20.

Robinson, E. J. and Whittaker, S. (in press) 'Children's conceptions of relations between messages, meanings and reality', *British Journal of Developmental Psychology*.

Ross, P. and Howe, J. A. M. (1981) 'Teaching mathematics through programming: ten years on'. In R. Lewis and D. Tagg (eds), *Computers in Education*, Amsterdam: North Holland.

Rozin, P., Bressman, B. and Taft, M. (1974) 'Do children understand the basic relationship between speech and writing? The mow-motorcycle test', *Journal of Reading Behaviour, 6*, 327–34.

Ruff, H. A. (1975) 'The function of shifting fixations in the visual perception of infants', *Child Development, 46*, 857–65.

Ryle, G. (1949) *The Concept of Mind*, London: Hutchinson.

Salapatek, P. (1968) 'Visual scanning of geometric figures by the human newborn', *Journal of Comparative and Physiological Psychology, 66*, 247–58.

Salapatek, P. (1975) 'Pattern perception in early infancy'. In L. B. Cohen and P. Salapatek (eds), *Infant Perception: From Sensation to Cognition*, Vol. 1, New York: Academic Press.

Salomon, G. and Perkins, D. N. (1987) 'Transfer of cognitive skills from programming: when and how?', *Journal of Educational Computing Research, 3*, 149–69.

Sandars, N. K. (1968) *Prehistoric Art in Europe*, Harmondsworth: Penguin.

Savić, S. (1980) *How Twins Learn to Talk*, London: Academic Press.

Scholl, D. M. and Ryan, E. B. (1975) 'Child judgments of sentences varying in grammatical complexity', *Journal of Experimental Child Psychology, 20*, 274–85.

Searle, J. (1983) *Intentionality*, Cambridge: Cambridge University Press.

Sedlak, A. J. and Kurtz, S. T. (1981) 'A review of children's use of causal inference principles', *Child Development, 52*, 759–84.

Self, J. (ed.) (1988) *Artificial Intelligence and Human Learning*, London: Chapman and Hall.

Selfe, L. (1977) *Nadia: A Case of Extraordinary Drawing Ability in an Autistic Child*, New York: Academic Press.

Shatz, M. (1978) 'The relationship between cognitive processes and the development of communication skills'. In B. Keas (ed.), *Nebraska Symposium on Motivation 1977*, University of Nebraska Press.

Shatz, M. and Gelman, R. (1973) 'The development of communication skills: modifications in the speech of young children as a function of listeners', *Monographs of the Society for Research in Child Development, 38*, Serial Number 152.

Shatz, M., Wellman, H. M. and Silber, S. (1983) 'The acquisition of mental verbs: a systematic investigation of the first reference to mental state', *Cognition, 14*, 301–21.

Shipley, E. F. and Kuhn, I. F. (1983) 'A constraint on comparisons: equally detailed alternatives', *Journal of Experimental Child Psychology*, 35, 195–222.

Shultz, T. R. (1980) 'Development of the concept of intention'. In W. A. Collins (ed.), *The Minnesota Symposium on Child Psychology, Volume 13*, Hillsdale, N.J.: Erlbaum.

Shultz, T. R. (1982) 'Causal reasoning in the social and nonsocial realms', *Canadian Journal of Behavioural Science*, 14, 307–22.

Shultz, T. R., Altmann, E. and Asselin, J. (1986) 'Judging causal priority', *British Journal of Developmental Psychology*, 4, 67–74.

Shultz, T. R. and Cloghesy, K. (1981) 'Development of recursive awareness of intention', *Developmental Psychology*, 17, 465–71.

Shultz, T. R. and Kestenbaum, N. R. (1985) 'Causal reasoning in children'. In G. J. Whitehurst (ed.), *Annals of Child Development, Volume 2*, 195–249.

Shultz, T. R. and Shamash, F. (1981) 'The child's conception of intending act and consequence', *Canadian Journal of Behavioural Science*, 13, 368–72.

Shultz, T. R. and Wells, D. (1985) 'Judging the intentionality of action-outcomes', *Developmental Psychology*, 21, 83–9.

Shultz, T. R., Wells, D. and Sarda, M. (1980) 'Development of the ability to distinguish intended actions from mistakes, reflexes, and passive movements', *British Journal of Social and Clinical Psychology*, 19, 301–10.

Simon, T. (1987) 'Claims for Logo: What should we believe and why?' In J. C. Rutkowska and C. Crook (eds), *Computers, Cognition and Development*, London: Wiley.

Sinclair, A., Jarvella, R. J. and Levelt, W. J. M. (1978) *The Child's Conception of Language*, Berlin: Springer.

Sinclair, J. M. and Coulthard, R. M. (1974) *Towards an Analysis of Discourse: The English Used By Teachers and Pupils*, Oxford: Oxford University Press.

Smith, F. (1978) *Reading*, Cambridge: Cambridge University Press.

Smith, N. V. (1973) *The Acquisition of Phonology: A Case Study*, Cambridge: Cambridge University Press.

Snyder, A. D. (1914) 'Notes on the talk of a two-and-a-half year old boy', *Pedagogical Seminary*, 21, 412–24.

Solomon, C. (1986) *Computer Environments for Children*, Cambridge, Mass.: MIT Press.

Somerville, J. (1983) 'Individual drawing styles of three children from five to seven years'. In D. Rogers and J. Sloboda (eds), *Acquisition of Symbolic Skills*, New York: Plenum Press.

Somerville, J. C. and Haake, R. J. (1985) 'The logical search skills of infants and young children'. In H. M. Wellman (ed.), *Children's Searching: The Development of Search Skill and Spatial Representation*, Hillsdale, N.J.: Erlbaum.

Sophian, C. (1986) 'Early developments in children's spatial monitoring', *Cognition*, 22, 61–8.

Sophian, C. and Huber, A. (1984) 'Early developments in children's causal judgments', *Child Development*, 55, 512–26.

Sophian, C. and Wellman, H. M. (1980) 'Selective information use in the development of search behaviour', *Journal of Developmental Psychology*, 4, 323–31.

Sperber, D. and Wilson, D. (1986) *Relevance*, Oxford: Blackwell.

Stanovich, K. E. (1980) 'Toward an interactive-compensatory model of individual differences in the development of reading fluency', *Reading Research Quarterly, XVI*, 32–71.

Stein, N. L. and Trabasso, T. (1982) 'Children's understanding of stories: a basis for moral judgement and dilemma resolution'. In C. J. Brainerd and M. Pressley (eds), *Verbal Processes in Children*, New York: Springer.

Straker, A. (1989) *Children Using Computers*, Oxford: Blackwell.

Stubbs, M. (1976) *Language, Schools and Classrooms*, London: Methuen.

Sugarman, J. (1983) *Children's Early Thought*, Cambridge: Cambridge University Press.

Sully, J. (1895) *Studies in Childhood*, London: Longman.

Suppes, P. and Morningstar, M. (1969) 'Computer-assisted instruction', *Science, 166*, 343–50.

Taeschner, T. (1983) *The Sun is Feminine: A Study on Language Acquisition in Bilingual Children*, Berlin: Springer.

Tolchinsky-Landsmann, L. and Levin, I. (1985) 'Writing in preschoolers: and age-related analysis', *Applied Psycholinguistics, 6*, 319–39.

Trabasso, T., Stein, N. L. and Johnson, L. R. (1981) 'Children's knowledge of events: a causal analysis of story structure'. In G. H. Bower (ed.), *The Psychology of Learning and Motivation*, Volume 15, New York: Academic Press.

Trehub, J. E. and Abramovitch, R. (1978) '*Less* is not *more*: further observations on nonlinguistic strategies', *Journal of Experimental Child Psychology, 25*, 160–7.

Tunmer, W. E. and Grieve, F. (1984) 'Syntactic awareness in children'. In W. E. Tumner, C. Pratt, and M. L. Herriman (eds) *Metalinguistic Awareness in Children*, Berlin: Springer.

Tunmer, W. and Herriman, M. (1984) 'The development of metalinguistic awareness: a conceptual overview'. In W. Tunmer, C. Pratt and M. Herriman (eds), *Metalinguistic Awareness in Children*, Springer: Berlin.

Tunmer, W. E., Pratt, C. and Herriman, M. L. (eds) (1984) *Metalinguistic Awareness in Children*, Berlin: Springer.

Van Sommers, P. (1983) *Drawing and Cognition: Descriptive and Experimental Studies of Graphic Production Processes*, Cambridge: Cambridge University Press.

Vinter, A. (1986) 'The role of movement in eliciting early imitations', *Child Development, 57*, 66–71.

Vurpillot, E. and Ball, W. A. (1979) 'The concept of identity and children's selective attention'. In G. A. Hale and M. Lewis (eds), *Attention and Cognitive Development*, New York: Plenum.

Vygotsky, L. S. (1962) *Thought and Language*, Cambridge, Mass.: MIT Press.

Vygotsky, L. S. (1978) *Mind in Society*, Cambridge, Mass.: Harvard University Press.

Vygotsky, L. S. (1981) 'The genesis of higher mental functions'. In J. V. Wertsch (ed.), *The Concept of Activity in Soviet Psychology*, Armonk, New York: Sharpe.

Wales, R. and Coffey, G. (1986) 'On children's comprehension of metaphor'.

In C. Pratt, A. Garton, W. Tunmer and A. Nesdale (eds), *Research Issues in Child Development*, Sydney: Allen and Unwin.

Walkerdine, V. (1982) 'From context to text: a psychosemiotic approach to abstract thought'. In M. Beveridge (ed.), *Children Thinking Through Language*, London: Edward Arnold.

Wannemacher, J. T. and Ryan, M. L. (1978) 'Less is not more: a study of children's comprehension of *less* in various task contexts', *Child Development*, 49, 660–8.

Weber, R. M. (1970) 'A linguistic analysis of first-grade reading errors', *Reading Research Quarterly*, V, 427–51.

Weiner, S. L. (1974) 'On the development of *more* and *less*', *Journal of Experimental Child Psychology*, 17, 271–87.

Wellman, H. M. (1985) 'The importance of studying children's searching'. In H. M. Wellman (ed.), *Children's Searching: The Development of Search Skill and Spatial Representation*, Hillsdale, N.J.: Erlbaum.

Wellman, H. M., Somerville, S. C. and Haake, R. H. (1979) 'Development of search procedures in real-life spatial environments', *Developmental Psychology*, 15, 530–42.

Wenger, E. (1987) *Artificial Intelligence and Tutoring Systems*, Los Angeles: Morgan Kaufman.

Wertsch, J. V. (1985) *Culture, Communication and Cognition: Vygotskyan Perspectives*, Cambridge: Cambridge University Press.

Willatts, J. (1983) 'Getting the drawing to look right as well as be right: the interaction between production and perception as a mechanism for development'. In W. R. Crozier and A. J. Chapman (eds), *Cognitive Processes in the Perception of Art*, Amsterdam: North Holland.

Willatts, J. (1987) 'Marra and pictures: an information-processing account of children's drawings', *Archives de Psychologie*, 51, 105–25.

Wimmer, H., Gruber, S. and Perner, J. (1984) 'Young children's conception of lying: lexical realism – moral subjectivism', *Journal of Experimental Child Psychology*, 37, 1–30.

Wimmer, H. and Perner, J. (1983) 'Beliefs about beliefs: representation and constraining function of wrong beliefs in young children's understanding of deception', *Cognition*, 13, 103–28.

Winner, E. (1982) *Invented Worlds: The Psychology of the Arts*, Cambridge, Mass.: Harvard University Press.

Winner, E., Blank, P., Massey, C. and Gardner, H. (1983) 'Children's sensitivity to aesthetic profiles of line drawings'. In D. Rogers and J. Sloboda (eds), *Acquisition of Symbolic Skills*, New York: Plenum Press.

Witelson, S. F. and Kristofferson, A. B. (1986) 'McMaster-Bauer Symposium on Consciousness', *Canadian Journal of Psychology*, 27, 122–82.

Wohlwill, J. F. (1962) 'From perception to inference'. In W. Kessen and C. Kuhlmann (eds), *Thought and the Young Child*, Society for Research in Child Development, Monograph Number 83, Volume 27.

Wragg, E. C. and Wood, E. K. (1984) 'Pupil appraisals of teaching'. In E. C. Wragg (ed.), *Classroom Teaching Skills*, London: Croom Helm.

Yuill, N. (1984) 'Young children's coordination of motive and outcomes in judgements of satisfaction and morality', *British Journal of Developmental Psychology*, 2, 73–81.

Zinchenko, V. F., Chzhi-Tsin, B. and Tarakanov, V. V. (1963) 'The formation and development of perceptual activity', *Soviet Psychology and Psychiatry*, 2, 3–12.

Zwanenburg, W. (1981) 'Le principe du blocage dans la morphologie derivationelle'. In S. Daalder and M. Gerritsen (eds), *Linguistics in the Netherlands 1981*, Amsterdam: North Holland.

Name Index

Subject Index